THE BEST TEST PREPARATION FOR THE

CLEP

College Composition Exams

With REA's TestWare® on CD-ROM

Rachelle Smith, Ph.D.
Associate Professor of English
Emporia State University
Emporia, Kansas

Dominic Marullo, M.A
Oriskany Junior/Senior High School
Oriskany, New York

Ken Springer, Ph.D.
Simmons School of Education &
Human Development
Southern Methodist University
Dallas, Texas

Research & Education Association
Visit our website at:
www.rea.com

Research & Education Association
61 Ethel Road West
Piscataway, New Jersey 08854
E-mail: info@rea.com

The Best Test Preparation for the
CLEP College Composition Exams
With TestWare® on CD-ROM

Printed in the United States of America

Library of Congress Control Number: 2010942245

ISBN 13: 978-0-7386-0889-1
ISBN 10: 0-7386-0889-0

Windows® is a registered trademark of Microsoft Corporation.

All other trademarks cited in this publication are the property of their respective owners.

CONTENTS

About Our Authors v

About Research & Education Association..................................vi

Acknowledgments...vi

CLEP Independent Study Schedule...vii

Part I: Introduction 1

About This Book and TestWare® 3

About the Exam 3

Format and Content of the College Composition and
College Composition Modular Exams....................................6

How to Use This Book and TestWare® 8

How the Exams Are Scored 9

Test-Taking Tips...9

The Day of the Exam 11

Part II: Multiple-Choice Questions 13

Chapter 1   Conventions of Standard Written English 15

Syntax...15

Parallelism..22

Agreement..23

Diction..31

Modifiers 39

Reference 43

Punctuation...45

Chapter 2   Revision Skills...55

Organization...56

Audience, Purpose, Tone...62

Evaluation of Evidence 62

Level of Detail..71

Coherence...72

Sentence Variety...74

Main Idea, Topic Sentence, Thesis Statement.................74

Rhetorical Effects...75

Use of Language 76
Transitions..77
How to Approach Revision Skills Questions 78

Chapter 3 Ability to Use Source Materials..............................87
Documentation of Sources 87
Evaluation of Sources 93
Integration of Resource Materials..100
Use of Reference Materials..112
How to Approach Ability to Use Source Materials Questions ..118

Chapter 4 Rhetorical Analysis 127
Critical Thinking 127
Understanding of Organization 140
Understanding of Style..147
Understanding of Audience, Purpose, and Tone 154
Understanding of Rhetoric...159
How to Approach Rhetorical Analysis Questions....................163

**Part III: The Essays: College Composition
and College Composition Modular Essays**...............................171

Chapter 5 The Essays..173
Overview of the CLEP College Composition Examination,
Including Modular Option 173
Basic Writing Strategies for Producing High-Scoring
CLEP Essays 175
Practice Writing the CLEP Argumentative Essays 182

Part IV: Practice Exams...191
College Composition Practice Test 1 193
Answer Key...213
College Composition Practice Test 2 221
Answer Key...239
College Composition Modular Practice Test 1.........................245
Answer Key...273
College Composition Modular Practice Test 2.........................281
Answer Key...308

Index...315

Installing REA's TestWare® 328

About Our Authors

Dr. Rachelle M. Smith has served as Director of Composition at Emporia State University for the last sixteen years. She did her doctoral work at Texas Christian University with a specialization in rhetoric and composition. She enjoys teaching science fiction written by women, as well as classic mysteries by Sir Arthur Conan Doyle, Wilkie Collins, and Agatha Christie.

Dominick Marullo, M.A. is currently a high school English teacher with a Bachelors degree in English/Education and a Masters in Writing. He has also taught a creative writing course at a local community college. Over the years, he has written for several educational publishers in the area of test preparation, as well as for high school and college review books. He has written several screenplays, one of which was a semi-finalist in a prestigious, worldwide competition. He also received the Utica Writers Guild award for fiction for a short story. In his spare time, he also performs as a musician, playing bass guitar and drums in various bands.

Dr. Kenneth Springer is a developmental psychologist. After receiving his Ph.D. from Cornell University in 1990, he served on the faculty of SMU's Psychology Department before moving to the Simmons School of Education and Human Development in 2002. Dr. Springer currently teaches undergraduate classes in educational psychology, as well as research methods and statistics for graduate students. Dr. Springer is active as a researcher, with more than 60 scientific publications and presentations, as well as three books, including *Educational Research: A Contextual Approach* (2010). His current research focuses on academic achievement among students from economically disadvantaged backgrounds. Dr. Springer's administrative work includes serving as chair of the SMU Institutional Review Board from 2005 to present, chair of the Faculty Ethics & Tenure Committee from 2008 to present, and secretary of the Faculty Senate from 2006 through 2008.

About Research & Education Association

Founded in 1959, Research & Education Association (REA) is dedicated to publishing the finest and most effective educational materials—including software, study guides, and test preps—for students in elementary school, middle school, high school, college, graduate school, and beyond.

Today, REA's wide-ranging catalog is a leading resource for teachers, students, and professionals.

We invite you to visit us at *www.rea.com* to find out how "REA is making the world smarter."

Acknowledgments

In addition to our authors, we would like to thank Larry B. Kling, Vice President, Editorial, for his overall guidance, which brought this publication to completion; Pam Weston, Publisher, for setting the quality standards for production integrity and managing the publication to completion; John Cording, Vice President, Technology, for coordinating the design and development of REA's TestWare®; Diane Goldschmidt, Senior Editor, for project management; Alice Leonard and Kathleen Casey, Senior Editors, for preflight editorial review; Heena Patel, Technology Project Manager, for design contributions and software testing efforts; Christine Saul, Senior Graphic Designer, for designing our cover; and Fred Grayson of American BookWorks Corporation for overseeing manuscript development and typesetting.

We gratefully acknowledge Sonja Mix of Thomas Dale High School, Richmond, Virginia, for technical review of the manuscript.

CLEP College Composition and College Composition Modular Independent Study Schedule

The following study schedule allows for thorough preparation for the CLEP College Composition and College Composition Modular exams. Although it is designed for six weeks, it can be condensed to a three-week course by collapsing each two-week period into one. Be sure to set aside enough time—at least two hours each day—to study. No matter which study schedule works best for you, the more time you spend studying, the more prepared and relaxed you will feel on the day of the exam.

Week	Activity
1	Read and study the Introduction of this book, which will introduce you to the CLEP College Composition and College Composition Modular exams. Take Practice Test 1 on CD-ROM for the particular CLEP College Composition exam you will be taking to determine your strengths and weaknesses. Start reading Chapter 1 that will introduce you to the Conventions of Standard Written English that will be tested on the exam.
2, 3, and 4	Finish reading Chapter 1. Continue to carefully read and study the CLEP College Composition and College Composition Modular review material included in Chapters 2 through 5 in this book.
5	Take Practice Test 2 on CD-ROM for the particular CLEP exam you will be taking and carefully review the explanations for all incorrect answers. If there are any types of questions or particular subjects that seem difficult to you, review those subjects by again studying the appropriate sections of the CLEP College Composition and College Composition Modular review chapters.
6	This last week affords you the opportunity to do more review work for the exam and ample time to re-take the practice tests that are printed in this book. This will help strengthen the areas in which your performance may still be lagging and build your overall confidence.

Part I

INTRODUCTION

Passing the CLEP College Composition/College Composition Modular Exams

ABOUT THIS BOOK AND TestWare®

This book will provide you with complete preparation for the *CLEP College Composition* and *College Composition Modular* exams. Inside you will find a targeted review of the subject matter, as well as tips and strategies throughout for doing well on either test. In addition we offer you two full-length tests for each of the specific exams. These tests are based on the official CLEP requirements. By answering all of the questions—both multiple-choice and essay questions—you will benefit from the basic rule of test preparation success: the more questions you answer before you take the test, the better your chances are for improving your score on the actual exam.

The practice exams in this book and software package are included in two formats: in printed format in this book, and in TestWare® format on the enclosed CD. **We strongly suggest that when you begin your preparation for the tests, that you start with the TestWare® practice exams.** The software provides the added benefits of instant scoring and enforced time conditions.

All CLEP exams are computer-based. As you can see, the practice tests in our book are presented as paper-and-pencil exams. However, the content and format of these exams faithfully mirror the actual subject tests.

ABOUT THE EXAM

Who takes CLEP exams and what are they used for?

CLEP examinations are typically taken by people who have acquired knowledge outside the classroom and wish to bypass certain college courses and earn college credit. The CLEP is designed to reward students for learning—no matter where or how that knowledge was acquired. The CLEP is the most widely accepted credit-by-examination program in North America, with almost 3,000 colleges and universities granting credit for satisfactory scores on CLEP exams.

Although most CLEP examinees are adults returning to college, many graduating high school seniors, enrolled college students, military personnel, veterans, and international students also take the exams to earn college credit or to demonstrate their ability to perform at the college level. There are no prerequisites, such as age or educational status, for taking CLEP examinations. However, because policies on granting credits vary among colleges, you should contact the particular institution from which you wish to receive CLEP credit.

There are two categories of CLEP examinations:

1. **CLEP General Examinations,** which are six separate tests that cover material usually taken as requirements during the first two years of college. CLEP General Examinations are available for College Composition and College Composition Modular, Humanities, College Mathematics, Natural Sciences, and Social Sciences and History.

2. **CLEP Subject Examinations** include material usually covered in an undergraduate course with a similar title. For a complete list of the subject examinations offered, visit the College Board website.

Who administers the exam?

The CLEP exams are developed by the College Board, administered by Educational Testing Service (ETS), and involve the assistance of educators throughout the United States. The test development process is designed and implemented to ensure that the content and difficulty level of the test are appropriate.

When and where is the exam given?

CLEP exams are administered each month throughout the year at more than 1,700 test centers in the United States and can be arranged for candidates abroad on request. To find the test center nearest you and to register for the exam, you should obtain a copy of the free booklets *CLEP Colleges* and *CLEP*

Information for Candidates and Registration Form. They are available at most colleges where CLEP credit is granted or by contacting:

> CLEP Services
> P.O. Box 6600
> Princeton, NJ 08541-6600
> Phone: (800) 257-9558 (8 A.M. to 6 P.M. ET)
> Fax: (609) 771-7088
> Website: *www.collegeboard.com/clep*

CLEP Options for Military Personnel and Veterans

CLEP exams are available free of charge to eligible military personnel and eligible civilian employees. All the CLEP exams are available at test centers on college campuses and military bases. In addition, the College Board has developed a paper-based version of 14 high-volume/high-pass-rate CLEP tests for DANTES Test Centers. Contact the Educational Services Officer or Navy College Education Specialist for more information. Visit the College Board website for details about CLEP opportunities for military personnel.

Eligible U.S. veterans can claim reimbursement for CLEP exams and administration fees pursuant to provisions of the Veterans Benefits Improvement Act of 2004. For details on eligibility and submitting a claim for reimbursement, visit the U.S. Department of Veterans Affairs website at *www.gibill.va.gov/ pamphlets/testing.htm.*

CLEP marks a special sweet spot with reference to the Post-9/11 GI Bill, which applies to veterans returning from the Iraq and Afghanistan theaters of operation. Because the GI Bill provides tuition for up to 36 months, racking up college credits by testing out of general introductory courses with CLEP exams expedites academic progress and degree completion within the funded timeframe.

SSD Accommodations for Candidates with Disabilities

Many test candidates qualify for extra time to take the CLEP College Composition and College Composition Modular exams, but you must make these arrangements in advance. For information, contact:

> College Board Services for Students with Disabilities
> P.O. Box 6226
> Princeton, NJ 08541-6226
> Phone: (609) 771-7137 (Monday through Friday, 8 A.M. to 6 P.M. ET)
> TTY: (609) 882-4118
> Fax: (609) 771-7944
> E-mail: ssd@info.collegeboard.org

FORMAT AND CONTENT OF THE COLLEGE COMPOSITION AND COLLEGE COMPOSITION MODULAR EXAMS

These exams are new, and were first administered in July 2010. These exams replaced three exams that have been discontinued:

- English Composition has been replaced by *College Composition Modular*.

- English Composition with Essay has been replaced by *College Composition*.

- Freshman College Composition has been replaced by *College Composition Modular*.

The two new College Composition examinations are designed to measure your writing skills that are taught in most first-year college composition courses. They consist of *Conventions of Standard Written English*, *Revision Skills*, *Ability to Use Source Materials*, and *Rhetorical Analysis*. In addition there are two essays on the College Composition and one or two on the College Composition Modular. (The number of essay questions in this test is determined by the institution.) Following is a breakdown of each test:

College Composition		
Type of Questions	**Number of Questions**	**Time**
Multiple-Choice Questions	50	50 minutes
Essays	2	70 minutes
TOTAL TIME		120 minutes
College Composition Modular		
Multiple-Choice Questions	90	90 minutes
Essays	2	70 minutes
TOTAL TIME		160 minutes

Each of these tests may contain additional multiple-choice questions that will not be counted toward your scores.

Within the multiple-choice section of each exam, the topics are broken down by the following percentages:

Conventions of Standard Written English (10%)

- Syntax (parallelism, coordination, subordination)

- Sentence boundaries (comma splice, run-ons, sentence fragments)

- Recognition of correct sentences

- Concord/agreement (pronoun reference, case shift, and number; subject-verb; verb tense)

- Diction

- Modifiers

- Idiom

- Active/passive voice

- Lack of subject in modifying word group

- Logical comparison

- Logical agreement

- Punctuation

Revision Skills, Including Sentence-Level Skills (40%)

- Organization

- Evaluation of evidence

- Awareness of audience, tone, and purpose

- Level of detail

- Coherence between sentences and paragraphs

- Sentence variety and structure

- Main idea, thesis statements and topic sentences

- Rhetorical effects and emphasis

- Use of language

- Evaluation of author's authority and appeal

- Evaluation of reasoning

- Consistency of point of view

- Transitions

- Sentence-level errors primarily relating to the conventions of standard written English

Ability to Use Source Materials (25%)

- Use of reference materials

- Evaluation of sources

- Integration of resource material

- Documentation of sources (including, but not limited to, MLA, APA and Chicago styles)

Rhetorical Analysis (25%)

- Appeals

- Tone

- Organization/structure

- Rhetorical effects

- Use of language

- Evaluation of evidence

These percentages are the same regardless of which of the two tests you take. However, some of the topics within those sections may be different. We have indicated them within the review chapters.

HOW TO USE THIS BOOK AND TestWare®

What do I study first?

To begin your studies, read over this introduction and our suggestions for test taking. Take Practice Exam 1 for the CLEP College Composition or CLEP College Composition Modular exam on CD-ROM to determine your strengths and weaknesses. Then study the course review material, focusing on your specific problem areas. The course review includes the information you need to know when taking the exam. Make sure to follow up your diagnostic work by taking the remaining practice exam printed in this book to become familiar with the format and feel of the CLEP College Composition or the CLEP College Composition Modular exam.

To best utilize your study time, follow our Independent Study Schedule, which you'll find in the front of this book. The schedule is based on a six-week program, but can be condensed to three weeks if necessary by collapsing each two-week period into one.

HOW THE EXAMS ARE SCORED

College English professors selected by the College Board score the essays for the CLEP College Composition exams. Each essay is read and graded by two or more faculty consultants and the grade is combined with the multiple-choice score. The result is reported as a scaled score of 20 to 80. You will receive your scaled score for the CLEP College Composition or College Composition Modular exam within three to four weeks of taking the exam.

The American Council on Education's (ACE) College Credit Recommendation Service recommends the awarding of six credit hours for a score of 50 on the CLEP College Composition examination. ACE recommends awarding of three credit hours for a score of 50 on the 90-minute multiple-choice College Composition Modular exam. If colleges elect to supplement the Modular version of the examination with an essay available from CLEP or with a writing assessment of their own, the credit recommendation is six credit hours for a score of 50.

When will I receive my score report?

The test administrator will print out a full Candidate Score Report for you immediately upon your completion of the exam (except for CLEP College Composition and College Composition Modular). Your scores are reported only to you, unless you ask to have them sent elsewhere. If you want your scores reported to a college or other institution, you must say so when you take the examination. Since your scores are kept on file for 20 years, you can also request transcripts from Educational Testing Service at a later date.

TEST-TAKING TIPS

Although you may not be familiar with computer-based standardized tests such as the *CLEP College Composition* or *College Composition Modular* exams, there are many ways to acquaint you with the type of examination and to help alleviate your test-taking anxieties. Following are some ways to help you become accustomed to the CLEP, and some tips to get you through the multiple-choice section.

Know the format of the test. CLEP computer-based tests are not adaptive but rather fixed-length tests. In a sense, this makes them similar to the familiar paper-and-pencil exam, in that you have the same flexibility to go back and review your work in each section. Moreover, the format isn't a great deal different from the paper-and-pencil CLEP. The TestWare® CD enclosed with this book should help you acclimate to the style and format.

Read all directions, questions, and response options carefully. For example, the *Conventions of Standard Written English* section will be described as a test of your knowledge of grammar, usage, diction, and idiom. You will not be asked to evaluate the accuracy or relevance of details given in the sentences of this section.

Use the process of elimination. As you prepare to answer each question, start by eliminating options you know to be incorrect. Often, you will be asked to choose the "best" option, or the one that is "most clear," or "most likely," and so on. These superlatives hint that that some of the options for a particular question may be partially correct, but that one particular option will be preferable. For example, suppose that one of the test questions asks you to choose the "best" revision of the underlined portion of the following sentence:

Santiago, in Ernest Hemingway's novel The Old Man and the Sea, *displays admirable courage and strength <u>in his fight with a great marlin, which is very symbol</u>.*

(A) when symbolically with a great marlin, fighting.

(B) in his fight with a great marlin, a symbolic fight.

(C) when he fights, with that great marlin, symbolic.

(D) in his fight with a very symbolic, great marlin.

(E) in his symbolic fight with a great marlin.

After reading the question, you should examine each option in turn. Option A can be eliminated right away, as it is clearly grammatically flawed. Option B is awkward, but not clearly ungrammatical, so you should make note of it as possibly correct before proceeding. Option C is clearly grammatically flawed and can be eliminated. Option D is awkward but not clearly ungrammatical, so it should be kept in mind (along with Option B) as possibly correct. Option E is sensible, grammatically correct, and not awkward in the way that Options B and D are. Thus, Option E is the correct answer.

Keep track of time as you work. Do not spend too much time on any one question. If you're not sure about a question after examining it briefly, mark it and return to the question later. (In the previous example, if Option B did not immediately strike you as problematic, you could consider both Options B and D as possibly correct and return to the question later.) However, if you're sure you don't know the answer to a question, make an educated guess. There is no penalty for incorrect answers.

Acquaint yourself with the computer screen. Familiarize yourself with the CLEP computer screen beforehand by logging on the College Board website. Waiting until test day to see what it looks like in the pretest tutorial risks injecting needless anxiety into your testing experience. Also, familiarizing yourself with the directions and format of the exam will save you valuable time on the day of the actual test. You will have only one minute to answer each multiple-choice question. Don't waste time trying to figure out what they're asking of you.

Be sure that your answer registers before you go to the next item. Look at the screen to see that your mouse-click causes the pointer to darken the proper oval. This takes less effort than darkening an oval on paper, but just be careful.

THE DAY OF THE EXAM

On the day of the test you should wake up early. Make sure you've had a decent night's sleep, and then eat a good breakfast. Check the weather and dress appropriately, but remember that you'll be taking the test indoors, so keep that in mind as you select your clothing. Try to arrive early at the test center. This will allow you to collect your thoughts and relax before the test. Keep in mind that no one will be allowed into the test session after the test has begun.

Before you leave for the test center, make sure that you have your admission form and another form of identification, which must contain a recent photograph, your name, and signature. Acceptable forms of identification are a driver's license, student identification card, or current alien registration card. If you do not have the proper identification, you will not be admitted to the test center.

You are permitted to wear a watch, but it should not make noise. Also, turn off your cell phone and put it away. You are not permitted to bring dictionaries, textbooks, notebooks, briefcases, or packages, and drinking, smoking, and eating are prohibited.

If you have spent your time working with this book, reading through the review chapters, answering the questions in the chapters and taking the tests, you should not have a lot of trouble with the exam. The more questions you answer before you take the test, the better your chances are for greatly improving your scores on the actual exam.

Good luck on the test!

Part II

MULTIPLE-CHOICE QUESTIONS

Chapter 1

Conventions of Standard Written English

In the Conventions of Standard Written English section, knowledge of English grammar, usage, diction, and idiom is tested. Each question in this section consists of a sentence in which four words or phrases are underlined. Your task is to choose the one underlined word or phrase out of the four that is ungrammatical or reflects some other error in the way it is written. If the sentence contains no errors, you can indicate that instead.

The skills tested in this section include knowledge of syntax, agreement, diction, modifiers, punctuation, idiom, and voice. The Revision Skills section (see Chapter 2) also tests many of these skills, and thus what you learn from each of these chapters may be tested in either section of the CLEP College Composition/College Composition Modular exams.

Among the skills mentioned above, idiom and voice are discussed in Chapter 4. The other skills are discussed in this chapter, followed by guidance on how to approach Conventions of Standard Written English questions, and some practice questions with answers and explanations.

SYNTAX

Syntax refers to the rules that govern sentence structure, particularly the order of words and phrases in sentences. For example, the rules of English syntax indicate that the first sentence below is grammatically correct, while the second sentence is grammatically incorrect:

"I have gone to the store."

"I have to the store gone."

Each language has its own syntactic rules. In German, for example, the first sentence above would be incorrect, while the second sentence would be correct.

Although the grammatically incorrect sentence "I have to the store gone" is more or less understandable, in the extreme case a syntactic error will change the intended meaning of the sentence. For example, the two sentences below consist of exactly the same words, but the meanings of the sentences are different because of the difference in the order of the words:

"The cat bit the dog."

"The dog bit the cat."

Simple Sentences

In written English, sentences usually must consist of a subject and a predicate. The predicate in turn must include a verb. Thus, the sentence "Marianna arrived" is grammatically correct, because it consists of a subject ("Marianna") and a verb ("arrived"). Sentences can be much longer and more elaborate than this one, of course.

A simple sentence consists of one subject and predicate, as in the following examples:

"Cecilia likes dark chocolate."

"The jaguar fell asleep in the only remaining secluded area of this once mighty rainforest."

"At 6:00 a.m. the alarm went off."

Each of the sentences above is a simple sentence, because it contains one subject ("Cecilia," "the jaguar," and "the alarm," respectively) and one predicate.

In any sentence, a subject and its predicate are referred to as a clause. A clause that functions as a complete sentence is an independent clause. Thus, by definition, a simple sentence consists of one independent clause. A clause that does not function by itself as a complete sentence is a dependent clause (also known as a subordinate clause). Examples of dependent clauses are given below:

"in the park beside the tallest elm tree"

"because he believed what his uncle had told him"

"after dinner, sitting in my chair"

As you can see, none of the clauses above functions as a complete sentence.

Compound Sentences

A compound sentence contains two or more independent clauses typically linked by a coordinating conjunction. Examples of coordinating conjunctions are as follows:

and
but
for
not
or
so
yet

"Coordination" refers to the combination of independent clauses to form a compound sentence. For example:

"John fell asleep, but Mary stayed up a little while longer."

In the sentence above, "John fell asleep" is one independent clause, while "Mary stayed up a little while longer" is a second independent clause.

Punctuation rather than conjunctions can be used between two independent clauses in some cases, as in the following examples:

"John fell asleep; Mary stayed up a little while longer."

"John fell asleep. Mary stayed up a little while longer."

Further details about punctuation are discussed throughout this chapter, and in the section on punctuation.

Complex Sentences

A complex sentence consists of an independent clause and one or more dependent clauses, as in the following example:

"I disliked the dessert that he brought."

In the sentence above, the clause "I disliked the dessert" is an independent clause. The clause "he brought" is a dependent clause. In this example, the word "that" connects the two clauses.

As noted earlier, dependent clauses are sometimes referred to as subordinate clauses. The reason for this is not simply that a dependent clause cannot stand alone as a sentence, but also because the details it provides will be subordinate to the information in the independent clause. That is, a dependent clause will simply provide additional information about the statement established by the independent clause. In the preceding example, the dependent clause "that he brought" simply helps identify which particular dessert it is that the writer dislikes.

In general, two kinds of words can be used to link the independent and dependent clauses in a complex sentence.

First, relative pronouns such as "that," "which," "who," and "whoever" can be used. For example:

"I am grateful to the person who invented pizza."

In this example, "I am grateful to the person" is the independent clause and "invented pizza" is the dependent clause.

Second, subordinate conjunctions can be used to link independent to dependent clauses, as in the following example:

"He always gets drowsy after eating a large dinner."

In the example above, the subordinate conjunction is "after." Other commonly used subordinate conjunctions are:

although	once
as	since
because	though
before	unless
how	whether
if	whenever

In the examples of complex sentences given thus far, the independent clause precedes the dependent clause, but it is also acceptable for the dependent clause to come first, as in the following revision of the previous sentence:

"After eating a large dinner, he always gets drowsy."

When a dependent clause precedes an independent clause, a comma will often be used to separate them, as in the example above. However, when the independent clause comes first, a comma may not be used.

In some complex sentences, the subject and predicate of the independent clause will be divided, as in the following example:

"The man who called yesterday is at the door now."

In this example, the word "who" links the dependent clause ("called yesterday") to the independent clause "The man is at the door now."

Notice that although the subject and predicate of the independent clause in the preceding example can be divided, the dependent clause cannot. Dependent clauses generally cannot be divided in this way.

Compound-Complex Sentences

A compound-complex sentence consists of at least two independent clauses and one or more dependent clauses. For example:

"The tree that grew near the house fell over yesterday, but the house was unharmed."

In this example, the first independent clause is "The tree fell over yesterday" and the second independent clause is "the house was unharmed." The dependent clause is "grew near the house."

Sentence Boundaries

Ordinarily a sentence cannot be grammatically correct unless it contains a subject and a predicate, and the predicate in turn contains a verb. The absence of any of these elements usually results in a sentence fragment. For example, the following fragments lack a subject:

"Ran the race in brand new shoes."

"Overcoming obstacles, one at a time."

The next two examples are fragments because each lacks a main verb:

"The parrot who suddenly flew away."

"A math teacher who perplexed the class.

Although each of the two fragments above contains a verb ("flew" and "perplexed," respectively), these verbs are part of phrases that modify the subject. In other words, each fragment above is actually a subject. "The parrot who suddenly flew away" is a subject that requires some sort of predicate, as in the following example:

"The parrot who suddenly flew away just returned."

In this example, "just returned" is the predicate associated with the subject "The parrot who suddenly flew away."

Notice that another approach to rendering the fragment about the parrot grammatically correct would be to simply remove the word "who," as follows:

"The parrot suddenly flew away."

This is a grammatically correct sentence. The subject is "The parrot" and the predicate is "suddenly flew away." The inclusion of the word "who" after the word "parrot" makes the sentence into a fragment of a more elaborate sentence. The purpose of this more elaborate sentence is not to simply indicate that a parrot flew away, but to say something else about a parrot who flew away.

Finally, here are two examples that are fragments because each one lacks a subject and a main verb:

"After a delightful stroll down to the beach followed by a dip in the ocean."

"Because she asked me to wait before knocking."

The preceding two examples are fragments, even though each one contains nouns and verbs, because neither fragment contains a noun that functions as a subject or a verb that would help complete the idea. Neither one of these fragments could be made into a complete sentence by adding only a noun or a verb; rather, what is needed would be an independent clause that contains both. This point is illustrated by the first example below. (The second example below illustrates how narrowing the scope of the fragment can result in a complete sentence.)

"Because she had asked me to wait before knocking, I decided to wait."

"She asked me to wait before knocking."

Notice that in some cases, the subject of a sentence will be implied rather than directly stated, as in the following sentence:

"Think about this issue carefully."

In the sentence above, the implied subject is "you." The sentence is grammatically correct even though the subject is implied rather than directly stated. In contrast, the following example is a fragment and thus grammatically incorrect because the subject is neither known nor implied:

"Thought about this issue carefully."

The examples given here illustrate the idea that sentence fragments are usually dependent clauses. A sentence fragment is usually a dependent clause treated as an entire sentence, in other words.

In many forms of writing, a sentence fragment may be acceptable when the structure and meaning of the complete sentence implied by the fragment is clear. For example, consider the following passage:

"Mr. Johnson was convinced that Smith had committed the crime. Absolutely certain."

In the passage above, the second sentence is actually a sentence fragment, as it lacks a subject. However, it is clear from the context established by the first sentence that Mr. Johnson is the subject.

The second sentence in the previous example could have been rewritten as a complete sentence, as illustrated by the following revision:

"Mr. Johnson was convinced that Smith had committed the crime. Mr. Johnson was absolutely certain of Smith's guilt."

Although the second sentence is now grammatically correct, it lacks the punch of the original version ("Absolutely certain.").

For the Conventions of Written English and Revision Skills sections of the CLEP College Composition and College Composition Modular exams, you should be careful not to assume that a sentence fragment is acceptable for stylistic reasons, even if the meaning is clear. For example, consider the following passage:

"Imran climbed the stairs leading up to the park's entrance and then paused. Because his girlfriend had asked him to wait before entering."

In the passage above, the second sentence is a fragment because it lacks a subject. Although the meaning and grammatical structure are clear from the context, you should not consider this a grammatically correct sentence.

Fragments occur when the writer does not produce a complete sentence. In contrast, run-on sentences occur when the writer joins two or more sentences within the same sentence without separating them appropriately. Consider the following example:

"Will admires the actor Meryl Streep, she is so talented."

Here two different independent clauses are joined by a comma, resulting in a grammatically incorrect run-on sentence referred to as a comma splice. In order to make the sentence grammatically correct, the writer could divide it into separate sentences, as follows:

"Will admires the actor Meryl Streep. She is so talented."

Alternatively, the writer could add an appropriate conjunction or form of punctuation between the clauses, as in the following examples:

"Will admires the actor Meryl Streep, because she is so talented."

"Will admires the actor Meryl Streep; she is so talented."

Not all conjunctions or forms of punctuation would be acceptable, as illustrated by the following grammatically incorrect sentences:

"Will admires the actor Meryl Streep, whereas she is so talented."

"Will admires the actor Meryl Streep, she is so talented."

This section has provided you with some information about the "mechanics" or basic rules of syntax. In Chapter 4, the contributions of syntax to a writer's style and rhetorical effectiveness are discussed.

PARALLELISM

Parallelism occurs when certain words or phrases in a sentence represent the same part of speech or other grammatical category. When words or phrases serve the same function in a sentence, they should reflect the same grammatical category. In such cases, parallelism is a requirement for grammatical correctness. Consider, for example, the following sentences:

"Suddenly he opened the desk drawer, retrieved a sheet of paper, and began to write the letter."

"Suddenly he opened the desk drawer, pulled out a sheet of paper, and there was a pen at the bottom of the drawer."

In the first sentence, parallelism can be seen across the verbs "opened," "retrieved," and "began." Because these verbs serve the same function in the sentence (i.e., to indicate a sequence of actions), they all reflect the same grammatical category (i.e., simple past tense), and thus the sentence is grammatically correct. In contrast, the second sentence is grammatically incorrect owing to the lack of parallelism between the final clause and those that preceded it.

The following sentences illustrate the need for parallelism across nouns or noun phrases:

"When doing this job, you should consider not only the product but also the process."

"When doing this job, you should consider not only the product but also enjoying your work."

In the first sentence, parallelism can be seen across the nouns "product" and "process." This parallelism is required by the "not only....but also" construction. The second sentence is grammatically incorrect, because what follows the "but also" is not a noun or noun phrase.

"Not only…but also" is an example of a correlative conjunction. Other examples include the following:

> both…and
> either…or
> just as…so
> neither…nor
> the more…the more
> whether…or

The use of any of these correlative conjunctions will require parallelism in what gets modified. Thus, the first sentence below is grammatically incorrect, while the second one is correct:

"Either you will love this movie, or obtain a refund for your ticket."

"Either you will love this movie, or you will be refunded for your ticket."

In Chapter 4, the use of parallelism to create rhetorical effects is discussed.

AGREEMENT

Grammatical agreement refers to relationships between words and/or phrases that are marked by changes in particular words. For example, in the sentence "Harriet, Letitia, and John are leaving," it is necessary to use the verb "are" rather than "is" because the subject of the sentence consists of more than one individual. This sentence illustrates agreement between subject and verb. If Harriet were the only person leaving, we would need to say that Harriet "is" leaving, so that we could maintain subject-verb agreement in the sentence.

As you can see, agreement is not the same as parallelism. Parallelism requires that different words or phrases reflect the same grammatical category – e.g., in the example above, the word that appears after "Harriet, Letitia, and…" should also be a proper noun or noun phrase. In contrast, agreement requires that whatever verb follows the list of people should take on plural form.

Types of agreement include agreement in number, gender, person, and case.

Agreement in Number

Agreement in number refers to the relationship between nouns, pronouns, verbs, and other parts of speech in a sentence according to whether the nouns are singular or plural. The general rule is that the pertinent words should agree in number. For example, consider the following pair of sentences:

"The bedroom was filled with toys."

"The bedrooms were filled with toys."

The sentences above are grammatically correct, in part because in each sentence there is agreement in number between subject and verb. The first sentence pertains to a single bedroom and thus the verb "was" is appropriate. The second sentence refers to more than one bedroom, and thus the plural form "were" is needed.

There are several kinds of agreement in number. For example, in each of the following sentences, you can see agreement in number between pronouns that have the same reference:

"His anger was revealed by the way he threw plates against the wall."

"Their anger was revealed by the way they threw plates against the wall."

In the first sentence above, "his" and "he" are singular, while in the second sentence, "their" and "they" are plural.

The following examples illustrate agreement in number between a quantifier and noun:

"I carried a box up the stairs."

"I carried some boxes up the stairs."

The examples below show agreement between nouns:

"Many families live in small houses."

"The students all sat down in their seats."

In practice, you may need to look closely in order to determine whether or not there is agreement in number. For example, consider the following sentence:

"Some dogs walk around in a small circle before lying down in their bed."

The sentence above is grammatically incorrect, because the subject ("some dogs") is plural but the final noun, "bed," is singular. The following sentence is incorrect for essentially the same reason:

"At the teacher's request, Yolanda, Crystal, Rebekah, and Sheronica all sat down in their seat."

In the sentence above, the subject ("Yolanda, Crystal, Rebekah, and Sheronica") is plural, and thus the word "seat" should be plural as well. (In the extremely unlikely event that Yolanda, Crystal, Rebekah, and Sheronica share one seat, it would be appropriate to refer to them as sitting down in their "seat." However, if each of these students has just one assigned seat, as is typically the case in a classroom, reference should be made to them sitting down in their "seats.")

Following is another sentence that is grammatically incorrect owing to a lack of agreement in number:

"If a person wants to do well in school, they should study hard."

In the sentence above, "person" is singular, and thus a singular pronoun should be used, as in the following grammatically correct revision:

"If a person wants to do well in school, he or she should study hard."

Particular caution is required in evaluating agreement when quantifiers such as the following are used:

all	many
each	most
every	much
few	no
little	some

For example, see if you can determine which of the following sentences is correct and which is incorrect:

"All drivers should glance at their tires periodically."

"Every driver should glance at their tires periodically."

The first sentence above is grammatically correct, in part because the plural subject ("all drivers") is in agreement with the pronoun ("their").

The second sentence above is incorrect, because the subject ("every driver") is singular, but the pronoun ("their") is plural. Following are two grammatically correct revisions of this sentence:

"Every driver should glance at his or her tires periodically."

"All drivers should glance at their tires periodically."

Notice that words like "each," "either," "every," and "everyone" seem to refer to more than one person, but they are in fact singular. Thus, the following sentence is grammatically correct in its use of the singular pronoun "his":

"Either John or Ricardo will be describing his science fair project at the end of class today."

Agreement in Gender

Writers are expected to use gender-neutral language, unless they are referring specifically to one gender. Thus, it is acceptable to write "All men should serve their country" if one specifically intends to target men. However, one should not write "Everyone should serve his country" if one happens to be referring to everyone of both sexes. In this case, one should choose a form or expression that reflects the gender-inclusiveness of the term "everyone," as in the following examples:

"Everyone should serve his or her country."

"All people should serve their countries."

(Notice, as per the earlier discussion of agreement in number, that because "everyone" is singular, the phrase "his or her" is used in the first sentence, while the pronoun "their" is used in the second sentence because "all people" is plural.)

The previous two examples illustrate that agreement in gender is required between the subject of a sentence ("everyone" and "all people") and the pronouns associated with the subject.

The requirement of gender neutrality can create grammatical difficulties in some cases. To return to an earlier example, suppose that a teacher informs her students that John may describe his science fair project at the end of class that day, but that if John is reluctant or does not appear to be ready, Mary may describe her science fair project at the end of the class instead. Each of the following descriptions of the situation is grammatically incorrect:

"Either John or Mary will be describing his science fair project at the end of class today."

"Either John or Mary will be describing her science fair project at the end of class today."

"Either John or Mary will be describing their science fair project at the end of class today."

"Either John or Mary will be describing his or her science fair project at the end of class today."

To describe this particular situation, the writer's only recourse would be to use a different sentence structure, as in the grammatically correct example below:

"Either John will be describing his science fair project at the end of class today, or Mary will be describing her project at that time."

Agreement in Person

Agreement in person pertains to the relationship between pronouns and verbs that are used to convey first, second, or third person in either singular or plural form. Generally speaking, pronouns and verbs should agree in person.

The fact that a verb is being used to convey first, second, or third person is often signaled by the particular pronoun that is used. Thus, we say "I go" to indicate first person singular and "you go" to indicate second person singular. (Nouns are always third person.) The form of the verb may change, as in the following sentence, which illustrates first, second, and third person usage, respectively:

"I am American, you are English, and she is Australian."

In other cases, the form of the verb does not change, and it is the pronoun or noun that signals person. For example:

"We are Americans, you two are English, and they are Australian."

Regardless of how person is conveyed, pronouns or nouns and the verbs they are associated with must agree in person. Thus, the following sentence is grammatically incorrect:

"If a student wants to do well in this class, you have to know when to approach the teaching assistants for guidance."

In this sentence, the phrase "a student" is third person, and it fails to agree with "you," which is second person. Each of the following is a grammatically correct revision of this sentence:

"If a student wants to do well in this class, he or she has to know when to approach the teaching assistants for guidance."

"If you want to do well in this class, you have to know when to approach the teaching assistants for guidance."

Notice that in order to determine whether the requirement of agreement in person has been met, you will need to determine which verb is associated with which pronoun or noun. Consider the following sentence:

"The captain, like his soldiers, is nervous."

This sentence can be considered grammatically correct. Although you might be tempted to say that "are" should be used in place of "is," the subject of the sentence is a singular noun ("the captain") and thus a third-person singular form of the verb ("is") must be used in order for the sentence to reflect agreement in person.

Agreement in Case

Case refers to the grammatical function of a pronoun or noun in a sentence. Three cases are typically marked in English sentences: Nominative, Accusative/Dative, and Possessive. Agreement in case refers to usage of the correct pronoun or noun form associated with each case.

In the nominative case, a pronoun or noun serves as the subject of a sentence, as illustrated by the words "I" and "we" in the sentences below:

"I was paid by the curator."

"We ate more mashed potatoes."

In the accusative/dative case, a pronoun or noun serves as the direct or indirect object in a sentence, as illustrated by the words "me" and "ourselves" in the following sentences:

"The curator paid me for the statue."

"We helped ourselves to more mashed potatoes."

In the possessive case, a pronoun or noun has a relationship of possession to another noun in the sentence, as illustrated by the words "my" and "our" in the sentences below:

"The curator paid for my statue."

"The waiter filled our plates with mashed potatoes."

In the examples above, a different pronoun is used for each case. Nouns do not change across nominative and accusative cases, but their form changes in the possessive case. Usually, possessive case is created by adding an apostrophe followed by the letter "s" to the end of a noun. Thus, the following sentences are grammatically correct with respect to the proper noun "Nicky":

"Nicky owns a hybrid car." (Nominative.)

"I bought Nicky a hybrid car." (Accusative.)

"This is Nicky's hybrid car." (Possessive.)

In some sentences, particular caution is needed to determine whether the requirement of agreement in case has been met. For example, consider the following sentences:

"Charlonda, Bethany, and I went to the store."

"Kendra gave Charlonda, Bethany, and me a ride."

"Charlonda, Bethany, and me went to the store."

"Kendra gave Charlonda, Bethany, and I a ride."

The first sentence is grammatically correct because the subject of the sentence is "Charlonda, Bethany, and I" and the nominative form of the pronoun ("I") is correctly used.

The second sentence is also grammatically correct. Here, "Charlonda, Bethany, and me" is the direct object, and the accusative form of the pronoun ("me") is correctly used.

The third sentence is grammatically incorrect because the accusative form of the pronoun ("me") is used, but this pronoun is part of the subject and should be expressed in nominative form (i.e., "I"). This sentence illustrates a lack of agreement between a pronoun and its grammatical case.

The fourth sentence is incorrect for an analogous reason: the accusative form of the pronoun ("I") is used, but this pronoun is part of the direct object and should be expressed in accusative form (i.e., "me").

If the first two sentences do not "feel" correct, and/or the last two sentences do not "feel" incorrect, try dropping all words from the subject or direct object except for the pronoun. The grammatical correctness or incorrectness of the sentences may seem clearer, as illustrated below:

"Charlonda and I went to the store." (Correct.)

"Kendra gave me a ride." (Correct.)

"Charlonda and me went to the store." (Incorrect.)

"Kendra gave I a ride." (Incorrect.)

Non-Agreement in Tense

A form of agreement that has not been discussed thus far is the requirement that the verbs used in a sentence should be consistent in tense, as in the following examples:

"Ricky fell off the slide, skinned his knee, and bumped his head."

"When you see him, tell him that I want an explanation."

"Lily is here and she feels hungry."

In the first sentence, simple past tense is used for each verb ("fell," "skinned," and "bumped"), while in the second and third sentences, present tense is used for each verb ("see," "tell," "want," "is" and "feels").

At the same time, verb tense will not always be consistent within sentences that are grammatically correct. Changes in tense typically occur across rather than within clauses, and there are many reasons why these changes are needed. For example, the writer may shift tenses simply because he or she is shifting focus to a different time period, as in the following sentences:

"Ricky fell off the slide, skinned his knee, and bumped his head, and now the tears are flowing."

"When you see him, tell him that I want an explanation for what happened yesterday."

"Lily is full now but she will feel hungry soon."

Causal explanations sometimes require a shift in tense, as in the following examples:

"Bob is in the living room because he had gotten tired of waiting in the hallway."

"Lily will feel hungry soon because she has not eaten lunch."

Another reason for shifting tense is that the infinitive form of a verb will be used in present tense when combined with another verb, regardless of the tense of the other verb. For example:

"Demetria saw Jim's new hat and began to laugh."

In this sentence, "saw" and "began" are simple past tense forms, but the in the infinitive phrase, "laugh" appears in its present tense form.

One more of the many possible examples is that in both scientific and narrative writing, a writer may use simple past tense when describing a sequence of events in chronological order, but switch to present tense when describing characteristics that are more generally true and not simply part of the chronology. Consider, for example, the following sentences:

"The first time Karima visited Shanghai, she looked around and noticed that the architecture in this great city reflects Western influences."

"The first time Karima visited Shanghai, she looked into a small mirror and noticed a pigeon reflected in the glass."

Both sentences relate an anecdote using simple past tense ("visited," "looked," "noticed"). However, in the first sentence, the present tense verb "reflects" is used because the characteristics of the architecture that suggest Western influence have always been part of that architecture. In other words, the architecture did not begin to reflect Western influences when Karima looked at it, only to lose those influences when she looked away. Rather, the architecture always reflects those influences. In the second sentence, however, the reflection of the pigeon is a momentary occurrence, and thus the past tense verb "reflected" is used. The pigeon is not always reflected in the glass. Rather, it was reflected for a moment, and the writer would indicate what happened next by means of other past tense verbs (e.g., "The pigeon then flapped its wings, rose into the air, and vanished.").

DICTION

Diction refers to choice of words. In Chapter 4, the contribution of diction to a writer's style, tone, and persuasiveness are discussed. For example, describing a particular person as a "criminal" as opposed to a "thief" reflects a difference in diction that may affect what the reader infers about the writer's attitudes. However, neither term is necessarily inaccurate. Diction is also important in the sense that the wrong word choice can render a sentence incorrect or ambiguous. The use of correct diction is the focus of this section.

In many cases, a writer's diction will be incorrect because the writer has confused words that are similar in form and/or meaning. Following are some of the more common examples of words that are confused:

Effect vs. Affect

The word "effect" can be used as a noun or a verb. As a noun, it refers to an outcome, as in the following sentences:

"Adding fertilizer to the garden had a positive effect on the gardenias."

"The effects of Internet addiction on children's well-being is a topic that psychologists are beginning to study."

As a verb, "effect" refers to creation of a change, as in the following sentence:

"The prime minister attempted to effect a change in public attitudes toward his family."

The word "affect" can also be used as a noun or as a verb. As a verb, it refers to the cause of a particular outcome, as in the following sentences:

"Exhaustion began to affect the boxer's ability to defend himself."

"A well-made movie always affects me emotionally."

Most sentences can be expressed using either "effect" or "affect," but the writer must be careful to use each term correctly. For example:

"Prior generations of flame retardants are known to affect endocrine system functioning."

"Prior generations of flame retardants are known to have an effect on endocrine system functioning."

In sum, when your behavior "affects" someone else, you can say that you have "affected" them, or had an "effect" on them, or "effected" a change in them. However, it is grammatically incorrect to say that you have "effected" someone else, or that you have had an "affect" on them or otherwise "affected" a change in them.

Imply vs. Insinuate vs. Infer

To imply is to hint at something. To insinuate is to hint at something negative. To infer is to draw a conclusion about something based on evidence. Thus, the following sentences are grammatically correct:

"The policeman implied that Brenda had committed the crime."

"The policeman's remark implied that Brenda had committed the crime."

"The policeman insinuated that Brenda had committed the crime."

"John inferred from the policeman's remark that Brenda had committed the crime."

In sum, when evidence "implies" a particular conclusion, someone who examines the evidence may "infer" that conclusion. However, the evidence does not "infer" the conclusion. When someone "insinuates" something negative by means of a remark, you may "infer" what the other person means. However, that other person has not "inferred" something. Rather, you are the one who has made the inference. Likewise, you may "imply" that you know a secret, and someone else may "infer" that you know it. However, in this situation you could not be said to "infer" that you know a secret, nor could someone else "imply" that you do.

Farther vs. Further

"Farther" and "further" are both comparative terms, but their meanings are different and thus they are not interchangeable. "Farther" indicates a difference in physical distance, while "further" is an abstract term that suggests a difference in quantity or extent. Thus, each of the following sentences is grammatically correct:

"Ruth consistently hit the ball farther than any other batter of his time."

"After finishing the lecture, Smith discussed auditory development further with her students."

"Brianna is further along in her studies than Bettina will ever be."

The term "further" can also be used to mean "foster" and "in addition," as illustrated by the first and second uses of the term, respectively, in the passage below:

"One of the main purposes of a high quality child care program is to further children's intellectual development; further, such programs are designed to promote children's physical, social, and emotional well-being."

Than vs. Then

"Than" is a conjunction that is used when making comparisons, as in the following sentences:

"Bolt has consistently run faster than any of his competitors."

"It is later than you think."

"Than" is always preceded by a comparative adjective or adjectival phrase. Often, the adjective has an "-er" suffix and immediately precedes "than," as illustrated in each of the examples above. However, in some cases neither condition is observed. In the sentence below, for example, the comparative adjective ("more") does not have an "-er" suffix, and it does not immediately precede "than."

"The governor seems more peaceful this year than she was last year."

"Then" is not used to make comparisons. It has four possible meanings, none of which is interchangeable with "than." Specifically, "then" could mean "at that point in time," "next," "in addition," or something roughly synonymous with "therefore." Each of these four meanings is illustrated in turn by the second through fifth sentences in the passage below:

"The late 1960's were difficult years for him. He was a high school student then in the most academically rigorous prep school in the state. Each day he would suffer through his classes and then return home to the tedium of homework. And then there were the chores his mother pestered him to do. He felt that if she would just stop asking him to do so many chores, then he could have concentrated more on the homework and done a better job."

Who vs. That vs. Which

As relative pronouns, "who," "that," and "which" serve similar functions in sentences. However, "who" refers to people, while "that" and "which" refer to groups, events, and things, as in the following examples:

"Celia is a person who believes strongly in community development."

"DCP is an organization that promotes community development."

"DCP, which is the organization where Celia works, has long promoted community development."

As relative pronouns, "that" and "which" are used in a similar way. The key difference is that "that" is used with restrictive clauses, while "which" is used with nonrestrictive clauses.

A restrictive clause limits the identity of the subject to which it refers. For example, in the second sentence above, the clause "that promotes community development" limits the identity of the organization it refers to. DCP is not just any organization, in other words. According to this sentence, it is an organization that engages in a certain kind of activity, i.e., the promotion of community development.

A nonrestrictive clause provides further information about the subject to which it refers, but it does not provide essential, limiting information about the nature of the subject. In the third sentence above, the clause "which is the organization where Celia works" tells us something about DCP, but this detail is not part of the essential nature of the organization. The fact that Celia works there does not limit the identity of the organization—it does not clearly distinguish the organization from others.

Another way to think about the distinction between restrictive and nonrestrictive clauses is to consider what would happen if they were dropped from the sentences in which they appear. Deleting a restrictive clause would make the sentence vague or difficult to understand, while deleting a nonrestrictive clause would not undermine the understandability of the sentence. This point can be illustrated by looking back at the previous example sentences concerning community development and DCP. The first two sentences contain restrictive clauses, because dropping those clauses would make the sentences vague (i.e., "Celia is a person" and "DCP is an organization"). The third sentence contains a nonrestrictive clause, because dropping that clause would not undermine the meaning of the sentence. That is, the resulting sentence would be: "DCP has long promoted community development."

The distinction between restrictive and nonrestrictive clauses is not always clear cut. In some cases the distinction reflects something about the writer's intentions. Consider the following two sentences that might be found near the beginning of a media article or essay:

"DCP is a community development organization that has been discussed frequently in the local news."

"DCP, which is the organization where Barack Obama worked before attending law school, has long promoted community development."

In the first sentence, the fact that DCP has been discussed frequently in the local news is not very limiting—DCP presumably does not exist for the purpose of being discussed in the local media, and it is probably not the only organization that the local media frequently discusses. Thus, this part of the sentence says little about the nature of DCP. Moreover, by dropping what appears to be the restrictive clause ("has been discussed frequently in the local news"), the sentence is still meaningful and conveys something essential about the organization. However, if the writer's purpose in the essay is to describe the kinds of local media attention that DCP has received, then the clause in question does function in a restrictive way. Media attention is part of what distinguishes the organization, according to the journalist.

In the second sentence, the fact that Barack Obama worked for DCP is quite distinctive, given that Mr. Obama is a highly recognizable public figure. However, the fact that Mr. Obama worked for DCP prior to attending law school is not part of the essential nature of the organization. Presumably the main purpose of the organization—to promote community development—would have been carried out regardless of whether or not Mr. Obama had spent time working for the organization. Thus the "which" clause in the second sentence merely provides interesting information about DCP rather than further details about the nature of the organization. Moreover, removing this clause does not prevent the sentence from being understandable. Thus, the clause in question is a nonrestrictive clause.

Who vs. Whom

"Who" and "whom" are both relative pronouns that refer to people. However, "who" is used in reference to a subject, while "whom" refers to an object. The distinction is illustrated in the following grammatically correct sentences:

"Cecilia is the person who I love the most."

"To whom did she send that last letter?"

There are two simple tests that can be used to determine whether "who" or "whom" is the appropriate pronoun to use in a particular sentence. Both tests are based on the assumption that because "who" refers to a subject, it will be synonymous with a nominative pronoun ("he" or "she"). But because "whom" refers to an object, it will be synonymous with an accusative/dative pronoun ("him" or "her").

The first test is that if the sentence is a statement, you can substitute "he" (or "she") and then "him" (or "her") for the pronoun and check which result is grammatically correct. For example:

"Cecilia is the person [who or whom?] I love the most."

"She is the person who I love the most."

"Her is the person who I love the most."

As you can see, the second sentence is grammatically correct but the third one is not. Because the grammatically correct substitution for "Cecilia" is "she," the correct relative pronoun will be "who."

The second test is that if the sentence is a question, you can imagine an answer in which "he" (or "she") and then "him" (or "her") is part of the answer, and then check which result is grammatically correct. For example:

"To [who or whom?] did she send that last letter?"

"She sent that last letter to he."

"She sent that last letter to him."

This time, the third sentence is grammatically correct but the second one is not. Because the appropriate pronoun is "him" rather than "he," the correct relative pronoun will be "whom."

There vs. Their vs. They're

"There," "their," and "they're" have different meanings and are thus not interchangeable. The primary meaning of the noun "there" is "that place." The pronoun "their" refers to something that belongs to or is in some way part of others. "They're" is a contraction that stands for "they are." Thus, the following sentences are grammatically correct:

"We should go there tonight for dinner."

"We should go to their house tonight for dinner."

"We should go to their house tonight. They're serving dinner."

Lie vs. Lay

One meaning of the verb "lie" is to recline. One meaning of the verb "lay" is to put or place. Thus, the following sentences are grammatically correct:

"I want to lie down on the bed."

"I want to lay my coat on the bed."

Strictly speaking, it would be incorrect to say, "I want to lay down on the bed" or "I want to lie my coat on the bed."

Confusion sometimes arises from the fact that the simple past test of "lie" is "lay," while the simple past tense of lay is "laid." Thus, the following sentences are grammatically correct:

"I lay on the bed."

"I laid my coat on the bed."

As you can see, the sentence "I lay on the bed" means that at some point in the past, I was reclining on the bed. It does not mean that I am now reclining on the bed. In order to indicate that I am now reclining on the bed, I must say, "I lie on the bed."

You can also see that the sentence "After work I lay my coat on the bed" does not mean that at some specific point in the past, I placed my coat on the bed after work. Rather, it means that I generally do so. If I want to indicate that I placed my coat on the bed after work one day (e.g., last Monday), I must say, "After work I laid my coat on the bed."

The present progressive verb tense indicates ongoing action, as in the phrases "I am singing" or "she is still sleeping." The present progressive form of lie is "lying," while the present progressive form of lay is "laying." Thus, the following sentences are grammatically correct:

"Hank is lying in bed."

"Hank is laying the coat on the bed."

The past participle tense indicates a previously completed action, as in the phrase "I have finished reading Bellow's last novel." The past participle of "lie" is "lain," while the past participle of "lay" is "laid." Thus, the following sentences are grammatically correct:

"I have lain in bed until noon more than once in my life."

"I have laid the coat on the bed already."

Other Commonly Confused Terms

A number of terms are commonly confused because they are similar or identical in pronunciation. Following are some examples.

"Accept" means "to receive," while "except" means "to exclude." Thus, one could say that Juan invited all of his friends to his birthday party, and that everyone accepted except for Steve, who has to work on the evening of Juan's party.

The term "elicit" means "to draw out," while the term "illicit" refers to something illegal. Thus, a teacher might speak very gently and carefully to a student in order to elicit information about illicit activities that have been carried out by one of the student's classmates.

The "capitol" is a building where a government is housed, while the "capital" is the locality (e.g., the city) where the government resides. Thus, one could say that in Rhode Island, the capitol building is located near downtown Providence, which is the state capital.

To "flaunt" is to show off, while to "flout" means to show contempt. Thus, a middle school student who wishes to flaunt his toughness might talk back to a teacher and otherwise flout class rules.

The term "principal" refers to something or someone that is important, while a "principle" is an important abstract truth. Thus, one could claim that the fundamental principle of management is to determine who has the principal authority for making decisions about hiring and firing.

"Stationary" means "standing still," while "stationery" refers to writing paper. Most people are stationary while writing something on stationery.

A "compliment" consists of verbal praise, while a "complement" is something that completes or enhances something else. Thus, one could speak of how Rachel complimented Matthias on his understanding of how white wine complements a good meal.

"Altogether" means "entirely" or "on the whole," while "all together" means "gathered in one place." Thus, one could say that altogether, John approves of the plan to bring the family all together at the restaurant next week.

"Discreet" means "tactful," while "discrete" means "separate." Thus, a psychiatrist who happens to encounter one of his patients in the grocery store will greet the patient discreetly, without referring to any of their private discussions in his office, because the psychiatrist is obligated to keep his professional interactions with patients discrete from any accidental personal contact with them.

A "disinterested" person is impartial, while an "uninterested" person is unengaged or bored. Thus, we hope that judges will be disinterested concerning the cases that they hear but not uninterested in those cases.

MODIFIERS

A modifier is any clause, phrase or word in a sentence that provides descriptive information about another part of the sentence. Among individual words, the two main types of modifiers are adjectives and adverbs.

Adjectives

Adjectives are words that modify nouns and pronouns. Typically, adjectives answer the following questions: What kind of? How many? Which? For example, in the sentence below, "long," "three," and "final" are adjectives:

"By the end of our surprisingly long hike, my brother had three blisters and could only walk slowly up the final hill."

The rules for use of adjectives are generally straightforward. However, certain adjectives can only be used with either count or mass nouns.

Count nouns are those that can be counted, as the name suggests, and thus written in plural form. Examples include "house," "birthday," "cloud," "person," "dynasty," and "idea."

Mass nouns cannot be counted. Examples include "sand," "grass," "food," "air," "money," and "peace." Whereas you can speak of one house, two houses, and so on, you cannot speak of one grass, two grasses, et cetera. Mass nouns can only be counted by means of some other noun that identifies a discrete unit. Thus, you can speak of one field of grass, two fields of grass, and so on.

Some adjectives, such as "some," "any," and "enough," can be used to modify both count and mass nouns. Others can only be used with one type of noun.

For example, "many" can only modify count nouns, while "much" can only modify mass nouns. Thus, the sentences below are grammatically correct:

"She keeps many horses in the barn."

"She keeps much hay in the barn too."

Likewise, "few" can only modify count nouns, while "little" can only modify mass nouns. Thus, the sentences below are grammatically correct as well:

"Her best friends only own a few horses."

"Her best friends keep very little hay in their barns."

Thus, it would be grammatically incorrect to refer to "much horses," "many hays," or "few hays." Reference to "little horses" is grammatically acceptable only when referring to size rather than quantity.

Adverbs

Adverbs are words that modify verbs, other adverbs, adjectives, and entire clauses. Typically, adverbs answer the question: How? For example, in the sentence below, "surprisingly" and "slowly" are adverbs:

"By the end of our surprisingly long hike, my brother had three blisters and could only walk slowly up the final hill."

Adjectives and adverbs are not interchangeable, although in many cases an adverb can be formed by adding the suffix -*ly* to an adjective, as in the following examples:

"He is a quick learner." (Adjectival form.)

"He learns quickly." (Adverbial form.)

"The end of the music was unexpected." (Adjectival form.)

"The end of the music came unexpectedly." (Adverbial form.)

Not all adverbs end in -*ly*, of course. Compare the following two sentences:

"The cat smells good."

"The cat smells well."

In the first sentence, "good" is an adjective that modifies the noun "cat." In the second sentence, "well" is an adverb that modifies the verb "smell." The second sentence indicates (somewhat awkwardly) that the cat has a good sense of smell. These two sentences highlight the importance of recognizing what word or phrase in a sentence is being modified when distinguishing between adverbs and adjectives. To take another example, compare the following sentences:

"I am sure he can cook the soup without making a mess in the kitchen."

"Surely he can cook the soup without making a mess in the kitchen."

In the first sentence, "sure" is an adjective because it modifies the initial pronoun "I." In the second sentence, "surely" is an adverb because it modifies the remainder of the sentence.

Misplaced Modifiers

The rules of syntax allow some flexibility in the location of a modifier in a sentence. For example, as you read the following sentences, notice how the location of the adjective "hot" changes in relation to the noun that it modifies ("summer"):

"We had a hot summer this year."

"The summer was hot this year."

"How hot the summer was this year!"

The following examples show flexibility in the location of an adverb ("quickly") in relation to the verb that it modifies ("found"):

"He found the missing keys quickly."

"Quickly he found the missing keys."

"He quickly found the missing keys."

Although syntactic rules allow some flexibility in the locations of modifiers, there are still many rules. Misplaced modifiers result in sentences that are misleading, ambiguous or incoherent.

A general rule is that modifiers should be close to what they modify. For example, consider the following sentence:

"The weather forecast called for heavy rain yesterday."

This sentence appears to state that according to some weather forecast, heavy rain was expected yesterday. However, if the writer meant that yesterday the weather forecast predicted heavy rain at some point in the future, then the modifier ("yesterday") should be located closer to the subject, as in the following examples:

"Yesterday the weather forecast called for heavy rain."

"The weather forecast yesterday called for heavy rain."

"Yesterday's weather forecast called for heavy rain."

Even when a modifier is right next to the word it modifies, the meaning may be compromised if it is on the wrong side. For example, suppose that Johnson arrives at a party and then asks nearly everyone else in attendance for money. Compare the following two descriptions of this unpleasant situation:

"Johnson asked almost everyone at the party to borrow money."

"Johnson almost asked everyone at the party to borrow money."

Although both sentences are grammatically correct, the first sentence accurately conveys the situation. However, in the second sentence, the misplacement of the modifier "almost" suggests incorrectly that Johnson did not ask others for money. Rather, it suggests that he considered asking everyone for a loan, but chose not to, or was otherwise prevented from doing so.

Notice that misplaced modifiers could consist of entire phrases rather than just words. Consider the following sentence:

"I heard that the governor decided to run for re-election while I was at Fiona's apartment."

It is not clear whether the governor made the decision to run for re-election during the time when the writer was at Fiona's apartment, or whether the writer learned while at Fiona's apartment that the governor had made this decision at some earlier time. If the latter is the case, then the sentence should be reordered as follows:

"While I was at Fiona's apartment, I heard that the governor decided to run for re-election."

Finally, here is one of Groucho Marx's more famous jokes:

"One morning I shot an elephant in my pajamas. How he got into my pajamas I'll never know."

This joke relies on the misplacement of the phrase "in my pajamas" in the first sentence. What Marx should have said, had this been a true story, would be something like "One morning, while I was still in my pajamas, I shot an elephant."

Squinting and Dangling Modifiers

A squinting modifier is one that has been misplaced in such a way that it could refer to the clause that precedes it or to the one that follows. For example:

"Running on concrete surfaces quickly leads to knee damage."

Owing to the squinting modifier "quickly," this sentence could mean that running at a high rate of speed on concrete surfaces leads to knee damage, or that running on concrete surfaces will very soon lead to knee damage. The writer would need to choose between revisions such as the following:

"Running quickly on concrete surfaces leads to knee damage."

"Running on concrete surfaces will quickly lead to knee damage."

The misplaced and squinting modifiers discussed so far are problematic because they modify the wrong word or phrase, or because it is ambiguous as to what they modify. However, in each case the correct word or phrase is present in the sentence. When a sentence does not contain the word or phrase that should be modified, the modifier that is used can be called a dangling modifier. For example:

"Walking to school this morning, the mosquitoes were everywhere."

In this example, the phrase "walking to school this morning" tells us something about the person who was walking. However, that person is not identified in the sentence. As a result, the sentence seems to indicate that it was the mosquitoes who were walking to school. An acceptable revision of the sentence would need to include an appropriate subject. For example:

"Walking to school this morning, I noticed that the mosquitoes were everywhere."

"As I walked to school this morning, I noticed that the mosquitoes were everywhere."

REFERENCE

The discussions of misplaced, squinting, and dangling modifiers illustrate the need for a writer to be clear about what is referred to by the modifiers that he or she uses. More generally, the writer must be clear about the reference of all words or phrases that are used to indicate some other word or phrase.

The particular type of reference discussed in this section is pronoun reference, or the use of pronouns to refer to nouns. In the following sentence, for example, it is clear that the pronoun "he" refers to the individual named "George":

"George rushed into the room, and he looked scared."

In the following sentence, however, the reference of "he" is unclear:

"George was fighting with Quinton and he looked scared."

Unless there are contextual cues, the reader cannot tell whether "he" refers to George or Quinton. Assuming that George is the one who appeared to be scared, here are a few of the many possible ways to fix the sentence:

"George was fighting with Quinton; George looked scared".

"George, looking scared, was fighting with Quinton."

"While fighting with Quinton, George looked scared."

Pronoun reference is important when using the demonstratives "this," "that," "these," and "those."

As adjectives, demonstratives direct the reader's attention toward particular nouns, as in the sentence below:

"This bird is a robin."

"I plan to install two more of these applications."

As pronouns, demonstratives are used in place of nouns, as illustrated by the following examples:

"This is an outstanding translation of Goethe's *Faust*."

"That was quite a party!"

Confusion sometimes occurs when beginning a sentence with a demonstrative pronoun, as illustrated by the passage below:

"The surface of the brain is compressed, highly wrinkled, and covered with layers of tissue such as the meninges. This makes it difficult to visually examine features just below the surface."

In this passage, the word "this" points to whatever it is that makes it difficult to examine certain features of the brain. However, it is unclear whether "this" refers to the layers of tissue such as the meninges, or whether it refers to all of the physical characteristics of the brain described in the first sentence. Assuming the latter, here are two more suitable versions of the passage:

"The surface of the brain is compressed, highly wrinkled, and covered with layers of tissue such as the meninges. These characteristics make it difficult to visually examine features just below the surface."

"The surface of the brain is compressed, highly wrinkled, and covered with layers of tissue such as the meninges. This set of characteristics makes it difficult to visually examine features just below the surface."

PUNCTUATION

Many different types of punctuation contribute to the form and grammatical meanings of sentences.

Periods, Exclamation Points, Question Marks

The end of a sentence can be indicated by a period, an exclamation point, or a question mark.

Periods are used to end complete sentences. For example, consider the following passage:

"Johnson criticized Milton's politics. But esteemed his poetic works most highly. Especially *Paradise Lost.*"

As the first sentence is complete, the period is appropriately placed. The second two sentences are fragments, and thus setting them off by means of periods is grammatically incorrect. Generally, periods should not be used at the end of dependent clauses. Following is one possible revision of the passage that would be grammatically correct:

"Johnson criticized Milton's politics, but he esteemed his poetic works most highly. Johnson especially admired *Paradise Lost.*"

Exclamation marks are used to emphasize ideas, or to convey strong attitudes or emotions such as admiration or astonishment. For example:

"You should never hitchhike!"

"Afterwards, the truck nearly exploded!"

"He worked on his first novel for seventeen years!"

Exclamation marks can also be used for exclamations and commands, as illustrated by the following:

"Extraordinary!"

"Stop!"

Question marks are used to convey both direct questions (e.g., "What should we do today?") and rhetorical questions (e.g., "What have they ever done for me?"). However, questions can be formed without using question marks, as in the case of the indirect question. For example:

"I want to know when someone will stand up and address our concerns."

The direct form of this question would be: "I want to know: When will someone stand up and address our concerns?" Alternatively, the direct form of the question could be: "When will someone stand up and address our concerns?"

Semicolons and Colons

Two of the more common ways to divide a sentence are the semicolon and the colon.

Semicolons are used to separate independent clauses. Consider, for example, the following sentences:

"Shonte came to school today; Anna stayed home."

"I really enjoy chocolate ice cream for dessert; unfortunately, there was no ice cream left in my freezer."

In each of these sentences, what comes before the semicolon and what follows it each consists of an independent clause. As you can see, each sentence consists of exactly two independent clauses. Sentences that contain more than two independent clauses are usually divided by commas rather than semicolons (see discussion of commas below for details).

A colon is used at the end of an independent clause. There are several grammatically correct options as to what can follow the colon, including lists, explanations, quotations, and so on.

First, the clause following a colon may be a list, as in the following example:

"For the lunch special, diners can choose among three entrees: pasta salad, fried fish, or steak."

Second, the clause following the colon may be an explanation or restatement of what preceded the colon. For example:

"The immunization program was a resounding success in the village: 100% of the children were immunized."

Third, the clause following the colon may consist of a lengthy quotation, as in the following example:

"Our society suffers from too much knowledge and not enough optimism about how that knowledge can be used. Camus stated this point in a sophisticated way: 'The modern mind is in complete disarray. Knowledge has stretched itself to the point where neither the world nor our intelligence can find any foothold. It is a fact that we are suffering from nihilism.'"

Notice that in each example above, the clause preceding the colon is an independent clause and thus stands alone as a complete sentence. Thus, the following sentences are grammatically incorrect, because what precedes the colon is a dependent clause:

"My favorite foods are: pizza, chocolate, and fried cheese."

"All I know is: you can't take it with you!"

In order to make either one of the sentences above grammatically correct, the writer would need to either revise the clause preceding the colon so that it becomes an independent clause, or simply remove the colon, as in the following grammatically correct examples:

"My favorite foods are as follows: pizza, chocolate, and fried cheese."

"My favorite foods are pizza, chocolate, and fried cheese."

"All I know is this: you can't take it with you!"

"All I know is that you can't take it with you!"

Commas

The comma is the form of punctuation used most frequently within sentences. Following are four of the more important purposes that commas serve.

First, a comma can be used to separate a sequence of two or more modifiers, as in the following sentences:

"The highway was long, dark, and surprisingly narrow."

"*Moby Dick* appeared to be a long, difficult book."

In sentences like these, the comma takes the place of the word "and." For example, the second sentence above indicates that the book appeared to be both long and difficult. Strictly speaking, the presence of the comma indicates that both adjectives modify the noun. It is the book that appears to be both long and difficult, in other words. The absence of a comma between a pair of modifiers indicates that the first modifier actually modifies the second one rather than the noun. Consider, for example, the following sentence:

"All day in the lab he was a cautious, quiet employee; in the evening, however, his wild side emerged, and he lived the life of a recklessly optimistic adolescent."

In the first clause, a comma is used between "cautious" and "quiet" because both words modify the noun "employee." In the final clause, no comma is used between "reckless" and "optimistic" because only "optimistic" modifies the noun "adolescent." "Recklessly" is an adverb that modifies "optimistic." The sentence is not saying that the person is a reckless adolescent. Rather, it is saying that his optimism is reckless.

Notice how the use of the semicolon in the example sentence above illustrates the earlier discussion of semicolons.

Second, commas will be used to separate a nonrestrictive modifier from the rest of the sentence in which it appears. Recall from the earlier discussion in this chapter that a restrictive modifier describes essential information, while a nonrestrictive modifier provides information that may be important but is not quite so essential to the nature of what it modifies and could be deleted without diminishing the coherence of the sentence. Following are some examples of nonrestrictive modifiers that are set off by the use of commas:

"The next document, dated November 14, clearly indicates the man's identity."

"Although he would be flying to Paris, the most romantic city in the world, the purpose of the trip was purely business."

In the first sentence above, the phrase "dated November 14" modifies "document." In the second sentence, the phrase "the most romantic city in the world" modifies "Paris." This phrase is actually an appositive. An appositive is a noun or noun phrase that renames or otherwise identifies an associated noun. Here is another example:

"On that morning his wife, Mrs. Jane Doe, checked into a downtown hotel and went straight to her room."

In this second sentence, "Mrs. Jane Doe" is the appositive for "his wife." Notice that the second sentence could have been rearranged as follows in order to make "his wife" the appositive:

"On that morning Mrs. Jane Doe, his wife, checked into a downtown hotel and went straight to her room."

In each of these sentences, commas are used to divide the noun from the appositive, and the appositive from the rest of the sentence. Notice, however, that not all appositives require commas. For example:

"It was Shaw's play *Major Barbara* that we saw together last spring."

In this sentence, the name of the play is the appositive for the noun "play," but no commas are needed.

Third, when a sentence begins with a dependent clause, and the sentence is sufficiently long, a comma will be used to divide the dependent clause from the rest of the sentence, as in the following examples:

"After a long and sleepless night, he roused himself and got ready for work."

"If you suspect that an insurance company is disreputable, you should avoid buying a policy from that company."

If there is more than one dependent clause, a comma will be used to divide each one from the rest. For example, the following sentence consists of three dependent clauses followed by an independent clause:

"If you visit the downtown area, tour the arts district, or swim in the lake, you should be careful."

Finally, notice that for short sentences beginning with a dependent clause a comma may not be needed, as in the following examples:

"After church they went out for brunch."

"In time governments may gain more humanity."

Fourth, as noted earlier, a comma should be used in a compound sentence (i.e., one that consists of two or more independent clauses) in order to separate the independent clauses. For example:

"The violist stood and stretched, but she still felt a bit of stiffness in her back."

Recall that a semicolon can also be used to divide independent clauses. The difference is that a semicolon must be used if there is no conjunction between the clauses, while a comma must be used if there is. Thus one can write, "The violist stood and stretched; she still felt a bit of stiffness in her back." However, the following two sentences would be grammatically *incorrect*:

"The violist stood and stretched, she still felt a bit of stiffness in her back."

"The violist stood and stretched; but she still felt a bit of stiffness in her back."

The grammatically correct version of this sentence ("The violist stood and stretched, but she still felt a bit of stiffness in her back.") reflects a common type of sentence that consists of independent clause-comma-independent clause. Notice that while a sentence consisting of dependent clause-comma-independent clause is also grammatically correct, a sentence consisting of independent-clause-comma-dependent clause will typically be incorrect. Thus the first sentence below is grammatically correct, but the second sentence is grammatically incorrect:

"After standing and stretching, the violist still felt a bit of stiffness in her back." (Dependent clause-comma-independent clause—correct.)

"The violist stood and stretched, but still felt a bit of stiffness in her back." (Independent clause-comma-dependent clause—incorrect.)

What would make the second sentence grammatically correct is either the inclusion of the word "she" in the dependent clause in order to make it an independent clause, or the removal of the comma. These two grammatically correct versions of the sentence are illustrated below:

"The violist stood and stretched, but she still felt a bit of stiffness in her back."

"The violist stood and stretched but still felt a bit of stiffness in her back."

Finally, notice that the rules for using commas to separate independent clauses in compound sentences are the same when the sentences contain more than two independent clauses, as illustrated by the following sentence:

"The violist stood and stretched, but she still felt a bit of stiffness in her back, and her neck still ached after that evening's performance."

Apostrophes and Possessives

Apostrophes are used for two different purposes: to create contractions such as "don't," "could've," and "let's," and to mark the possessive case, as shown in the following sentences:

"This is John's book."

"Nature's path is one of mystery and beauty."

"The administration's position on this matter is quite clear."

The possessive form of a singular noun is usually created by adding an apostrophe and then an "s" to the end of the noun, as in the examples above. When a noun is plural, the possessive is created by adding the apostrophe after the "s," as you can see in the following example:

"The performance of any team is ultimately the players' responsibility."

There are some exceptions to the rule for plurals. For example, "children" and "men" are both plural, but the possessive forms are created by adding an apostrophe and then an "s" to the end of each word ("children's," "men's), as if they were singular.

Possessive pronouns constitute an important exception to the rules concerning use of apostrophes and other changes to indicate possession. Possessive pronouns include the following:

my	hers
mine	its
your	our
yours	their
his	theirs
her	whose

When these pronouns are used as modifiers, they do not change. For example:

"Everyone wondered where she left her book."

"This is their first trip to Nicaragua."

The forms of most of these pronouns change when they are used on their own. For example:

"This is my book."

"This book is mine."

"My suitcase weighs nine pounds; how heavy is your suitcase?"

"My suitcase weighs nine pounds; how heavy is yours?"

As these examples illustrate, "my" becomes "mine" when used by itself, while "you" becomes "yours." In addition, "her" becomes "hers" and "their" becomes "theirs." "His" and "its" do not change.

"Its" and "it's" are commonly confused. "It's" is a contraction for "It is." "Its" is the possessive pronoun. Compare the following two sentences:

"My old car still sounds ragged when I start it up, and so I think its time for me to look at it's carburetor."

"My old car still sounds ragged when I start it up, and so I think it's time for me to look at its carburetor."

Because the writer means to say that "it is" time to examine the car's carburetor, the first sentence contains two grammatical errors ("its" and "it's"), but the second sentence is grammatically correct.

How to Approach Conventions of Standard Written English Questions on the CLEP Exams

All of the questions in the Conventions of Standard Written English section have the same format. These questions consist of individual, stand-alone sentences in which certain parts are underlined. For example:

A person <u>can become</u> very <u>susceptible to</u> colds if <u>they do</u> not get <u>enough</u>
           A   B   C   D

rest. <u>No error</u>
      E

Your task is to choose the underlined part of the sentence that is *incorrect*. Not factually incorrect, that is, but incorrect with respect to grammar and other aspects of language discussed in this chapter. If there is no mistake in the sentence, you should choose option E. In the sentence above, the correct answer is C. The subject of the sentence ("a person") is singular, and thus a singular form of the verb phrase (e.g., "he or she does") should have been used. (You are not asked for revisions in the Conventions of Standard Written English section.)

Questions in the Conventions of Standard Written English section will test your knowledge of the skills discussed in this chapter. In addition, some of the skills discussed in chapter 2 will be tested in this section, and vice versa.

The directions you can expect to see for the Conventions of Standard Written English section are reproduced here from the CLEP College Composition/ College Composition Modular Examination Guide:

"The following sentences test your knowledge of grammar, usage, diction (choice of words) and idiom. Note that some sentences are correct, and no sentence contains more than one error.

"Read each sentence carefully, paying particular attention to the underlined portions. You will find that the error, if there is one, is underlined. Assume that elements of the sentence that are not underlined are correct and cannot be changed. In choosing answers, follow the requirements of standard written English.

"If there is an error, select the one underlined part that must be changed to make the sentence correct.

If there is no error, select 'No error.'"

Thus, for Conventions of Standard Written English questions, your task is to look for errors. As you consider each underlined portion of the sentence in turn, you can rule out those that reflect correct grammar and usage. However, it may be best if you read the entire sentence first before ruling out options, as the correctness of some options cannot be determined without examining other parts of a sentence. You do not have unlimited time, of course. But few of the sentences will be extremely lengthy, and in some cases you might even be able to spot an error as you read before systematically weighing each option.

Sample CLEP Questions

The questions provided in this section draw upon the skills discussed throughout this chapter. The format of the questions is exactly what you will find in the Conventions of Standard Written English section of the CLEP College Composition and College Composition Modular exams. Here we will work through the questions together.

Consider first this short and relatively simple sentence:

<u>On Tuesday</u> the German <u>army</u> advanced, <u>the</u> Russian army <u>retreated</u>. <u>No error</u>
     A   B   C   D   E

When you first encounter this sentence, Option A might not seem to be incorrect, but you should still read further to determine whether anything else in the sentence might call for a different opening. Option B does not seem to be incorrect either, regardless of what follows. As for option D, by the time you reach the end of the sentence it should be clear that this option is not a source of error. Option C is the correct answer. Because the first clause ("On Tuesday the German army advanced") is an independent clause, it needs to be separated from the second clause by means of a semicolon or by the addition of a conjunction, as illustrated by the following sentences, each of which is grammatically correct:

"On Tuesday the German army advanced; the Russian army retreated."

"On Tuesday the German army advanced, but the Russian army retreated."

"On Tuesday the German army advanced while the Russian army retreated."

Next, consider this more elaborate sentence:

In order to <u>determine</u> whether someone <u>is eligible for</u> admission to <u>this</u> academy,
              A   B   C
our admissions officer will first check <u>their</u> credentials and administer several
                                      D
assessments. <u>No error</u>
            E

As you read through this sentence, the only option that appears to reflect an error should be option D. "Their" refers to the word "someone" in the previous clause. But because "someone" is singular, the pronoun "their" does not reflect agreement in case. Thus, D is the correct answer. The word "their" would need to be replaced by "his or her," for example, in order for the sentence to be grammatically correct.

Now consider a somewhat longer sentence:

Picasso was indispensible to the emergence of cubism, and he <u>was</u> the cubist
A
movement's <u>principle advocate</u>, but the role of other artists in the <u>movement's</u>
B   C
development should not be downplayed simply because <u>they</u> were lesser
D
geniuses than Picasso. <u>No error</u>
E

As you read through this sentence, what you will find is an error of diction rather than grammar. In option B, the word "principle" is used instead of "principal," which would mean "main" or "primary."

The next sentence is relatively simple:

Mary stayed in the car <u>while</u> John <u>went</u> to the door; <u>I</u> found <u>this</u> very
A   B   C   D
confusing. <u>No error</u>
E

Here the problem with the sentence is that the pronoun reference is unclear. "This" could refer to Mary's behavior, John's behavior, or the behavior of both individuals considered simultaneously. Thus option D is the correct answer.

Finally, a somewhat challenging sentence:

Criticism of Cheever's short stories <u>is</u> misguided, in my view, as it stems from
A
malicious <u>insinuations</u> that <u>he</u> knew nothing of life <u>beyond the suburbs</u>. <u>No error</u>
B   C   D   E

The correct answer this time is E. There are no errors in this sentence. Regarding option A, agreement is required between the verb "is" and "criticism," not between "is" and "short stories." Regarding option B, "insinuations" is an acceptable term here (as opposed to, say, "inferences"). Regarding option C, it is clear that "he" refers to "Cheever." Likewise, there is nothing ungrammatical about option D. Thus E is the correct answer.

Chapter 2

Revision Skills

In the Revision Skills section, your understanding of how to revise sentences and passages is tested. In the CLEP College Composition exam, all of the Revision Skills questions will refer to passages. In the CLEP College Composition Modular exam, most of the Revision Skills questions will refer to passages but some will refer to stand-alone sentences. In each exam, each Revision Skills question will ask you to choose the best revision to some part of a passage or sentence. All of the questions are multiple-choice and consist of five options.

The Revision Skills section is the longest of the four multiple-choice sections in the CLEP College Composition and College Composition Modular exams. To some extent, this section tests your ability to apply the skills tested in other sections of these exams. You will find that many of the skills tested in the Revision Skills section are also tested in the Conventions of Standard Written English and Rhetorical Analysis sections, which are covered in Chapters 1 and 4 of this book, respectively. Thus, you should expect that the material reviewed in any one of these chapters may be tested in a section of the CLEP exam.

The skills tested in this section are described in the College Composition/College Composition Modular Examination Guide as follows:

- Organization
- Evaluation of evidence
- Awareness of audience, tone, and purpose
- Level of detail
- Coherence between sentences and paragraphs
- Sentence variety and structure
- Main idea, thesis statements, and topic sentences
- Rhetorical effects and emphasis
- Use of language

- Evaluation of author's authority and appeal
- Evaluation of reasoning
- Consistency of point of view
- Transitions
- Sentence-level errors

Each of these skills is discussed in this chapter and/or in another chapter. (If a skill is not discussed in this chapter, you will be guided to the chapter where the discussion can be found.) The discussion of skills in this chapter will be followed by guidance on how to approach Revision Skills questions, and then some practice questions with answers and explanations.

ORGANIZATION

In writing, organization refers to the order in which information is presented. Several factors contribute to effective organization.

First, by considering the nature of the audience (i.e., the likely readers), the writer can organize the information in a way that is consistent with the audience's interests and expertise.

Second, by arranging sentences and paragraphs in a logical order, the writer can organize the information in a coherent and understandable way.

Third, by clearly introducing and later summarizing key points and themes, the writer can help the reader follow the argument that is being developed.

Fourth, by providing transitions between topics and themes, the writer can prevent the reader from becoming confused.

Fifth, by sticking to a particular type of organization, the writer can provide the reader with expectations about how various details will be organized. There are several types of organization that characterize most works of non-fiction. These include chronological, emphatic, generality, comparison, and cause-effect organization. This section includes a brief introduction to each type of organization, with emphasis on how they can be recognized. Additional examples, and the role of each type of organization in creating rhetorical effects, are given in Chapter 4.

Chronological Organization

Chronological organization consists of a sequence of events presented in order of occurrence. For example, readers should be able to quickly spot the chronological organization of the following passage:

"The United States became a free and sovereign nation following a number of interrelated events. First, European explorers discovered the North American continent while trying to find shorter trade routes to Asia. Then, as more and more Europeans immigrated to the New World, colonies began to form, and a desire to be self-governed increasingly took root among the populace..."

Chronological organization is suggested by the first sentence of the passage, and by key words such as "First" and "Then." Other terms that suggest chronological organization include "afterward," "beginning with," "later," "next," and so on. As you can see, someone reading a passage such as this one will almost immediately expect to see a chronology of events, and any significant departure from this form of organization will be potentially confusing.

For example, in the following version of the passage, the third sentence ("Trade is one of the contributors to cultural interdependence") is out of place, because it delves into a topic (i.e., causes of cultural independence) that is not relevant to the chronology of the passage. The third sentence would need to be deleted in a revision of the passage:

"The United States became a free and sovereign nation following a number of interrelated events. First, European explorers discovered the North American continent while trying to find shorter trade routes to Asia. Trade is one of the contributors to cultural interdependence. Then, as more and more Europeans immigrated to the New World, colonies began to form, and a desire to be self-governed increasingly took root among the populace..."

Emphatic Organization

Emphatic organization consists of information that is presented in order of importance from greatest to least importance (or vice versa). For example, readers should be able to quickly see that information in the following passage is organized in terms of greatest to least importance.

"The main reason that Jones and Yamaguchi obtained different results is that their experiments relied on slightly different methodologies for DNA sampling. The fact that Jones and Yamaguchi run different labs located in different parts of the world may have also played a role..."

Here the use of terms such as "main reason" and "also played a role" hint that emphatic organization is being used. The reader will be able to see that a methodological difference is the main reason for the two scientists having obtained different results, and that other information in the passage will cover lesser contributors and other minor details. Any departure from this organization will be confusing, because the opening sentence has already led the reader to expect that no other contributor to the difference in results will be as important as the difference in methodologies that each lab uses for its DNA sampling. For example, in the following version of the passage, the final sentence is out of place, because its assertion about what is most important contributor seems inconsistent with what is asserted in the first sentence. The final sentence would need to be deleted in a revision of the passage.

"The main reason that Jones and Yamaguchi obtained different results is that their experiments relied on slightly different methodologies for DNA sampling. The fact that Jones and Yamaguchi run different labs located in different parts of the world may have also played a role. But the most important reason for the difference in results is the use of a different statistical procedure for analyzing the data."

In the passage above, the writer may have in mind a distinction between the "main reason" (first sentence) and the "most important reason" (final sentence), but in the absence of further information the final sentence is problematic because "main" and "most important" can be construed as synonymous.

Emphatic organization does not always present information from greatest to least importance. Following is a passage that presents details in order of increasing importance:

"In order to engage in formal debate, a debater must research the topic ahead of time and become familiar with pertinent facts. More importantly, the debater must understand how to use these facts to support his or her own position. Winning a debate, however, does not rely solely on how the debater makes use of his or her knowledge. Ninety percent of communication consists of body language and delivery. Most important to successful performance in a debate is the ability to express oneself by means of passionate, persuasive delivery."

Here the reader will only gradually realize that the information is being presented in order of increasing importance. Once the reader does come to this realization, departures from this least-to-greatest importance organization will make the passage more difficult to follow. For example, consider what happens when one word—the first word of the second sentence—is changed:

"In order to engage in formal debate, a debater must research the topic ahead of time and become familiar with pertinent facts. Most importantly, the debater must understand how to use these facts to support his or her own position. Winning a debate, however, does not rely solely on how the debater makes use of his or her knowledge. Ninety percent of communication consists of body language and delivery. Most important to successful performance in a debate is the ability to express oneself by means of passionate, persuasive delivery."

The passage is now confusing because the second sentence and the final sentence each point to a different factor as most important to successful debate performance. Given that the passage places so much emphasis on delivery, it seems clear that the writer means to say that delivery is the most important factor. Thus, the best revision to the passage would be to change the phrase "Most importantly" at the outset of the second sentence. The phrase could be changed back to "More importantly," for example, or simply deleted altogether.

Generality Organization

Generality organization consists of information presented in order of specificity, either from general to specific, or from specific to general. For example, readers will quickly recognize that the following passage begins with a broad theme that becomes progressively narrower:

"Put simply, our legal system is in disarray. Criminal trials in particular drag on much longer than they should. *People v. Simpson* is a classic example. This most famous of trials began in Los Angeles County Superior Court on January 29, 1995 and lasted until October 3, 1995, a period of over seven months..."

Following a very general opening statement, each sentence in the passage above provides a more specific discussion of the idea introduced in the previous sentence. By the end of the passage, the reader will be expecting to see more details about the actual trial.

Following is the same passage rewritten in order to reflect specific-to-general organization:

"On January 29, 1995, in Los Angeles County Superior Court, the most famous trial in American history got underway. This trial, *People v. Simpson*, lasted more than seven months and represents a classic example of how criminal trials in our country drag on much longer than they should. Our legal system, put simply, is in disarray."

Here, the organization of the passage suggests that the writer may continue with a discussion of certain problems that plague our legal system.

In writing that reflects either general-to-specific or specific-to-general organization, shifts away from the organizational structure can be confusing. For example, consider the following passages:

"Put simply, our legal system is in disarray. *People v. Simpson* is a classic example. Criminal trials drag on much longer than they should. This most famous of trials began in Los Angeles County Superior Court on January 29, 1995 and lasted until October 3, 1995, a period of over seven months..."

"Put simply, our legal system is in disarray. *People v. Simpson* is a classic example. Criminal trials such as this drag on much longer than they should. This most famous of trials began in Los Angeles County Superior Court on January 29, 1995 and lasted until October 3, 1995, a period of over seven months..."

In the first passage above, the third sentence ("Criminal trials drag on much longer than they should") is out of place, because it is a general statement that appears in the midst of an increasingly specific discussion. (It is also out of place because it interferes with reference of the pronoun "This" at the outset of the fourth sentence to the subject "*People v. Simpson*" in the second sentence.) Thus, one way to revise this passage would be to relocate the third sentence so that it comes after the first one.

In the second passage above, the third sentence ("Criminal trials such as this drag on much longer than they should") may still seem somewhat out of place owing to its generality, but its placement is not a glaring problem. The reader can still see a general-to-specific progression in the passage.

Comparison Organization

Comparison organization consists of information about things or ideas that is presented in order to compare and contrast them. For example, readers will quickly spot the comparison drawn in the following passage:

"The most influential political leaders are both articulate as well as passionate. Two such figures are John F. Kennedy and Fidel Castro. Although the two men differed greatly in the ideals they represented, both had the capacity to inspire and motivate the citizens of their respective countries through their speeches and other public appearances."

The organization of this particular passage suggests that the writer will go on to focus on similarities between the two men. Other uses of comparison organization may focus on differences. In either case, substantial departure from comparative discussions may undermine the coherence of the writing. For example:

"The most influential political leaders are both articulate as well as passionate. Two such figures are John F. Kennedy and Fidel Castro. Castro is still alive but has stepped down as President of Cuba. Although the two men differed greatly in the ideals they represented, both had the capacity to inspire and motivate the citizens of their respective countries through their speeches and other public appearances."

In this passage, the third sentence ("Castro is still alive but has stepped down as President of Cuba") is informative but out of place, because the purpose of the passage is to discuss similarities between the two men. The simplest and most effective revision of this passage would be to simply remove the third sentence.

Cause-Effect Organization

Cause-effect organization consists of information about the relationship between a cause or causes and the effects produced by the cause(s). The writer may identify some cause, such as a historical event, and then discuss its various effects, or the writer may identify some effect and focus on discussing various causes. For example:

"From April 6 through April 12, 1968, rioting broke out in the city of Baltimore. The immediate cause of the rioting was the assassination of Dr. Martin Luther King, Jr. in Memphis on April 4. However, it seems unlikely that the assassination of any one figure, no matter how beloved, would have spurred rioting had there not already been decades of frustration and outrage concerning race relations in the U.S. The Baltimore Riot of 1968 reflected a sudden explosion of pent-up frustration, one that echoed rioting which had already taken place in other American cities by April 6."

In this passage, the effect is the Baltimore Riot, and the author discusses two causes (the assassination of Dr. King and deep frustration among citizens). The author also hints that rioting in other cities may have played a causal role.

The organization of this passage suggests that the author will describe and analyze causes of a particular historical event. Significant departure from this organizational structure could be confusing, as illustrated by the following version of the passage:

"From April 6 through April 12, 1968, rioting broke out in the city of Baltimore. Baltimore is a prominent eastern city. The immediate cause of the rioting was the assassination of Dr. Martin Luther King, Jr. in Memphis on April 4. However, it seems unlikely that the assassination of any one figure, no matter how beloved, would have spurred rioting had there not already been decades of frustration and outrage concerning race relations in the U.S. The Baltimore Riot of 1968 reflected a sudden explosion of pent-up frustration, one that echoed rioting which had already taken place in other American cities by April 6."

Here, the second sentence ("Baltimore is a prominent eastern city.") is somewhat out of place, because it provides a descriptive detail that does not contribute to an understanding of the causes of the Baltimore Riot of 1968. A revision of this passage would benefit most from the removal of this sentence.

AUDIENCE, PURPOSE, TONE

The audience consists of the individuals who will be reading a written work. Authors must keep their audience in mind when considering topic, depth of coverage, organization, word choice, and tone.

"Purpose" refers to the main reason for creating a written work. The author's purpose will be closely matched to the intended audience.

"Tone" refers to the author's underlying attitudes, which may or may not be detected by readers. An author's tone will be influenced by his or her purpose as well as the nature of the audience.

Extensive discussion of these concepts can be found in the "Understanding of Audience, Purpose, and Tone" section of Chapter 4.

EVALUATION OF EVIDENCE

Evidence consists of observations, references to scholarly works, quotations, logical analysis. and other kinds of information that are used by writers to bolster their arguments. There are several different types of evidence.

Observations

One type of evidence consists of the observations that the writer himself or herself has made, as illustrated in the following passage:

"The effects of global warming are even apparent in regions that seem to experience very little by way of carbon emissions. Outside of Lhasa, for example, cliffs that were heavily forested as little as two decades ago are now barren and dusty, as I discovered on my return to the area last year."

In this passage, the writer is presenting his or her own observations of erosion in the cliffs as evidence of climate change.

Observational evidence can be relatively informal and anecdotal, as in the previous example, or it can be formal, as in a scholarly paper in which a scientist reports the observations he or she made during a study.

In some contexts, scientific observations are preferable as evidence to informal, anecdotal observations. For example, compare the following passages:

"In my research I find that males who have been smoking for more than a decade were twice as likely to have developed cardiovascular disease than nonsmokers. Hence I discourage young people from taking up smoking."

"My uncle Rick smoked for almost thirty years and then had a heart attack one day, so I discourage young people from taking up smoking."

Assuming that the writer's goal is to provide evidence concerning the relationship between smoking and heart disease, and to then discourage people from taking up smoking, the first passage provides better evidence than the second one. The first passage describes scientific observations of numerous people, while the second passage describes an anecdote about one person.

At the same time, combining the two passages does not automatically yield better evidence:

"In my research I find that males who have been smoking for more than a decade were twice as likely to have developed cardiovascular disease than nonsmokers. My uncle Rick smoked for almost thirty years and then had a heart attack one day. Hence, I discourage young people from taking up smoking."

In this passage, the credibility of the writer is undermined somewhat by the anecdote, and by the ambiguity of the word "Hence" in the third sentence. "Hence" could mean that the writer's conclusion is based on his or her own research evidence as well as Uncle Rick's heart attack, or it could mean that the conclusion is based primarily on the demise of Uncle Rick. One way to improve the passage would be to remove the reference to Uncle Rick. Another way to improve it would be to clarify the relationship between the evidence and the conclusion, as follows:

"In my research I find that males who have been smoking for more than a decade were twice as likely to have developed cardiovascular disease than nonsmokers. I can also tell you that my uncle Rick smoked for almost thirty years and then had a heart attack one day. Although Rick is just one person, the findings from my research are clear and lead me to discourage young people from taking up smoking."

Although scientific observation is preferred as a source of evidence about scientific topics, there are two reasons that it is not automatically preferred.

First, scientific observation does not work well for supporting certain kinds of arguments. A writer who wishes to argue for the merits of a particular musician or genre of music, for example, is not likely to find much support for the argument in scientific research. The same could be said about arguments about the moral character of a particular public figure.

Second, scientific evidence is not infallible. The fact that evidence is scientific implies that it is grounded in systematic observation, but not that it is automatically accurate or unbiased.

Findings

Another form of evidence consists of findings described previously by someone other than the writer. These findings may consist of theoretical claims, observations, or statistics. In order to use these findings as evidence, the writer will typically either paraphrase or quote the original source.

Statistics are often given great respect as a source of evidence, and indeed percentages and other kinds of statistical information may constitute good evidence for or against a particular argument. However, statistics are not infallible. Moreover, as a reader, you must be cautious about misuse of statistics as a form of evidence. Some kinds of misuse can be detected as part of the process of evaluating a piece of writing. Consider, for example, the following passage:

"In 2009 the dropout rate in our city was 67.7%. In 2008 the dropout rate was 62.1%, and the year before that it was exactly 60%. The dropout rate in our city is increasing, in other words, and it will continue to increase until someday soon commencement exercises all across the city will be cancelled because there aren't any graduates."

Although the statistics do show a rise in the dropout rate, it does not follow that the dropout rate will reach 100% "someday soon." A suitable revision to this passage would qualify the final sentence in some way. For example:

"In 2009 the dropout rate in our city was 67.7%. In 2008 the dropout rate was 62.1%, and the year before that it was exactly 60%. The dropout rate in our city is increasing, in other words, and judging from the statistics we can expect it to continue to increase."

The next passage illustrates a number of fallacies that can occur when arguments are based on statistical information.

"Abstinence-only programs do not work. A recent study showed that when abstinence-only programs are available to high school students during freshman year, only 48% of the students who participate remain abstinent throughout their remaining high school years. Thus, the best way to reduce the rate of teenage pregnancy is for school districts to shut down abstinence-only programs and focus on teaching high school students safe-sex practices."

Here are three fallacies in the passage that even non-statisticians can recognize:

First, the assertion that abstinence-only programs do not work is based on the finding that "only" 48% of students remain abstinent following participation in such programs during their freshman year. Perhaps this statistic does show that abstinence-only programs do not work. We cannot be sure, however, because we do not know what the rate of abstinence would be if students had not participated in these programs. There is no comparison group. In other words, we need more statistical information. If roughly 48% of students who do not participate in abstinence-only programs actually remain abstinent, then we could conclude that the programs do not work. If the figure were 68% or 78%, we would have evidence of the programs' effectiveness.

Second, given that participation in abstinence-only programs appears to be optional, perhaps the statistical results are influenced by who chooses to participate or not to participate. Perhaps students who are quite convinced they will remain abstinent during high school see no reason to participate, while students who are experiencing inner conflict about the issue are more likely to participate. If this were true, then any effectiveness that the abstinence-only programs have would be underestimated owing to the fact that students who are more susceptible to engaging in sex participate in the programs in the first place.

Third, even if we did conclude that abstinence-only programs are ineffective, it does not follow that school districts should focus on teaching safe-sex practices. Perhaps they should develop better abstinence-only programs. Perhaps there is another solution. The only thing the statistics could tell us would be whether the abstinence-only programs are effective. The statistics themselves do not suggest alternatives here.

Authority

A third type of evidence consists of authority, including the authority of experts, groups, organizations, scholarly works, and testimonials. For example, consider the following sentence:

"As the U. S. Surgeon General has observed, alcohol should not be consumed during pregnancy."

Because the Surgeon General is a highly respected source, the fact that this individual has made a particular health-related recommendation has been used by the writer as evidence for that recommendation. This is an appeal to authority that differs somewhat from an appeal to the evidence provided by an authority or authorities, as in the following example:

"Alcohol should not be consumed during pregnancy, owing to a substantial number of studies showing that even low levels of alcohol consumption can harm the developing fetus."

This sentence illustrates an appeal to findings rather than to authority per se, even though we assume the writer believes that the studies he or she is citing are authoritative.

Appeal to authority can constitute good evidence for an argument, so long as the reader understands that authorities are not infallible—and that sometimes their views are not accurately depicted by writers. Appeals to authority will be effective if a specific authority is identified, and if the reader recognizes the authority as an expert and credible source. Consider the following sentences:

"As the U.S. Surgeon General has observed, chocolate milk should be avoided during pregnancy."

"As a reputable expert has observed, chocolate milk should be avoided during pregnancy."

"As my sister Clarissa has observed, chocolate milk should be avoided during pregnancy."

In the first sentence, the fact that the Surgeon General is the source of the recommendation constitutes some evidence for that recommendation, for the reasons noted earlier.

In the second sentence, the source is described as reputable but is not named. The fact that the recommendation came from a "reputable expert" does not constitute strong evidence in favor of the recommendation. Thus, a good way to revise this sentence would be to identify the expert who has made this observation.

In the third sentence, the source is named but does not appear to be authoritative. Unless Clarissa happens to be the Surgeon General or some other known expert, the fact that she advocates against drinking chocolate milk during pregnancy does not itself constitute strong evidence for the recommendation. Thus, the sentence requires some sort of revision.

For example, evidence could be introduced into the sentence, and the distinction between the evidence and the anecdote about Clarissa could be made more clearly, as in the following example:

"Scientific studies show that chocolate milk should be avoided during pregnancy, as my sister Clarissa likes to recommend."

In the sentence above, studies are cited as the main evidence for the recommendation, and Clarissa's views are simply described as consistent with the evidence.

The original sentence ("As my sister Clarissa has observed, chocolate milk should be avoided during pregnancy") could also be revised to simply remove any hint that evidence is being presented. For example:

"My sister Clarissa and I believe that chocolate milk should be avoided during pregnancy."

Reasoning

In some cases, evidence consists of applications of logic in order to yield information that the reader may not have anticipated.

The mere use of logic does not in itself provide much evidence. For example, consider the following recommendation:

"In spite of the fact that flame retardants are used in mattresses, one should not smoke in bed. If you smoke while reclining in bed, you may fall asleep, and the burning cigarette you drop may then cause the mattress to catch fire. A burning mattress will in turn have negative consequences."

The final sentence of the passage yields little evidence in favor of the writer's main thesis. Since all readers presumably know that it is undesirable for one's mattress to be on fire, the writer does not help advance his or her argument by drawing out that inference for us. Thus, a desirable revision to this passage would be to delete the final sentence (or to revise it in some way—e.g., to include statistics on the rate of injury or death resulting from smokers' mattresses catching fire).

In other cases, the writer may apply logic in such a way that the information revealed does constitute evidence, because the reader may not have considered this information before. For example, consider the following revision of the previous passage:

"In spite of the fact that flame retardants are used in mattresses, one should not smoke in bed. If you smoke while reclining in bed, you may fall asleep, and the burning cigarette you drop may then cause the mattress to catch fire. Since you would be asleep at this point, your ability to escape from the fire will be somewhat diminished."

Here, the final sentence provides evidence in support of the writer's main thesis. Although the inference conveyed by this sentence is not deeply insightful or reflective of something that readers could not figure out on their own, it does present an observation that readers may not have been considering at that particular moment.

Another example of how logic can be used to yield evidence is in the use of analogy. A writer will sometimes make an assertion about a particular scenario, and then point out similarities between this scenario and another one as evidence for the assertion. For example:

"In a recent editorial, an anonymous writer called upon Americans to voluntarily reduce their energy consumption. This appeal, however laudable, will accomplish nothing. If you want people to reduce their energy consumption, simply asking them to do so will never work. It didn't work in the 1970's when

President Carter presented the same appeal to the American people, and it will not work now."

In this example, the writer's sole evidence that the appeal to voluntarily reduce energy consumption will not accomplish anything is that the appeal did not accomplish anything on a prior occasion.

As you can see, the strength of the evidence here rests on two assumptions: first, that the writer accurately portrayed the prior occasion accurately, and second, that the two situations are analogous. Arguably, they are not. For example, one could argue that attitudes toward energy consumption were much different in the 1970's than they are now. A suitable revision of this passage might consist of adding a sentence that contains additional evidence, such as:

"In a recent editorial, an anonymous writer called upon Americans to voluntarily reduce their energy consumption. This appeal, however laudable, will accomplish nothing. If you want people to reduce their energy consumption, simply asking them to do so will never work. It didn't work in the 1970's when President Carter presented the same appeal to the American people, and it will not work now. Survey data suggest that contemporary Americans have the same sense of entitlement with respect to energy consumption that we did in the 1970's."

Dimensions of Evaluation

When a writer attempts to make a point or otherwise convey some idea, the reader should evaluate whatever evidence the writer presents in favor of the idea. The evidence presented should be relevant and logical.

Although wildly irrelevant statements may be relatively easy to spot, in some cases the reader will need to judge the relevance of particular evidence very carefully. For example, consider the following passage:

"The role of women in Chinese society has been explored at length in recent fiction by authors such as Amy Tan and Maxine Hong Kingston. For example, in *Woman Warrior*, Kingston writes about her mother's struggles as a Chinese immigrant in the U.S."

Although the passage is sensible, it is not clear how the second sentence constitutes evidence for the first one. The struggles of a female immigrant may not reveal something about the role of women in the home country, depending on how the writer treats the topic, but it is not immediately clear that such a discussion would explore the topic "at length." Thus, a revision is needed to the preceding passage in order to increase its coherence. For example:

"The experiences of women immigrants from China has been explored at length in recent fiction by authors such as Amy Tan and Maxine Hong Kingston. For example, in *Woman Warrior*, Kingston writes about her mother's struggles as a Chinese immigrant in the U.S."

Finally, writers must develop logical connections between the evidence they present and the conclusions they draw. Although illogical statements may be easy to spot, in some cases the reader must evaluate the writer's logic carefully. For example, consider the following passage:

"Thomson argues that the laws against possession of recreational drugs should be made more lenient in order to reduce the burden on law enforcement and to help the legal system focus on rehabilitation rather than punishment. The problem with this point of view is that if we allow people to take recreational drugs without negative consequences, the rates of addiction in this country will skyrocket and we will see an epidemic of drug-related crime."

This passage illustrates a logical fallacy called a "straw-man argument," in which the writer distorts a particular point of view before criticizing it. The result is that the writer criticizes the "straw man" (i.e., the distorted view) rather than the actual view. As you can see from the first sentence in the passage above, Thomson is not arguing that there should be no negative consequences for taking recreational drugs. Rather, the argument is that the negative consequences should be lessened. However, the writer does not attack this claim. Rather, the attack focuses on the straw man claim that we should allow people to take recreational drugs without negative consequences whatsoever. This is an easier claim to attack than Thomson's actual claim. The second sentence of the passage requires revision. For example:

"Thomson argues that the laws against possession of recreational drugs should be made more lenient in order to reduce the burden on law enforcement and to help the legal system focus on rehabilitation rather than punishment. The problem with this point of view is that if we diminish the negative consequences for taking recreational drugs, the rates of addiction in this country will skyrocket and we will see an epidemic of drug-related crime."

This revision is not ideal, because the writer is making predictions (skyrocketing addiction rates and a drug-related crime epidemic) that are not supported by evidence. However, the writer has at least paraphrased Thomson's view appropriately rather than attacking a straw man.

Another kind of logical fallacy is the circular argument, in which a conclusion is assumed as part of its own premises. Thus, the conclusion is not suggested by evidence and reasoning; rather, the conclusion is already assumed. For example:

"Sir Winston Churchill is known as a mesmerizing speaker because his speeches to huge crowds in Whitehall and elsewhere had a riveting effect on the public."

In the sentence above, evidence for the conclusion that Churchill was a mesmerizing speaker is that his speeches were riveting. In short, because "mesmerizing" and "riveting" are very similar in meaning, the writer is saying, in effect, that Churchill was mesmerizing because he was mesmerizing. This reflects a circular argument. The evidence presented in support of the conclusion in fact reflects that very conclusion. One of the many possible non-circular revisions of the preceding sentence would be as follows:

"Sir Winston Churchill is known as a mesmerizing speaker because his speeches to huge crowds in Whitehall and elsewhere caused audiences to stare, slack-jawed, and then erupt in shouts and peals of applause."

A third type of logical fallacy is called the false analogy, because it characterizes an argument in which an analogy is drawn between elements that are not truly analogous, or analogous in a merely superficial or irrelevant way. For example:

"The CEO of a large industrial chemical company recently argued that his company's newest product should not have been banned by the EPA simply because of evidence that proper use of the chemical resulted in several fatalities. 'According to that line of reasoning,' the CEO scoffed, 'the use of automobiles should be banned, because they cause fatalities too. Nobody in their right mind would suggest that we actually pass a law banning automobiles.'"

In this passage, the CEO presents the following argument:

1. Use of my company's new product results in fatalities.
2. Use of automobiles results in fatalities.
3. The new product is therefore analogous to automobiles.
4. Since automobiles should not be banned, the new product should not be banned.

The analogy between the product and automobiles can be considered a false analogy because the commonality between them is not very relevant. The use of many things can potentially cause fatalities. However, the proper use of automobiles, according to some reasonable definition of the term "proper," would not result in fatalities. In contrast, the company's product seems to do so even when used properly.

Several other types of logical fallacy are discussed in Chapter 4.

LEVEL OF DETAIL

The author of a written work must choose the level of detail that is appropriate to the interests and expertise of the audience. This is a requirement that pertains to the entire work. In addition, the author must convey specific points with enough detail that these points are understandable and persuasive. Missing details undermine the coherence of an argument, as discussed in the previous section as well as in the one that follows. To take just one example, consider the following passage:

"Thomson argues that the laws against possession of recreational drugs should be made more lenient in order to reduce the burden on law enforcement and to help the legal system focus on rehabilitation rather than punishment. Thomson has presented this argument in six different scholarly publications and uncounted numbers of editorials and interviews. The problem with this point of view is that if we diminish the negative consequences for taking recreational drugs, the rates of addiction in this country will skyrocket and we will see an epidemic of drug-related crime."

This passage contains too much detail on one point and too little on another. The second sentence ("Thomson has presented this argument in six different scholarly publications and uncounted numbers of editorials and interviews") may be accurate, but these details have no bearing on either the substance of Thomson's view or the substance of the writer's objections to that view. In a suitable revision of this passage, the second sentence would be removed.

Although too detailed about Thomson's publications and media activity, this passage is not detailed enough concerning the link between diminished consequences for drug use and changes in rates of addiction and drug-related crime. The addition of a sentence describing this link would be helpful, as in the following revision:

"Thomson argues that the laws against possession of recreational drugs should be made more lenient in order to reduce the burden on law enforcement and to help the legal system focus on rehabilitation rather than punishment. The problem with this point of view is that if we diminish the negative consequences for taking recreational drugs, drug use will rise because users will be less afraid of getting caught. As a result, the rates of addiction in this country will skyrocket and we will see an epidemic of drug-related crime."

Although the argument in this passage may still not be very strong, the addition of further details has now made it more explicit.

COHERENCE

Coherence refers to the clarity and connectedness of written information. Writing can be judged coherent when the reader is able to understand the individual elements (phrases, sentences, paragraphs, ideas, and themes) as well as the connections between these elements. For example, consider two of the factors that contribute to the coherence of a paragraph: the topical focus of the paragraph, and the extent of connectedness between sentences.

Topical Focus

The coherence of a paragraph is determined in part by its focus on a single point or idea. Coherence is undermined when more than one point or idea is developed in a paragraph. Consider, for example, the following:

"The use of bottled water is irresponsible. Water is readily available from taps and public fountains. In addition, water from taps and fountains is free. Bottled water costs us time and money to purchase, and the plastic from discarded water bottles is a major source of environmental pollution. Studies now show that all kinds of plastics break down quickly in the ocean, resulting in microscopic particles that make their way into the food supply via plankton and other tiny creatures; fish eat the plankton, we eat the fish, and thus our health is imperiled."

In some respects this paragraph is quite coherent. The main point is conveyed in the opening sentence, and the remainder of the paragraph provides evidence in support of that point. Moreover, each individual sentence in the paragraph is understandable.

In spite of these positive qualities, the coherence of the paragraph is diminished by the final sentence. The main point of the paragraph is that use of bottled water is irresponsible. However, the final sentence of the paragraph is concerned with a related but separate point—i.e., the impact of plastics pollution on human health. Removal of this sentence would increase the coherence of the passage.

Sentence-Level Connections

An additional contributor to the coherence of a paragraph is the extent of connectedness between individual sentences. Coherence in this sense can be created by a number of methods.

First, repetition of a word across sentences can link the sentences together. Consider, for example, the following pairs of sentences:

"Marijuana has been praised for its relaxing and euphoric qualities. Users should also recognize that slower reaction times and moderately impaired judgment are possible."

"Marijuana has been praised for its relaxing and euphoric qualities. Users of marijuana should also recognize that slower reaction times and moderately impaired judgment are possible."

Although the first pair of sentences is understandable, the second pair is more closely interconnected owing to the repetition of the term "marijuana."

Second, rather than literally repeating a word, the writer can use a synonym, antonym, or pronoun that refers to a word in the previous sentence and thereby links the sentences together. Words that are merely close in meaning rather than synonymous can also be effective in this way. Compare the following examples:

"Marijuana has been praised for its relaxing and euphoric qualities. Users of the nostrum should also recognize that slower reaction times and moderately impaired judgment are possible."

"Marijuana has been praised for its relaxing and euphoric qualities. Users of the drug should also recognize that slower reaction times and moderately impaired judgment are possible."

Here again, the first pair of sentences is understandable, because the reader will recognize that "nostrum" is a reference to marijuana, but the coherence of the second pair of sentences is greater owing to the clearer relationship in meaning between "drug" and "marijuana."

Third, the writer can simply use a word that tends to be associated with a word in the previous sentence, and in this way, link the sentences together. Consider the following passages:

"Through his binoculars Francis saw the lion rise to its feet. Suddenly he heard a loud sound."

"Through his binoculars Francis saw the lion rise to its feet. Suddenly he heard a loud roar."

The link between the sentences is clearer in the second passage, because of the association that readers naturally make between lions and roaring.

Fourth, the writer can use parallelism to connect sentences. (Parallelism is discussed at length in Chapters 1 and 4.)

Fifth, transitions between sentences can help connect them. This topic is discussed further under the Transitions section below.

SENTENCE VARIETY

In the section on syntax in Chapter 1, you read about different sentence structures, which include simple, compound, complex, and compound-complex. Writing that does not include a mix of these structures quickly becomes tedious. To illustrate, compare the following two passages:

"Joe DiMaggio is one of the most well-known celebrities in American history. Marilyn Monroe is one of America's most famous celebrities too. Joe was a great baseball player. Marilyn was an actress. Joe and Marilyn met in 1952. They got married in 1954. They divorced less than one year later. Journalists followed their marriage and divorce closely. Joe and Marilyn did not like having so much media attention on their marriage. They were patient about the extent of media attention they received."

"Joe DiMaggio and Marilyn Monroe are two of the most well-known celebrities in American history. Joe was a great baseball player, while Marilyn was an actress. The couple met in 1952. Married in 1954, they divorced less than one year later. Both disliked the fact that journalists followed their marriage and divorce very closely, but they were patient about the media attention they received."

The first passage seems stilted, or awkward, because every one of its sentences is a simple sentence.

In contrast, the second passage is an improvement over the first one, because there is more variety in sentence structure. Here is the passage again, accompanied by labels indicating each sentence's type:

"Joe DiMaggio and Marilyn Monroe are two of the most well-known celebrities in American history [simple sentence]. Joe was a great baseball player, while Marilyn was an actress [compound sentence]. The couple met in 1952 [simple sentence]. Married in 1954, they divorced less than one year later [complex sentence]. Both disliked the fact that journalists followed their marriage and divorce very closely, but they were patient about the media attention they received [compound-complex sentence]."

MAIN IDEA, TOPIC SENTENCE, THESIS STATEMENT

The main idea is the most important point developed in a paragraph, passage, or work of writing in its entirety. The thesis statement is the author's opinion on a topic. Although all coherent written works have a main idea, not all writing contains a thesis statement. A description of a historical event, for example, will not contain a thesis statement if the author simply wishes to state the facts.

A topic sentence summarizes the main idea of a paragraph. The main idea is developed by means of each sentence in the paragraph, and it is summarized in the topic sentence. In some cases, the topic sentence is the first sentence of the paragraph, while in other cases it is the final paragraph.

In the following description of a research study, you can see that the first sentence is the topic sentence, in that it captures the main idea of the study. The final sentence of the paragraph consists of a thesis statement.

"In this study we showed that parenting style has an impact on children's honesty. All 83 parents whose children attended a local Montessori school were observed during brief interactions with their preschoolers on the school playground. Based on these interactions, each parent was labeled as authoritative, authoritarian, permissive, or uninvolved. Ten parents representing each style were chosen to participate in the lab phase of the study. In the lab phase, each child played cards with an experimenter while the parent waited in a separate room. During the card game, the experimenter left the room for ten minutes, placing his cards face down on the table before leaving. While he was gone, a hidden camera recorded whether or not the child cheated by looking at the cards. We found that the incidence of cheating was greatest among children with authoritarian parents but least among those with authoritative parents. Thus, we believe that parents who exhibit authoritarian styles should be encouraged to shift to a more warm and receptive style of parenting."

RHETORICAL EFFECTS

Rhetoric consists of the use of language in an effective and persuasive way. Following Aristotle, three general approaches to persuasion have been identified: ethos, pathos, and logos.

Ethos refers to an appeal to the writer's own authority. For example, a writer can increase his or her persuasiveness by claiming to be knowledgeable, to be recognized by others as an authority, or simply to be an honest and reliable person.

Pathos refers to an appeal to the audience's emotions. A writer can increase his or her persuasiveness by engaging readers' interest in a topic by amusing readers, by eliciting a sense of moral outrage among readers, and so on.

Logos refers to an appeal to the audience's reason. A writer can increase his or her persuasiveness by getting readers to think about a topic by presenting compelling evidence for an argument, by pointing out logical fallacies in an opposing argument, and so on.

The rhetorical approach that will be most effective depends on the audience as well as the writer's purpose. Logos will tend to be most effective when presenting a scholarly theory to scholars, for example, but when presenting the same theory to the general public, a writer will need to make use of ethos (in order to convince the audience to trust his or her rendition of the theory) as well as pathos (to help maintain audience interest). At the same time, overreliance on logos would be counterproductive if it makes the writer seem distant or it fails to capture audience interest. Typically, a combination of approaches is needed, for the reasons given below.

First, exclusive reliance on ethos will often be counterproductive, because the writer is asking the reader to accept a particular idea simply because the writer is smart and credible. At the same time, written works are often unpersuasive when readers doubt the writer's authority and credibility, and thus ethos is generally needed.

Second, exclusive reliance on pathos will be counterproductive if readers wonder about the writer's authority or feel they need some sort of rationale for what is being asserted. At the same time, written works are often unpersuasive when they lack any sort of emotional appeal.

Third, as noted, exclusive reliance on logos can be counterproductive if the audience senses a lack of emotional engagement on the author's part, or if the writing is so dry and logical that the audience fails to connect with it.

Specific rhetorical devices are discussed in the "Understanding of Rhetoric" section of Chapter 4.

USE OF LANGUAGE

As discussed in Chapter 4, a writer's diction (i.e., choice or words and phrases) has a powerful influence on the coherence and persuasiveness of his or her writing. Following are some uses of language that should be avoided:

First, writers should avoid diction that is overly formal, or not formal enough, for a particular audience. Consider the following passage:

"The assassination of Abraham Lincoln was a national tragedy. The loss of this great man was an unexpected blow to the spirit of a nation already wounded by a bloody civil war. Lincoln's family was upset too."

In this passage, the final sentence is much too informal given what preceded it. Deleting this sentence would improve the overall diction of the passage.

Second, writers should avoid jargon. For example:

"Jack made one unwise investment after another, and not one of these ventures paid off. As his assets quickly dwindled, his wife began to realize that she had married a bad ball hitter."

In the passage above, the baseball term "bad ball hitter" is used to indicate that Jack pursues investments that are unlikely to pay off (in the manner of a hitter who swings at a ball that he is unlikely to hit). However, if it seems likely that the audience will not recognize this particular piece of jargon, the writer should replace "bad ball hitter" with a more understandable phrase, as in the following revision:

"Jack made one unwise investment after another, and not one of these ventures paid off. As his assets quickly dwindled, his wife began to realize that she had married an unwise or unlucky risk taker."

Third, writers should avoid slang. For example:

"Following his conviction for embezzlement, the embattled congressman was sentenced to three years in the slammer, with the possibility of parole after six months."

In this sentence, "the slammer" is overly slang and should be replaced by a term that suits the overall diction of the sentence, such as "prison."

Finally, as noted in Chapter 1, writers should avoid gender-biased diction.

TRANSITIONS

As discussed earlier, transition terms and phrases contribute to the organization and coherence of writing. Following are some examples of these terms and phrases organized by the purposes they serve.

Adding to a Previous Statement

also	furthermore
again	in addition
as well as	likewise
besides	moreover
coupled with	similarly

Describing a Consequence of a Previous Statement

accordingly	otherwise
as a result	so then
consequently	subsequently
for this reason	therefore
for this purpose	thus
hence	

Illustrating a Previous Statement

chiefly	markedly
especially	namely
for example	particularly
for instance	specifically
including	such as
in particular	to illustrate

Restating or Summarizing a Previous Statement

all in all	in short
briefly	in sum
in conclusion	in brief
in essence	on the whole
in other words	that is
namely	to put it simply

Contrasting with a Previous Statement

at the same time	nevertheless
but	on the contrary
however	rather
in contrast	similarly
instead	yet

HOW TO APPROACH REVISION SKILLS QUESTIONS ON THE CLEP EXAMS

All of the Revision Skills questions on the CLEP College Composition exam and most of those on the College Composition Modular exam pertain to passages. Usually there are three to five questions per passage. These passages may concern virtually any topic. Each passage may represent an introduction or a conclusion, or it may represent the body of a piece of writing. Some of the passages will be factual, while others will be theoretical or speculative. Many of the passages will be expository, while others will primarily attempt to persuade the reader to adopt a particular point of view.

The directions you can expect to see for the Revision Skills section are reproduced here from the CLEP College Composition/College Composition Modular Examination Guide.

First, here are the instructions for passage-based questions. (All of the Revision Skills questions on the College Composition exam and most of the Revision Skills questions on the College Composition Modular exam are passage-based.)

"The following passages are early drafts of essays.

"Read each passage and then answer the questions that follow. Some questions refer to particular sentences or parts of sentences and ask you to improve sentence structure or diction (word choice). Other questions refer to the entire essay or parts of the essay and ask you to consider the essay's organization, development or effectiveness of language. In selecting your answers, follow the conventions of standard written English."

Second, here are the instructions for the Improving Sentences questions that are included in the Revision Skills section of the College Composition Modular exam:

"The following sentences test correctness and effectiveness of expression. In choosing your answers, follow the requirements of standard written English: that is, pay attention to grammar, diction (choice of words), sentence construction and punctuation.

"In each of the following sentences, part of the sentence or the entire sentence is underlined. Beneath each sentence you will find five versions of the underlined part. The first option repeats the original; the other four options present different versions.

"Choose the option that best expresses the meaning of the original sentence. If you think the original is better than any of the alternatives, choose the first option; otherwise, choose one of the other options. Your choice should produce the most effective sentence—one that is clear and precise, without awkwardness or ambiguity."

Sample CLEP Questions

The questions provided in this section draw upon the skills discussed in this chapter, as well as in chapters 1 and 4. The format of the questions below closely matches what you will find in the Revision Skills section of the CLEP College Composition and College Composition Modular exams. That is, the questions pertaining to passages are organized into sets of about three to five questions each. The sentences within each passage are numbered, in order to make it easier to identify them in the questions. Five answer options are given for each question, and you are asked to choose the best option. In addition, you will find some Improving Sentences questions of the sort that are included in the Revision Skills section of the CLEP College Composition Modular exam.

We will work through the first set of questions together, once you have read the following passage.

(1) Why do people voluntarily relocate to a large city? (2) First of all, a large city will offer a wide variety of job opportunities owing to the variety of its businesses. (3) Given that rural areas suffer from high unemployment, low wages, and the workers are not satisfied, more and more people are choosing to relocate to the large metropolis in search of work. (4) The populations of large cities have continued to grow in recent years, partly due to an influx of people from rural areas.

(5) The public services in cities are superior. (6) For example, because public transportation is plentiful and efficient, residents waste less time in transit between locations. (7) The A-line bus is the one I use most frequently. (8) Medical services are more plentiful and supported by the latest technological improvements, there is access to modern hospitals too. (9) Educational opportunities in large cities are also quite advanced. (10) Along with public schools, it is relatively easy to find private schools and charter schools in these cities.

First, consider the following question about sentence 1. As is often the case in the Revision Skills section, the sentence to which the question refers is reproduced in italics beneath the question.

In context, which of the following versions of sentence 1 (reproduced below) is best?

Why do people voluntarily relocate to a large city?

(A) Why do people voluntarily relocate to the large city?
(B) Why do people voluntarily relocate to the large cities?
(C) Why does a person voluntarily relocate to large cities?
(D) Why do people voluntarily relocate to large cities?
(E) Why does a person voluntarily relocate to the large cities?

Options A and B reflect a change in article from "a" to "the," and thus both options are incorrect. Specifically, option A is incorrect because the passage concerns cities rather than one particular city. Option B is incorrect because a particular set of large cities has not been identified.

Options C and E reflect a change in noun from "people" to "person." Both options are thus incorrect because of the lack of agreement between "person," which is singular, and the plural "cities." (Details concerning agreement were discussed in the previous chapter.)

Option D is correct. The article has been removed, and "people" agrees with "cities."

The next question asks you to consider a revision to just one part of a sentence rather than the entire sentence.

Which of the following would be the best revision to the underlined portion of sentence 2 (reproduced below)?

First of all, a large city will offer a wide variety of job opportunities <u>owing to the variety of its businesses</u>.

- (A) Leave it as it is.
- (B) Change "owing to" to "because of."
- (C) Change it to "owing to a wide variety of its job market."
- (D) Change "owing to the" to "in the."
- (E) Delete it.

Sentence 2 reflects what is referred to in this chapter as circular reasoning. The sentence says, in effect, that the fact that a wide variety of jobs is available can be attributed to the fact that there are a wide variety of jobs. Thus, option A is incorrect. Option B doesn't fix the problem, because it simply replaces one word phrase indicating causality with another one. Option C is simply grammatically incorrect, while option D is incoherent. Option E is the correct answer. By simply deleting the underlined phrase, the circular reasoning is removed.

The next question is analogous to the previous one but concerns a grammatical problem rather than circularity:

Which of the following would be the best revision to the underlined portion of sentence 3 (reproduced below)?

Given that rural areas suffer from high unemployment, low wages, <u>and the workers are not satisfied</u>, more and more people are choosing to relocate to the large metropolis in search of work.

- (A) Leave it as it is.
- (B) Change it to "and dissatisfied workers."
- (C) Change it to "and that the workers are not satisfied."
- (D) Change it to "and workers are not satisfied."
- (E) Delete it.

In sentence 3, the parallelism of "high unemployment" and "low wages" is not continued in the final phrase of the sentence. The sentence must be revised in some way to preserve this parallelism, and thus option A is incorrect. Likewise options C and D do not make the final phrase parallel to the ones that preceded it. Option E would yield a sentence that is grammatically incorrect. Option B is the correct answer, because it replaces the underlined phrase with one that matches the parallelism of other phrases in the sentence.

The next question pertains to the organization of the passage and requires you to consider several sentences rather than just one.

Where would be the best place to relocate sentence 4?

(A) Before sentence 1
(B) Before sentence 2
(C) Before sentence 3
(D) Before sentence 6
(E) Before sentence 7

This passage reflects cause-effect organization. That is, the causes for people relocating to large cities is discussed. Sentence 4 is out of place because it introduces the effect in the midst of a discussion of causes. By moving this sentence to the beginning of the essay, it no longer disrupts the organization of the essay, and it provides a strong introduction, and thus option A is correct.

The next question also requires you to compare several sentences rather than focusing on just one.

Deleting which of the following sentences would most improve the coherence of the passage?

(A) sentence 3
(B) sentence 5
(C) sentence 7
(D) sentence 9
(E) sentence 11

Unless you have already spotted a sentence that clearly does not belong the passage, the best approach to a question like this is to consider each option in turn.

Although the removal of sentence 3 would not substantially undermine the coherence of the passage, doing so would not improve the passage's coherence; thus, option A is incorrect.

The removal of sentence 5 would diminish the coherence of the passage, since it would be unclear what the "For example" in sentence 6 refers to, and thus option B is not correct.

Sentence 7 is out of place because it relates an anecdote that has no relevance to the writer's purpose (i.e., to explain why people relocate to large cities). Removing this sentence clearly improves the coherence of the passage, and thus option C is the correct answer.

When evaluating each option in turn, if you have any doubts about the option you have identified as correct, you should consider the remaining options. Here, an examination of options D and E will reinforce the choice of option C as the correct answer.

As with sentence 3, the removal of sentence 9 would not diminish the coherence of the passage, but nor would its removal increase the passage's coherence, and so option D is not correct.

Sentence 11, like sentences 3 and 9, could be deleted without undermining the coherence of the passage, but its removal would not improve the passage, and so option E is not correct.

The next question pertains to transitions, but it requires you to think about the organization of the passage as well as the writer's purpose:

In context, which is best to add to the beginning of sentence 5?

    (A) Clearly
    (B) However,
    (C) We all know
    (D) Second,
    (E) Occasionally

Option A is incorrect, because it is not immediately clear that public services in cities are superior. The word "clearly" would be appropriate here only if the writer had previously given evidence for the superiority of public services in cities, or if that superiority were immediately recognizable to all readers (which is unlikely).

Option B is incorrect, because the transition term "however" introduces a contrast or qualification that does not reflect the organization of the passage. The writer is engaged in describing causes for a particular effect. The assertion that public services in cities are superior is one more cause for the reader to consider. Thus, a transitional phrase like "In addition" would be more appropriate than "however."

Option C is incorrect for essentially the same reasons that option A is incorrect.

Option D seems correct because sentence 5 constitutes the second cause that the writer is discussing.

Option E is incorrect because the term "occasionally" would introduce a qualification that undermines the writer's purpose. If public services in cities were only occasionally superior, it would be less clear why public services would be one of the reasons people relocate to cities.

In sum, we can be confident that option D is the correct answer.

The next question pertains to a comma splice in one of the sentences:

Which of the following revisions to sentence 8 (reproduced below) is best?

Medical services are more plentiful and supported by the latest technological improvements, there is access to modern hospitals too.

(A) Medical services are more plentiful and supported by the latest technological improvements, and access to modern hospitals.

(B) Medical services are more plentiful and supported by the latest technological improvements; and there is access to modern hospitals too.

(C) Medical services are more plentiful and supported by the latest technological improvements, and there is access to modern hospitals too.

(D) Medical services are more plentiful and supported by the latest technological improvements, access to modern hospitals.

(E) Medical services are more plentiful and supported by the latest technological improvements; access to modern hospitals there.

An independent clause is needed following the comma in sentence 8, and thus option A is incorrect.

Regarding option B, the conjunction "and" should not be used following the semicolon, and thus this option is incorrect too.

Option C is the right answer because it is the only grammatically correct option.

Option D is incorrect because it has the same kind of comma splice as in the original sentence. That is, the comma separates an independent clause from the dependent clause that follows. As discussed in the previous chapter, the dependent clause would need to be independent in order for the sentence to be grammatically correct.

Option E is incorrect because the clause following the semicolon is dependent, and the reference for the term "there" is ambiguous.

The next question asks to you make an inference about diction, or word choice, in one of the sentences.

In context, which is best to do with the word "advanced" in sentence 9 (reproduced below)?

Educational opportunities in large cities are also quite advanced.

(A) Leave it as it is.
(B) Replace it with "large."
(C) Replace it with "urban."
(D) Replace it with "helpful."
(E) Replace it with "plentiful."

As you read sentences 8 through 10, it becomes clear that the writer's emphasis here is on the quantity, diversity, and accessibility of public services (transportation, medical, and educational) available to residents of large cities. Since nothing is said about educational opportunities until sentence 9, the word "also" in this sentence provides a hint that what will be said about education here is similar to what has been said about other services. Thus, you can assume that the correct answer will be one that reflects something about the quantity, diversity, and/or accessibility of educational opportunities.

"Advanced" is a vague term in this context, and thus option A is incorrect.

Option B is incorrect simply because it would render the sentence grammatically incorrect. "Opportunities" cannot be said to be "large."

Option C is incorrect because "urban" means "pertaining to cities," and thus the term would not clearly contribute any information about educational opportunities in large cities.

Option D is incorrect because the observation that educational opportunities are "helpful" in some way would not be consistent with the writer's point which, as noted earlier, pertains to the quantity, diversity, and accessibility of public services.

Option E is correct. By replacing "advanced" with "plentiful," the relationship between sentences 9 and 10 becomes clearer, and the word "also" in sentence 9 can be understood to indicate that not only are medical services plentiful (see sentence 8), but educational opportunities are plentiful too.

Next is a question that asks you to consider the meaning and purpose of the entire passage:

Which of the following would be the best sentence with which to end the passage?

(A) In sum, the advantages of city life outweigh the disadvantages.
(B) In sum, more jobs and better schools are the main reasons people prefer large cities.
(C) In sum, the attractions of rural life cannot compete with the advantages of cities.
(D) In sum, there are several reasons why people voluntarily relocate to large cities.
(E) In sum, education is the primary reason that people choose to relocate to large cities.

Option A is incorrect because the writer did not discuss the disadvantages of city life. This passage is not a comparison essay, in other words.

Option B is incorrect because it only mentions two of the reasons that the writer discusses. Option B would be an acceptable closing sentence only if it also included reference to medical services.

Option C is incorrect because the attractions of rural life are not discussed in the passage. In fact, the only mention of rural life focuses on its relative disadvantages.

Option D seems correct because it accurately summarizes the content of the passage. However, it would be best for you to examine all options before deciding which one would be best as a closing sentence.

Option E is incorrect because it is not indicated anywhere in the passage that education is the "primary" reason that people relocate to large cities. Rather, it is just one of three reasons discussed by the author. Thus we can be confident that option D is the correct answer.

Finally, here is one more question that asks you to consider the meaning and purpose of the entire passage:

Which of the following would make the most logical title for the passage?

(A) "The perils of country living"
(B) "Relocation to the city"
(C) "The advantages of city life"
(D) "Employment in the big city"
(E) "Why people relocate to cities"

After reading the passage, it should be clear that option E is the best choice of titles among the available options. None of the other options capture the main idea of the passage quite so accurately.

Chapter 3

Ability to Use Source Materials

In the Ability to Use Source Materials section, knowledge of basic reference and research skills is tested through both passage-based and stand-alone questions. The skills tested in this section include documentation of sources, evaluation of sources, integration of resource materials, and use of reference materials. Each of these skills is discussed below, followed by guidance on how to approach Ability to Use Source Materials questions, and then some practice questions with answers and explanations.

DOCUMENTATION OF SOURCES

The ability to evaluate non-fiction writing includes an understanding of why writers provide documentation for some of the statements they make. Three reasons for documenting the source of a statement are to enhance the credibility and persuasiveness of the statement, to provide readers with additional resources, and to meet ethical requirements.

Enhancing Credibility and Persuasiveness

To illustrate how the documentation of a source can enhance a writer's credibility and persuasiveness, consider the following passage:

"Currently about a fifth of the world's electricity comes from hydroelectric power generated by dams. The largest of these dams, the Three Gorges Dam in southern China, is expected to become fully operational in 2011. This is an exciting development. Hopefully greater reliance on energy sources such as dams will reduce our reliance on fossil fuels."

In this passage, the first two sentences convey facts, while the final two sentences convey the writer's personal reaction to the construction of the Three

Gorges Dam and to the broader implications of reliance on hydroelectric power. No authority is needed to justify these last two sentences. If the writer claims to feel a certain way about hydroelectric power, the reader will probably accept this as an accurate description of the writer's feelings. In this particular passage, there is no other source of information about the writer's feelings other than the writer's own expression of them.

In contrast, the reader could question the accuracy of the factual information that the writer provides. Thus, in order to increase credibility and persuasiveness, the writer could provide evidence for the factual assertions. Not direct evidence, of course. The writer of the passage would not attempt to prove that the Three Gorges Dam is the largest dam in the world by flying readers from dam to dam in order to take measurements. However, the writer might choose to mention other writers who have indeed taken such measurements, or who have at least collated the results of published measurements. For example:

"Currently about a fifth of the world's electricity comes from hydroelectric power generated by dams, according to John Smith in *Hydroelectric Power*."

Adding a reference to Smith's book increases the credibility and persuasiveness of the sentence, as it suggests that the writer of the passage is relying on an expert rather than simply guessing about the extent to which the world's electric power is generated by dams. The writer might even add some details about the source in order to directly promote its credibility, as in the following examples:

"Currently about a fifth of the world's electricity comes from hydroelectric power generated by dams, according to hydroelectric engineering expert John Smith in *Hydroelectric Power*."

"Currently about a fifth of the world's electricity comes from hydroelectric power generated by dams, according to John Smith in his authoritative classic *Hydroelectric Power*."

"Currently about a fifth of the world's electricity comes from hydroelectric power generated by dams, according to recent estimates provided by hydroelectric energy expert John Smith."

The reader must be cautious, of course. The mere fact that a writer has cited a source does not guarantee that the source is accurate, complete, or reputable, even if the writer has praised its authoritativeness. This notion is discussed further below under the Evaluation of Sources section.

In sum, documentation of sources is one way to increase the credibility and persuasiveness of a piece of writing.

Providing Readers with Additional Resources

By documenting their sources, writers provide readers with a way of obtaining additional information about a topic. For example, in the passages at the end of the previous section, the reader is alerted to Dr. Smith's book as a resource for further information about hydroelectric power.

When referring to a source, the writer may choose to give the reader information about what can be found in the source, as in the following example:

"Currently about a fifth of the world's electricity comes from hydroelectric power generated by dams, according to John Smith in his authoritative classic *Hydroelectric Power*, which provides a comprehensive overview of the contribution of dams to the world's energy supply."

Alternatively, the writer may simply name a source, and the reader will understand that the source may be consulted for further information. Mentioning sources also allows the reader to verify the accuracy and completeness of what has been written, if the reader so chooses.

Specific information about how writers use bibliographic details to cite sources is given below under the Integration of Resource Materials section.

Ethical Requirements

Most outlets for non-fiction writing, whether scholarly journals, popular magazines, or news media, have rules concerning the documentation of sources.

The main reason that a writer is expected to document a source is to ensure that that the source rather than the writer gets credit for particular statements or ideas. This represents a courtesy to the individuals who originally presented the statement or idea. Moreover, documentation is needed because the use of a source without proper documentation is considered plagiarism, an unethical and, in some circumstances, illegal practice. Plagiarism is illustrated in the following passage:

"I believe that democracy is the most enduring form of government. Government of the people, by the people, and for the people, will not perish from the earth, in my view."

The second sentence of the passage is copied almost verbatim from Abraham Lincoln's Gettysburg Address. By failing to attribute this sentence to Lincoln, the writer appears to be taking credit for having written the sentence himself, and he would therefore be guilty of plagiarism. One way to revise this passage so that it contains no plagiarism would be as follows:

"I believe that democracy is the most enduring form of government. As Abraham Lincoln put it, 'Government of the people, by the people, for the people, shall not perish from the earth.'"

Usually, any quotation included in a piece of writing must be indicated by quotation marks or italics and attributed to a source. Doing so ensures that credit for the quotation is properly attributed. Notice that changing a quotation slightly does not obviate the need to provide a source. For example, compare the two quotations below:

"...government of the people, by the people, for the people, shall not perish from the earth."

"A government that is created from the people, by the people, and for those very people, will never perish from the earth."

The first passage is quoted verbatim from the Gettysburg Address. The second passage would be considered a plagiaristic rendering, if not attributed to Lincoln, even though some of the words are different.

In practice, it can be difficult to determine whether or not a quotation is being used in a plagiaristic way. If the writer assumes that a particular quotation is highly recognizable, the writer may not feel obligated to provide the source. In some cases, a statement is so obviously a quotation, and the source of the quotation is so well-known, that nobody would expect the writer to provide a source. For example:

"As a highly religious person and a holder of public office, I *do* believe that we are one nation under god."

In this passage, the phrase "one nation under god" is taken verbatim from the Pledge of Allegiance, but the writer would not be considered to have committed plagiarism. For one thing, there is no ambiguity about the source. Because virtually every American has memorized the Pledge of Allegiance, virtually every American would recognize the Pledge rather than the writer as the origin of the phrase "one nation under god." Moreover, by using the phrase "I *do* believe," the writer implies that the concept of being one nation under god has already been proposed by someone else, and that the writer himself or herself chooses to embrace the concept.

In other cases, a writer will use a phrase or sentence that others may have used, but the phrase or sentence is so commonplace that no plagiarism can be said to have been committed. Following are some examples:

"Barack Obama was born on August 4, 1961."

"The blue whale is the largest animal in the world."

"The weather today was lovely."

"Children need our love and guidance."

These sentences are likely to have been used more than once already in written works, but using any one of them again would not constitute plagiarism. The first two sentences are simple statements of widely-known facts. There is nothing particularly distinctive about the manner of expression. In fact, it would be hard for a writer to come up with a simpler and more direct way of expressing such facts. The second two sentences convey opinions, but they are not particularly distinctive opinions, and there are not many alternatives for expressing these opinions quite so succinctly. In contrast, consider the following:

"The weather today was as lovely as an unspoiled lake at the foot of the Swiss alps."

If the sentence above already appears in a published work somewhere, using it again without documenting the source would constitute plagiarism, because the expression is highly distinctive. Although many writers have described the weather as lovely, it is not commonplace to compare the weather to an alpine lake. Such expressions should not be quoted with attribution to a source.

Documentation of sources is critical not only for quoted material. Sources must also be provided for ideas and facts. However, an idea or fact that is common knowledge need not be attributed to a source. A writer will not be asked to provide a source for the statement that Atlanta is the capital of Georgia, that Georgia is one of the United States, or that the United States is a major geopolitical power. However, the writer might be required to do provide a source for the assertion that as of 2009, the population of Atlanta was 540,922.

Generally, documentation of sources will be required for three types of material.

First, documentation of sources should be provided for ideas that are highly distinctive owing to their originality. Consider, for example, the following passage:

"Human beings experience considerable internal conflict. The primitive urges of the id clash with the moral restraints of the superego, while the ego does the best it can to compromise between them."

A source is not needed for the first sentence of the passage because this sentence does not convey a particularly distinctive idea. Although you may not agree with the idea, you would recognize it as a generalization that many people accept on some level depending on how the words "considerable" and "internal conflict" are interpreted. In contrast, the idea expressed in the second sentence should be attributed to its source, which happens to be the psychologist, Sigmund Freud. Freud held that the human psyche consists of the id, the ego, and the superego, and that these three entities interrelate in the way described in the passage. As this is a very distinctive idea, it should be attributed to the individual who proposed it.

Second, documentation of sources is needed for ideas or facts that are not commonly known, as in the following example:

"There are more than 400,000 species of beetle, and this year 25 new species were found in oak trees in the south of Turkey."

In this example, the number of species of beetle may be "common" knowledge in the sense of being commonly reported in textbooks and other reference materials, but the discovery of 25 additional species is a new scientific development, and thus in most cases documentation of the source of information about this discovery would be required. The documentation might consist of reference to a scholarly journal, a magazine article, a newspaper report, or some other source.

Third, documentation of sources is needed for ideas and facts that are difficult to verify, as in the following example:

"Parrot Jungle was one of the most popular tourist attractions in South Florida during much of the second half of the twentieth century, but it has since vanished without a trace."

In this example, the fact that the writer is discussing something that no longer exists calls for documentation of sources. In brief, the writer should indicate exactly where he or she has obtained information about this tourist attraction.

The need for documenting a source is not always as clear cut as in the previous examples. When an idea that was originally distinctive becomes widely accepted, or at least widely known, the source may or may not need to be identified. For example:

"Most bacteria die when exposed to antibiotics. However, a small number of bacteria have mutations that make them resistant to antibiotics. These bacteria survive and reproduce. Thus, through natural selection, the next generation of bacteria will be primarily antibiotic-resistant."

This passage contains reference to facts about bacteria that were discovered in the 20th century and are now considered to be well-established. Although an undergraduate writing a term paper may be required to provide sources for these facts, a journalist writing a newspaper article may not have such a requirement. Editorial policy may or may not require the journalist to provide specific citation. Alternatively, the journalist may be able to refer to the sources in a general way (e.g., "Experts agree that most bacteria die when exposed to antibiotics.") An additional consideration is the journalist's own level of expertise. The need for a citation may be relaxed for a journalist who is a doctor, or writes regularly about scientific topics.

The passage above also contains reference to natural selection, a distinctive concept formulated by Charles Darwin in the 19th century. In some cases, the writer of this passage would be required to cite Darwin. In other cases, natural selection could simply be mentioned without reference to a source. Although not everyone accepts the phenomenon of natural selection, the concept is widely assumed among scientists and taught as a core concept in biology classes. Here again, the expertise of the journalist may be taken into account.

EVALUATION OF SOURCES

As noted earlier, documentation of sources increases their credibility and persuasiveness, but in some cases a source may be inaccurate, unreliable, or used in a misleading way by a writer. Thus, the ability to evaluate non-fiction writing depends in turn on the ability to analyze and evaluate a writer's sources.

Readers can evaluate a source by examining it, or at least by examining bibliographic information given by the writer who cites the source. Some of the dimensions on which sources can be evaluated include date of publication, edition, type of source, credibility of source, credibility of author, relevance and scope of coverage, and objectivity of coverage.

Date of Publication

When evaluating a source, readers should consider when the source was published or created.

For some topics, such as science, technology, and current events, up-to-date sources can be critical. Consider the following two passages written in 2010:

"The great philosopher Aristotle was born in Stageira in 384 B.C. (Jones, 1990)."

"At present a silicon microprocessor chip may contain as many as a million transistors (Smith, 1990)."

In each case, a publication from 1990 is cited as a source. The fact that the source is 20 years old does not seem problematic with respect to the biographical details of a famous philosopher. However, the age of the source does seem problematic as a basis for information about current microprocessor technology. The assertion made by Smith (1990) may have been accurate 20 years ago, but it is almost certainly inaccurate regarding the present state of the field, given the rapidity of scientific and technological change.

Edition

Another characteristic that contributes to the credibility and persuasiveness of a source is its edition.

The first edition of a source represents the original publication. If the source is revised in some way and then released again for publication, the revision will be referred to as a "revised edition" or "new edition," or it will be referred to by number (e.g., "second edition," "third edition," and so on).

The importance of information about edition is that later editions of a work are often considered more authoritative than earlier ones. The fact that a publisher chooses to produce further editions beyond the first one suggests that that work has been well-received. Moreover, with each successive edition the author will have the opportunity to correct mistakes, make improvements, incorporate new developments and otherwise improve the quality of the work. However, not all subsequent editions contain substantial revisions.

Type of Source

To the greatest extent possible, the reader should identify and evaluate the types of sources that a writer provides. In particular, the reader should consider whether each source is primary or secondary, and peer reviewed or non-peer reviewed.

Primary sources consist of original findings, observations, ideas, or creations. Examples of primary sources include scientific reports in which the authors describe the findings of their research, eyewitness accounts of events, original theoretical statements, and authoritative documents (e.g., the U.S. Constitution).

Secondary sources consist of summaries, analyses, or commentaries regarding primary sources. Examples of secondary sources include literature reviews (i.e., reviews of research and/or theory on a particular topic), critical analyses, textbooks, and guides to particular works of scholarship or art. The purpose of a secondary source is to help readers understand, integrate, and/or judge a primary source or sources.

Primary and secondary sources are not inherently different in the extent of their accuracy or completeness. However, they differ in other important ways. A primary source is a firsthand account. The author of a primary source may be inaccurate, biased, or incomplete in his or her assertions, but the author will be the most direct source of information about what he or she asserts. A secondary source can provide background information and analysis that makes a primary source clearer, or that helps the reader understand biases and other limitations of the primary source. However, the secondary source is one step removed from the primary source, and may reflect its own limitations and biases.

The importance of distinguishing primary from secondary sources can be illustrated by comparing an eyewitness account of a historical event to a later description of the event in which eyewitness accounts are summarized. The eyewitness is in a unique position as to how it feels to have experienced or observed an event. However, if the eyewitness does not happen to be a historian, he or she may not be the best source of information about the historical context for the event. Rather, the historian writing a secondary source may be a better source of information about historical developments leading up to the event. In short, an eyewitness account may be a good source to cite when describing what it was like to experience a particular event. A historical analysis might be a preferable source to cite for an analysis of the causes of the event.

Along with the primary-secondary source distinction, another key distinction that readers can make is between peer reviewed and non-peer reviewed sources.

Peer review refers to the process by which a small number of experts in a particular field review a manuscript and make a recommendation as to whether it should be published. Typically, an editor will then make a decision as to whether the manuscript should be published as is, published with revisions, or rejected. Although peer review does not guarantee that a source is accurate and complete, peer reviewed publications are typically considered more reliable than those that are not peer reviewed owing to the quality control provided by the review process. Thus, in discussing the causes of economic distress, a peer-reviewed journal article will be a more credible source than a blog or a letter to the editor of a local newspaper.

The distinction between peer reviewed and non-peer reviewed sources roughly corresponds to a distinction between scholarly and popular sources. However, not all scholarly publications are peer-reviewed, and some popular sources do have a rigorous editorial process. Thus, the reader should also consider whether the intended audience of a source is primarily scholars, some other specialist group, or the general public.

Credibility of Source

For the reader who does not have expertise in a particular area, it can be difficult to ascertain the credibility of sources representing that area. Peer review confers some degree of credibility but does not guarantee that a source is accurate or complete. The same can be said for university presses and government agencies, whose publications are generally considered to be reputable but are by no means infallible. Type of source is nonetheless an important detail that the reader should consider when evaluating credibility.

As noted, scholarly sources tend to be considered more credible than popular sources. However, popular sources vary widely in this dimension. News sources such as *The New York Times* or *The Washington Post* are highly respected, for example. At the other end of the spectrum, a blog written by someone with an extreme political agenda is likely to be a less credible source of information.

Evaluation of credibility can be aided by locating critical reviews of the source through a reference work such as *Book Review Index, Book Review Digest,* or *Periodical Abstracts*. The reader can then determine whether reviews tend to be positive, whether the source is respected, whether the source includes points that are controversial or widely considered false, and whether the reviews point to other sources that are considered more authoritative.

An important consideration when evaluating credibility is the possibility of bias. The reader should consider who publishes the source and for what purpose. For example, a source published by a particular corporation may tend to reflect that corporation's interests. A source published by a group with a specific political or social agenda may reflect that agenda both in the range of topics covered and in the treatment of those topics.

In some cases, the possibility of bias will be evident from the name of a source. For example, the following (fictional) sources would probably not be unbiased sources of information about the debate over gun control:

Proceedings of the Biennial Meeting of the Mandatory Gun Ownership Society

The Annual Newsletter of the Consortium for the Worldwide Banishment of Firearms

Judging from their titles, neither one of these fictional sources would be likely to provide an unbiased look at the gun control debate. They may be useful sources of information about extreme positions in the debate, but they are unlikely to provide an unbiased overview.

In other cases, the reader may need to evaluate the possibility of bias by examining the contents of a source. Even without expertise in a particular area, the reader may be able to determine that only certain kinds of topics or perspectives are reflected in the source. This point is discussed further in the Objectivity section below.

Credibility of Author

Although it is also difficult for non-experts to appraise the credibility of an author, when evaluating a source the reader should consider the author's credentials and institutional affiliation, as well as any evidence as to the author's area of expertise, publication record, and professional reputation. Whether or not the author has been paid for the work, or has a professional affiliation with the organization that publishes the work, should also be considered.

By cross-referencing information in a source with information from other sources, the reader can determine the extent of convergence between an author's views and that of others who have written about the same topic. The credibility of an author may be diminished if he or she disagrees with the majority on basic facts (although, of course, the majority is not always right). Certainly the credibility of the author is undermined if he or she makes claims that are easily refuted through cross-referencing. For example, if an author claims that no studies have been conducted on a particular topic, but you discover studies on that topic, you should question whether the author's view of the topic can be trusted.

Information about authors can also be obtained from publications, Internet searches, and biographical sources such as *American Men and Women of Science* and *Contemporary Authors*. Although even the most well connected and highly esteemed authors make mistakes and exhibit biases, generally speaking the more widely respected the author, the more credible and persuasive the source created by that author will tend to be.

Relevance of Coverage

When documenting a statement, the sources that a writer provides should support that particular statement. For example, suppose that a writer is discussing the characteristics of Arenal Volcano in Costa Rica and wishes to document the dates of significant eruptions since the outset of the 20th century. A scholarly work on Arenal would be a credible source of information, but not if the work exclusively pertains to the formation of the volcano, the nature of seismological processes inside the volcano, or the economic impact of the volcano as a source of tourism. Rather, the writer would need a source that specifically discusses the recent history of Arenal's eruptions. Unless the reader is already familiar with a source, the main way of determining its relevance is to examine the source.

As this example suggests, the breadth of coverage in a source can impact its credibility and persuasiveness. Sources that focus on highly specific topics can enhance the credibility of specific statements about such topics, but they do not serve well to support broader statements. Sources that treat topics more broadly can provide stronger support for broad assertions. However, a source that is very broad, such as an introduction or an overview of a topic, may not be very authoritative if the content sacrifices depth for breadth.

Objectivity

The objectivity of the writing in a source has some impact on its credibility and persuasiveness. Even if the reader is not an expert on the topic discussed in the source, the reader may be able to evaluate objectivity if he or she is able to examine the source. The reader can look for evidence as to whether the writer's point of view is more or less impartial or biased. If the writer promotes a particular theory or takes a particular side in a debate, the reader can check whether the writer presents all sides of key arguments and acknowledges potential limitations to the views that he or she favors. The reader can check whether the writer has omitted key details—particularly those that do not seem to support the writer's own particular point of view. The reader can also evaluate the quality of argumentation and whether the source itself provides additional sources, if appropriate.

To illustrate how objectivity can be evaluated even in the absence of expertise regarding a topic, consider the following passages:

"Although numerous studies in which socioeconomic status (SES) is measured rely on single-item indicators of SES, SES is clearly a multidimensional construct, and different dimensions differentially affect families and children. For example, children's academic achievement is affected by parent education levels more strongly than by family income, regardless of some misguided claims to the contrary."

"Although numerous studies in which socioeconomic status (SES) is measured rely on single-item indicators of SES, evidence indicates that SES is a multidimensional construct, and that different dimensions differentially affect families and children (Conger & Dogan, 2007). For example, recent studies show that children's academic achievement is affected by parent education levels more strongly than by family income, although not all studies support this contention."

Even without knowledge of this particular area of research, the careful reader can detect that the writing of the first passage is less objective than that of the second one. The writer's tone is quite definitive, and his or her use of the term "clearly" as well as the phrase "regardless of some misguided claims to the contrary" seem dismissive of alternative points of view. In contrast, the second passage conveys similar points with a greater degree of impartiality. Rather than stating that SES "is clearly" multidimensional, the writer notes that "evidence indicates" as much, and the writer then provides a reference to an additional source (work by Conger & Dongan, 2007). In the final sentence, the writer supports his or her point through reference to "recent studies" and acknowledges that not all studies support the point. On the whole, the second passage seems less biased, and thus constitutes a more credible source. The second passage contains more documentation of the assertions that are made, and more acknowledgment of alternative points of view.

One of the most important clues to bias is word choice. When evaluating a source, the reader should be attentive to the particular words and phrases that are used, as they reveal something about the writer's attitudes. Certain words and phrases clearly indicate a biased perspective. For example, consider the following descriptions of the same individual:

"The manager hired a short order cook who had been convicted previously of theft."

"The manager hired a short order cook with a criminal record."

"The manager hired a short order cook who was a hardened criminal."

"The manager hired a short order cook who was not only a cook but a crook!"

"The manager hired a short order cook who had been prosecuted for committing a crime."

In the first two sentences, the cook's criminal history is described in an impartial way. The writer of each sentence might turn out to be biased, of course, but no bias is revealed in these particular sentences (at least when considered out of context), because they are merely statements of fact. In context, the phrase "hardened" in the third sentence conveys a negative judgment. The possibility of bias is suggested by use of this phrase rather than a more factual description of the person. In the fourth sentence, reference to the cook with the slang phrase "crook" suggests even more strongly that the writer is negatively biased against the cook. Here, the writer seems more concerned with judging the cook unfavorably (and attempting to be witty by exploiting the similarity between "cook" and "crook") than providing an accurate description of the person. Finally, the fifth sentence seems to reflect positive bias, in that the writer acknowledges that the cook had committed a crime but also indicates that the cook had been "prosecuted" for the crime. Through the use of the term "prosecuted," the writer appears to be taking the cook's side, an impression that would not be conveyed if the writer had chosen a more neutral term such as "convicted."

INTEGRATION OF RESOURCE MATERIALS

Citations

There are many ways to integrate sources into a particular piece of writing. Reference to a specific source in the main text of a piece of writing is referred to as a citation. You have seen an example of a citation already in the following sentence from the previous section:

"Although numerous studies in which socioeconomic status (SES) is measured rely on single-item indicators of SES, evidence indicates that SES is a multidimensional construct, and that different dimensions differentially affect families and children (Conger & Dogan, 2007)."

In this sentence, two authors whose last names are Conger and Dogan are cited. The context of the citation suggests that Conger and Dogan are scholars, and that the work cited is scholarly rather than a popular source. The reader cannot tell, however, whether the citation is a book, a journal article, or some other kind of publication. As discussed in the references section below, full bibliographic details will typically also be provided to the reader, either in a footnote, or in a separate reference list. By looking at that footnote or reference list, the reader will be able to find the details of what "Conger & Dogan, 2007" refers to.

Now consider again the following statement about hydroelectric power:

"Currently about a fifth of the world's electricity comes from hydroelectric power generated by dams."

Let us suppose that the writer wishes to cite a source for this particular fact. Suppose too that an internationally-renowned expert on hydroelectric power named John Smith has published a book in 2007 entitled *Hydroelectric Power,* and that pages 342 and 343 of this book include detailed and highly credible information about how much of the world's electricity comes from hydroelectric power and other technologies. Following are just a few of the approaches that could be used to integrate Smith's work into this sentence by means of a citation:

"As John Smith observes in *Hydroelectric Power*, currently about a fifth of the world's electricity comes from hydroelectric power generated by dams."

"*Hydroelectric Power* tells us that currently about a fifth of the world's electricity comes from hydroelectric power generated by dams."

"Currently about a fifth of the world's electricity comes from hydroelectric power generated by dams, according to an authoritative source."

"Currently about a fifth of the world's electricity comes from hydroelectric power generated by dams (Smith, 2007)."

"Smith (2007) indicates that currently about a fifth of the world's electricity comes from hydroelectric power generated by dams."

"Smith indicates that currently about a fifth of the world's electricity comes from hydroelectric power generated by dams (342-343)."

"Currently about a fifth of the world's electricity comes from hydroelectric power generated by dams (Smith 342-343)."

"Currently about a fifth of the world's electricity comes from hydroelectric power generated by dams (Smith 2007, 342-343)."

"Currently about a fifth of the world's electricity comes from hydroelectric power generated by dams, according to John Smith.[2]

When citing sources in a text, and providing full bibliographic details in a footnote or reference section, writers do not do so haphazardly. Rather, they are expected to systematically adhere to a set of rules. Three of the most prominent sets of rules are referred to as APA style, MLA style, and Chicago style. As you will see, each of these styles embodies a large number of highly specific rules, all of which reflect a common purpose: to facilitate access to sources. That is, the rules for citing sources and providing bibliographic details all help ensure that readers have the information they need to readily locate those sources.

Following are the rules governing citations in APA, MLA, and Chicago styles.

APA Style Citation

The American Psychological Association (APA) publishes a book entitled "Publication Manual of the American Psychological Association." This book is widely used in the social sciences as a comprehensive guide to scientific writing, and thus writers are often required to conform to APA style (or "APA format").

In APA style, sources are cited in the text of a piece of writing, and full bibliographic details are given in a separate reference section. Following are some of the rules for citations in APA style. (Rules governing reference lists are discussed in the References section below.)

First, citations in the text typically consist of the last name(s) of the author(s) of a source and the year of publication. For example:

"Smith and Jones (2006) found that many students dislike homework."

"It has been found that many students dislike homework (Smith & Jones, 2006).

The first sentence illustrates what is known as an in-text citation, while the second sentence contains a parenthetical citation of the same source. Notice that the word "and" is used to link author names in the in-text citation, while the use of an ampersand (&) is used to link their names in the parenthetical citation. This illustrates the great specificity of the rules in APA style (as can also be observed in the other two styles discussed here). This section does not provide comprehensive list of rules, but rather concentrates on describing those rules that a reader would need to know in order to understand the information that is given in citations and reference lists.

When more than one source appears in a parenthetical citation, the sources are listed alphabetically by the first letter of the last name of the first author, and each source is separated by semicolons, as in the following example:

"It has been found that many students dislike homework (Smith & Jones, 2006; Thomson, 2001; Yoon, Hong, Kwan, & Li, 2010)."

In the example above, three sources are mentioned. Smith and Jones (2006) is the first source, Thomson (2001) is the second source, and Yoon, Hong, Kwan and Li (2010) is the third source.

When a source has three to six authors, the writer must cite all authors the first time the source is identified in the text. In later references to the source, the writer should cite the last name of the first author, followed by the phrase "et al.", which is Latin for "and others." For example, notice the two citations of a work by Lassiter, Rynor, and Kilbretz in the following passage:

"Lassiter, Rynor, and Kilbretz (1997) found that many students dislike math homework more than other types of homework. Williams (1995) obtained similar findings. Lassiter et al. (1997) also found that the difference between attitudes toward math homework versus other types is stronger among high school students as compared with their middle school peers."

When a source has more than six authors, the writer only needs to cite the first six authors when the source is first identified in the text. All subsequent identifications of the source can consist of the last name of the first author followed by the phrase "et al."

When a source is an organization rather than an individual or group of individuals, the writer should cite the organization's name in the text, as illustrated in the following sentence:

"Reading research that relies on experimental or quasi-experimental designs continues to play a prominent role in the field (U. S. Department of Education, 2009)."

When a source is quoted, the page number(s) from which the quotation is drawn should also be provided, as in the following examples:

"Many students recognize the importance of homework even though they dislike spending time on homework assignments" (Brooks, 2004, p. 37).

"As Brooks (2004) points out, "Many students recognize the importance of homework even though they dislike spending time on homework assignments" (p. 37)."

When a source within a source is cited, both are included in the citation, as in the following example:

"Khan (2005) found a greater percentage of oaks than elms in this particular region (as cited in Jerrison, 2001)."

In this example, Khan (2005) is likely to be a primary source that is discussed in Jerrison (2001).

Other rules govern the citation of sources without authors, articles in non-scholarly sources such as newspapers and magazines, personal communications such as e-mails and letters, theses and dissertations, and non-print materials such as audio recordings and videotapes.

When a source is an Internet resource, the rules for citation in the text are generally the same as for print publications. That is, the citation will consist of the last name of the author(s) and the year of publication. However, in some cases a writer will cite a website but not a specific document on that website. In such cases, the writer should provide the Internet address, as in the following example:

"The Bureau of Ocean Energy Management, Regulation, and Enforcement is the federal agency that oversees development of energy and mineral resources on the outer continental shelf (http://www.boemre.gov/aboutBOEMRE)."

MLA Style Citation

The Modern Language Association (MLA) publishes a book entitled "The MLA Style Manual and Guide to Scholarly Publishing." This book is widely used in the humanities as a comprehensive writing guide, and thus writers are often required to conform to MLA style.

MLA style differs from APA style in the rules governing citation of sources in the main text.

First, citations in the main text typically consist of the last name of the author(s) and the page number(s), as in the following examples:

"Smith and Jones found that many students dislike homework (47-48)."

"It has been found that many students dislike homework (Smith and Jones 47-48)."

If reference is made to an entire source, page numbers need not be included. If page information is included and reference must be made to more than one page or sequence of pages, the page numbers are separated by commas, as below:

"It has been found that many students dislike homework (Smith and Jones 47-48, 50, 52-54)."

As with APA style, semicolons are used to separate sources when more than one source is included in a parenthetical citation. For example:

"It has been found that many students dislike homework (Smith and Jones 47-48; Thomson 22; Yoon, Hong, Kwan, & Li 33, 35-36)."

When a source has more than three authors, MLA style allows the writer to either name all authors, or simply name the first three followed by the designation "et al." When the source is an organization, the organization name is used along with page number, if page information is needed. If the source is part of a multi-volume set, the volume number is also included in the citation in the text, separated from the page number(s) by a colon, as in the following example:

"Boys tend to dislike homework more than girls do (Mattingly 2: 166)."

In this example, page 166 of volume 2 in a multi-volume series is cited.

When a source within a source is cited, both are included in the citation, as in the following example:

"Khan found a greater percentage of oaks than elms in this particular region (cited in Jerrison 67)."

If the source within a source is quoted, the abbreviation "qtd." is used, as follows:

According to Khan, "oaks predominate in this particular region (qtd. in Jerrison 67)."

As with APA style, other rules govern the citation of sources without authors, articles in non-scholarly sources such as newspapers and magazines, personal communications such as e-mails, theses and dissertations, and non-print materials such as audio recordings and videotapes.

The MLA rules for citation of Internet sources are similar to those for print sources. The citation should include the first item that appears in the reference list (referred to as the Works Cited section). Often this will be the first author's last name, but it may be the name of an article or website. No page numbers are needed unless a separate article is downloaded. If citing a website, the entire

URL is not needed. Rather, a domain name or some other phrase that will direct the reader to the correct entry in the Works Cited section will be acceptable.

Chicago Style Citation

The *Chicago Manual of Style* (CMS) is older than the APA and MLA manuals and, unlike those two manuals, it was not created by a professional organization. It is, however, widely used as a guide to all aspects of writing, and thus writers are often required to conform to Chicago style.

Chicago style allows writers to choose between two different systems for citations and full bibliographic details. One system is referred to as notes and bibliography, while the other is called author-date. Each system is roughly allied with different areas of scholarship. Scholars in the arts and humanities often use the notes and bibliography system, while scholars in the physical and social sciences often use the author-date system.

In the notes and bibliography system, each source cited in the text is marked by a superscript at the end of each sentence in which the source is mentioned, as in the following example:

"Garcia also found that the amount of homework assigned by middle-school teachers varies widely from school to school, even within the same district[1]."

Full bibliographic details are then provided in a footnote or endnote, as discussed below in the references section.

In the author-date system, citations in the main text generally consist of author(s), date of publication, and page number(s), as in the following example:

"High-achieving students do not necessarily like homework more than their less accomplished peers do, but they seem to value it more (Smits and von Kaampen 2002, 354)."

As with the APA and MLA styles, Chicago style includes other rules that govern the citation of sources without authors, articles in non-scholarly sources such as newspapers and magazines, personal communications such as e-mails and letters, theses and dissertations, non-print materials such as audio recordings and videotapes, and Internet resources.

References

In order to examine a source that has been cited, the reader will need the complete bibliographic details for the source. Along with names of author(s), date of publication, and title, the reader will also need to know the publisher and edition (if the source is a book), or the journal name and volume (if the source is a journal).

If the source is obtained from a website, the reader will need the URL and possibly also the DOI, if available.

The URL or Universal Resource Locator is the Internet address that uniquely identifies an electronic resource such as the page of a website. An example of a URL would be the home page of The New York Times: http://www.nytimes.com.

The DOI or Digital Object Identifier is a character string that uniquely identifies an electronic resource. Although not all resources on the Internet have a DOI, for those that do, the particular DOI will be permanent. URLs, in contrast, may change.

APA Style References

APA style requires that the writer create a separate list of references that contain full bibliographic details for all works cited in the main text. The works cited will be listed in alphabetic order in the reference list according to the first letter of the (first) author's last name.

Along with alphabetization of sources, there are many other rules governing how bibliographic details are presented in the APA style reference list. As a writer, you would need to consult the most recent edition of the "Publication Manual of the American Psychological Association" in order to conform to APA style in creating a reference section. As a reader, what is critical is that you understand what kinds of information are available from each part of a full citation. Following are example citations for four of the most common types of scholarly sources, as would be found in an APA style reference section:

Springer, K. (2010). *Educational research: A contextual approach*. New Jersey: Wiley.

Springer, K. (1999). How a naive theory of biology is acquired. In M. Siegal and C. Peterson (Eds.) *Children's understanding of biology and health* (pp. 45-70). Cambridge: Cambridge University Press.

Springer, K. (2001). Perceptual boundedness and perceptual support in conceptual development. *Psychological Review, 108*, 691-708.

Springer, K. (1997). Conceptual coherence in children's understanding of kinship. Invited paper presented at the 7th annual meeting of the European Association for Research in Learning and Instruction, Athens, Greece.

The first source is a book. The author is Springer and the publication date is 2010. The title is given in italics, followed by the place of publication (New Jersey) and the name of the publisher (Wiley).

The second source is a chapter from an edited book published in 1999. The author of the chapter is Springer and the chapter title is "How a naïve theory of biology is acquired." This chapter appeared in a book edited by Siegal and Peterson entitled "Children's understanding of biology and health." The chapter occupies pages 45 through 70 of the edited book. The edited book was published in Cambridge by Cambridge University Press.

The third source is a journal article. The author is Springer, the publication date is 2001, and the title is given immediately following the publication date. The name of the journal is *Psychological Review*. The volume number of the journal is 108. The article occupies pages 691 through 708 in the journal.

The fourth source is a conference presentation. The author is Springer, the date of the conference is 2007, and the title is given immediately following the conference date. The type of presentation is invited paper (as opposed to symposium paper, poster, keynote address, etc.). The name of the conference is the 7th annual meeting of the European Association for Research in Learning and Instruction, and the conference location is Athens, Greece.

For sources with more than six authors, only the first six need to be included in the reference list, as in the following example:

Dolan, L., Kellam, S., Brown, C., Werthamer-Larsson, L., Rebok, G., Mayer, L., et al. (1993). The short-term impacts of two classroom-based preventive interventions on aggressive and shy behaviors and poor achievement. *Journal of Applied Developmental Psychology, 14,* 317-345.

Sources that are organizations are cited in the reference list in much the way as publications by specific authors. For example:

National Assessment of Educational Progress. (1999). *Reading report card for the nation and state.* Washington, DC: National Center for Education Statistics, Office of Education Research and Improvement, U.S. Department of Education.

For sources other than books and articles, the type of source will be clearly identified in the reference section, as in the following examples:

Doe, J. M. (2010). *Family conflict and stress.* Unpublished manuscript.

Smith, P. M. (2005). *Compliance with style guides in the creation of reference lists: A mixed-methods study* (Doctoral Dissertation). University of Terner, Joliet, FL.

Most of the discussion thus far has focused on scholarly sources. APA style references for non-scholarly sources are similar but not identical. For example, the following is a reference list entry for a magazine article:

King, R. D. (1997, April). Should English be the law? *Atlantic Monthly, 279*, 55-64

For resources obtained from the Internet, a stable URL should provided along with a DOI (if available). If the URL is not stable, the home page of the website from which the source was retrieved should be provided. The date should be given for the final version of a work that is dated, but if the work has no date or the date changes (as in the case of an electronic encyclopedia article), then the date that the source was retrieved should be provided. Following are some examples:

Sanchez, D., & King-Toler, E. (2007). Addressing disparities consultation and outreach strategies for university settings. *Consulting Psychology Journal: Practice and Research, 59*(4), 286-295. doi:10.1037/1065- 9293.59.4.286

Miller, B. M. (2003). Critical hours: After-school programs and educational success. Retrieved 14 June 2006, from http://www.nmefdn.org/CriticalHours.htm.

Center for Prevention Research and Development. (2004). Teen REACH: Annual evaluation report. Retrieved from http://www.cprd.uiuc.edu/research/highrisk-pubs/TRAnnualReport04.pdf.

MLA and Chicago Style References

In MLA style, bibliographic information appears in a separate Works Cited section, similar to the reference section used in APA style.

As noted earlier, Chicago style allows writers to choose between the author-date (A-D) versus the notes and bibliography (NB) systems for citations and references.

In the A-D system, each source is cited in the text (as described in the Chicago style citations section), and full bibliographic details are given in a separate reference list similar to the reference section in APA style.

In the NB system, each source is cited in the text by means of a superscript number wherever the source is mentioned or quoted. Full bibliographic details are then provided by number in footnotes or endnotes. (Endnotes are a separate section located at the end of a chapter or document.)

The information provided for each source differs somewhat in content and order across the three styles. For example, here is how the same book would be referenced in APA, MLA, Chicago A-D, and Chicago NB styles:

APA style:

Springer, K. (2010). *Educational research: A contextual approach.* New Jersey: Wiley.

MLA style:

Springer, Ken. *Educational research: A contextual approach.* New Jersey: Wiley, 2010. Print.

Chicago A-D style:

Springer, Ken. 2010. *Educational research: A contextual approach.* New Jersey: Wiley.

Chicago NB style:

Ken Springer, *Educational research: A contextual approach.* (New Jersey: Wiley, 2010).

Along with variability in order of information, further differences between styles can be illustrated with reference to this single-author book.

First, unlike the other styles, MLA style requires that the type of source (print, audiovisual, electronic, etc.) be specified. Thus, in the MLA reference above, the word "Print" at the end of the reference indicates that the source is available through hard copy only.

Second, in Chicago NB style, if a source is cited more than once, each subsequent reference to the source after the first one can be abbreviated. For example, suppose that Springer's book referenced above is cited in an article on pages 4 and 12. Recall that each citation will be given in the text by means of a superscript number. In a footnote on page 4, the full reference to Springer's book will be provided. However, the footnote on page 12 can simply consist of the following abbreviated reference: Springer, *Educational Research.*

Third, if the writer wishes to quote from or otherwise refer to a specific page or pages in a source, APA and MLA styles require the writer to give the page number(s) in the text. In Chicago NB style, the page number may be given at the end of the bibliographic entry, as in the following example:

First citation:

Ken Springer, *Educational research: A contextual approach.* (New Jersey: Wiley, 2010), 27-28.

Subsequent citations:

Springer, *Educational Research*, 27-28.

Other differences between the styles can be seen in the following references to the same scholarly journal article. (Note that "Fall, 1995" is part of the title of the article rather than date of publication. The date of publication is 1997):

APA style:

Brod, R., & Huber, B. J. (1997). Foreign language enrollments in United States institutions of higher education, Fall 1995. *ADFL Bulletin, 28*(2), 55-61.

MLA style:

Brod, Richard, and Bettina J. Huber. "Foreign Language Enrollments in United States Institutions of Higher Education, Fall 1995." *ADFL Bulletin* 28.2 (1997): 55-61. Print.

Chicago A-D style:

Brod, Richard, and Bettina J. Huber. 2009. "Foreign Language Enrollments in United States Institutions of Higher Education, Fall 1995." *ADFL Bulletin* 28: 55-61.

Chicago NB style:

Richard Brod and Bettina J. Huber, "Foreign Language Enrollments in United States Institutions of Higher Education, Fall 1995," *ADFL Bulletin* 28 (1997): 55-61.

There are many other specific differences between these styles guiding the way reference lists, footnotes and endnotes are written, and thus authors should consult the appropriate style manual for guidance. As a reader, however, this section of the chapter should have provided you enough information to be able to decipher most of the information you would encounter in reference lists, footnotes, or endnotes. However, you will also need to know the meanings of various abbreviations and acronyms that are used in bibliographic entries.

Abbreviations in Bibliographic Entries

Following are some of the abbreviations commonly used in bibliographic entries in one or more of the three styles discussed here. (Note that some of these abbreviations may be capitalized in an entry.)

Abbreviation	Definition
chap.	Chapter
dir.	Director
diss.	Dissertation
doi	Digital Object Identifier, or DOI; the character string that uniquely identifies an electronic resource
ed.	Editor or edition
eds.	Editors
et al. Et alia.	A Latin phrase meaning, literally, "and others." Used to indicate additional authors
ibid.	Ibidem. A Latin term meaning, literally, "the same place." Used to indicate that a citation refers to the immediately preceding source
lib.	Library
n.d.	No date available for the source
n.p.	No publisher or place of publication available for the source
n.pag.	No page numbers available for the source
no.	Number. As in volume number, section number, et cetera
P	Press; a publishing house
para.	paragraph
p.	Page
p.p.	Pages
prod.	Producer
pt.	Part
qtd.	Quoted
rep.	Report
rev.	Revision or Reviewer
rpt.	Reprint
sec.	Section
s.v. Sub voca.	A Latin phrase meaning, literally, "under the word." Used to refer to a particular section of a bibliographic entry. For example, if the source is a discussion of thermodynamics in an encyclopedia, bibliographic details will be given for the encyclopedia, followed by "s.v. Thermodynamics."
trans.	Translator
U	University. For example, "U Texas P" stands for "University of Texas Press."
URL	Universal Resource Locator. The Internet address that uniquely identifies an electronic resource.
vol.	Volume
writ.	Writer

USE OF REFERENCE MATERIALS

Types of Reference Materials

Readers have access to many different kinds of reference materials. These materials are sources of factual information. When the facts are in dispute, as for certain topics discussed in an encyclopedia, for example, the coverage will be balanced and objective. Following are some key examples of reference materials:

An **almanac** is a book that consists of useful factual information. The information is presented in the form of lists, facts, tables, charts, timelines, and so on. Almanacs may pertain to a particular field or to the entire world. The organization may be topical or chronological. The reader might consult an almanac for astronomical data such as the times of sunrise and sunset, meteorological data such as forecasts, agricultural data such as information for gardeners, cultural data such as the dates of religious holidays and festivals, political data such chronologies of international events, and so on.

An **atlas** is a set of maps. A particular atlas may provide information about the layout of the solar system or the geographic features of a particular planet. At atlas may provide information about the physical geography of the entire world, one country, and/or one city. An atlas may identify boundaries that are economic, social, cultural, or natural. An atlas may consist of national or local transportation routes such as road maps. Although the main information in an atlas is graphic, presented in the form of maps, statistical information may also be included.

A **bibliography** is a list of writings organized by a particular topic or author. A bibliography provides citation information for sources such as books and articles. The reader may consult the bibliography to find sources for a particular topic or sources created by a particular author. In an annotated bibliography, information about each source such as a summary or a critical evaluation will also be provided.

A **citation index** is a list of citations for known sources. The citation index contains bibliographic information for later sources that cite each particular earlier source. The reader will consult the citation index to identify later sources that cite a particular book, article, and/or author. In this way the reader can find out where that book, article, or author has been discussed.

A **concordance** is an alphabetical list of significant words used in a written work or set of works. The concordance includes information such as page number indicating where each word is used. The reader will consult a concordance in order to determine all usages of a particular word in a source or set of sources that share a common element such as authorship. In a topical concordance, an alphabetical list of significant topics rather than words is presented.

A **dictionary** is an alphabetized list of words in a language that provides each word's definition. Information about pronunciation, part of speech, origin, alternative forms, and/or usage may also be provided. Special kinds of dictionaries include foreign language dictionaries, picture dictionaries, and dictionaries for particular topics such as literary terms, phrases used in a particular body of work, quotations, and so on. Further details about dictionaries are described below.

An **encyclopedia** is an alphabetically arranged set of entries covering a broad range of topics. Each entry provides an overview and summary of a topic. Encyclopedias may be pertain to all areas of human knowledge, or focus on topics in one particular area such as science and technology. The reader will consult an encyclopedia in order to obtain an introduction to a particular topic.

A **thesaurus** is an alphabetized list of words in which synonyms for each word are provided. Homonyms and antonyms may be provided as well. The reader will consult a thesaurus in order to identify different terms that convey the same concept.

Use of Dictionaries and Thesauri

Most reference materials include instructions for use. This section contains information about how to make use of dictionaries and thesauri.

Following is an example of a dictionary entry:

bi·as (bī 'əs) *n.* 1. A line cutting diagonally across the grain of fabric. 2. Preference or inclination that inhibits impartiality; prejudice. *-adv.* On a diagonal; aslant. *-v.* **-ased** or **-assed**, **as·ing** or **as·sing**. To cause to have a bias; prejudice. [< OFr. biais, oblique.]

This entry provides information about pronunciation, part of speech, meanings, grammatical forms, and etymology. (Etymology refers to the history of a word, including its origins and important changes in usage and form over time.)

First, pronunciation is indicated by the two renderings of the word "bias" in the entry: "bi·as (bī 'əs)". The dot that divides the first rendering in half indicates a syllable break. The accent mark that divides the second rendering in half indicates that the first syllable is stressed. The sounds of the consonants and vowels in the word are given in the second rendering.

Next, part of speech is indicated by the italicized "n," which tells the reader that the word is a noun.

Following the "n" is a description of two different meanings for the noun. As you can see, the first meaning is concrete, while the second meaning is abstract.

Information is also provided about different inflections such as "biased" and "biasing". From this entry you can see, for example, that "biasing" is a verb, that "biassing" is an alternative spelling of the word, and that there is a syllable break between the "as" and the "ing."

Finally, information is provided in brackets about the etymology of the word. Apparently the word "bias" originates from an Old French word "biais."

In the previous example, the literal meanings of the word "bias" are provided. The literal meaning of a word is referred to as its **denotation**. In contrast, the **connotation** is the subjective, suggested meaning of a word. For example, the words "slim" and "scrawny" can both refer to a particular body type, but "slim" has a positive connotation while "scrawny" has a negative one. A dictionary will typically include the connotations of a word, if it has any, along with the denotation, as in the following example of an entry for the word "vixen":

1. A female fox.
2. A woman regarded as quarrelsome, shrewish, or malicious.

In the example above, the first meaning is the denotation, while the second conveys a connotation.

Following are two examples of thesaurus entries from the third edition of *Webster's New World Thesaurus*:

instigate, *v.* - *Syn.* prompt, stimulate, induce, incite; see **incite, urge** 2.

See Synonym Study at INCITE.

green, *n.* **1.** [A color] - *Syn.* greenness, verdure, virescence, emerald, chlorophyll, verdantness, greenhood, viridity.

2. [A grass plot] - *Syn.* lawn, field, park; see **grass** 3, **long green*, folding green***- *Syn.* bills, paper money, greenbacks; see **money** 1.

The entry for each word provides information about part of speech, synonyms, and where to look in the thesaurus for additional information about synonyms for the word. The entry for the second word ("green") also provides information about different meanings of the word, as well as usage.

In the first entry, the italicized "v" indicates that the word "instigate" is a verb. The abbreviation "Syn." indicates that what follows is a list of synonyms for the word.

The reader is also referred to two closely related sets of synonyms, one given in the entry for "incite," and the other given in the second entry for "urge." Finally, the reader is informed that additional information is given in a "Synonym Study" section under the entry for "incite."

In the second entry, the italicized "n" indicates that "green" is a noun. Synonyms for two different meanings of "green" are provided—the first is "green" in the sense of green color and the second is "green" used in reference to a grass plot. Under the second set of synonyms, the asterisks indicates that the usage is slang, colloquial, archaic, or unusual in some other way.

Abbreviations for Parts of Speech

Following is a list of abbreviations often used in dictionaries and thesauri for identifying different parts of speech:

abbr. - Abbreviation	interrog. - Interrogative
adj. - Adjective	modif. - Modifier (adjective or adverb)
adv. - Adverb	n. - Noun. (Also: neuter)
conj. - Conjunction	prep. - Preposition
fem. - Feminine	pron. - Pronoun
interj. - Interjection	sb. - Substantive

Abbreviations for Grammatical Information

Following are a few of the abbreviations used in dictionaries and thesauri to provide information about the grammatical structure or usage of words:

acc. - Accusative	m. - Masculine
appos. - Appositive	nom. - Nominative
comp. - Compound	pa. t. - Past tense
compar. - Comparative	poss. - Possessive
compl. - Complement	pple. - Participle
dat. - Dative	pf. - Perfect
dem. - Demonstrative	pl. - Plural
der. - Derivation	pref. - Prefix
dim. - Diminuitive	refl. - Reflexive
fem. - Feminine	reg. - Regular
gen. - Genitive	sing. - Singular
imp. - Imperative	subj. - Subject
ind. - Indicative	suff. - Suffix
inf. - Infinitive	superl. - Superlative
intr. - Intransitive	trans. - Transitive
irreg. - Irregular	

Abbreviations for Usage and Etymology

Finally, here are a few of the abbreviations used in dictionaries to provide explanations for usage and etymological information:

Abbreviation	Definition
Amer.	American
app.	Apparently
bef.	Before
Brit.	British
c.	Century (Also, "cent.")
ca.	Circa. A Latin term meaning, literally, "approximately." This term is used in reference to dates. For example, "ca. 1945" means "around 1945."
cf.	Confer. That is, "compare." For example, the phase "cf. oak" in a particular entry would ask the reader to compare the current entry to the entry for "oak."
colloq.	Colloquial. (A colloquial term is causal and/or conversational rather than used in formal speech and writing.)
def.	Definition
dial.	Dialect
Eng.	English
esp.	Especially
etym.	Etymology
euphem.	Euphemism. (A euphemism is a polite phrase used in place of one that might be considered offensive. For example, "I need to go powder my nose" is a euphemism for "I need to use the toilet.")
fig.	Figuratively
freq.	Frequently
gen.	Generally
Gr.	Greek
Heb.	Hebrew
hist.	Historical
IE	Indo-European

Abbreviation	Definition
L	Latin
lang.	Language
lit.	Literally
ME.	Middle English
mod.	Modern
mythol.	In mythology
obs.	Obsolete
occas.	Occasionally
OE	Old English
opp.	Opposite
orig.	Originally
phr.	Phrase
poet.	Poetic
pop.	Popularly
pr.	Present
q.v.	Quod vide. A Latin phrase meaning, literally, "which see." Indicates that the reader should consult the source or entry just provided for additional information. The meaning is similar to "cf." (above)
rel.	Related to
rev.	Revised
sp.	Spelling
spec.	Specifically
unkn.	Unknown
usu.	Usually
var.	Variant of
viz.	Videlicit. A Latin word meaning, literally, "it may be seen." Indicates that what follows adds to what preceded it by providing a clarification, an example, or an omitted term.
wd.	Word

HOW TO APPROACH ABILITY TO USE SOURCE MATERIALS QUESTIONS ON THE CLEP EXAMS

Some of the questions in the Ability to Use Source Materials section will be stand-alone questions while others will be organized around passages. Some of the passage-based questions will test some skills that fall under the headings of Revision Skills and Rhetorical Analysis. For the most part, each question in the Ability to Use Source Materials section will test your knowledge of the four types of skills discussed in this chapter (documentation of sources, evaluation of sources, integration of resource material, and use of reference materials).

The directions you can expect to see for the Ability to Use Source Materials section are reproduced here from the CLEP College Composition/College Composition Modular Examination Guide:

"The following questions test your familiarity with basic research, reference, and composition skills. Some questions refer to passages, while other questions are self-contained. For each question, choose the best answer."

Sample CLEP Questions

The questions provided in this section draw upon the skills discussed throughout this chapter. The format of the questions closely matches what you will find in the Ability to Use Source Materials section of the CLEP College Composition and College Composition Modular exams. That is, the questions pertaining to passages are organized into sets of roughly three to five questions each. Five answer options are given for each question, and you are asked to choose the best option. We will work through these questions together.

The first three questions pertain to the following citation:

Caine, Franklyn. "How Not to Prepare for a Test." *Educators Monthly*: Sept. 2009. 112. Print.

Consider the following question about one detail given in the citation:

In the citation, what is "*Educators Monthly*?"

(A) A book
(B) A website
(C) A journal
(D) A newspaper
(E) A database

For most multiple-choice questions, you will need to read each option carefully before choosing your answer. For this question, as for some of the others you are likely to see concerning citations, you can determine the correct answer prior to examining the individual options. Based on the details of MLA style discussed in this chapter, you should be able to recognize that *Educators Monthly* is the name of a journal in which an article entitled "How Not to Prepare for a Test" appeared, and thus option C is the correct answer.

Here is another question about a detail in the citation:

How many pages in length is the source?

(A) 1
(B) 11
(C) 112
(D) 2009
(E) Unknown

Here again, you can determine the answer on the basis of what you know about MLA style. Option A is the correct answer, because the source is one page in length. That is, the source will appear in its entirety on page 112 of the September 2009 volume of *Educators Monthly*.

Following is a third question about the citation:

Which of the following best describes the authorship of this source?

(A) There is one author named Caine Franklyn.
(B) There is one author named Franklyn Caine.
(C) There are two authors, one named Caine and the other named Franklyn.
(D) There are three or more authors, including Caine and Franklyn.
(E) No author information is provided.

As per the requirements of MLA style, the first piece of information in a single-author source consists of the author's last name and then first name, with a comma separating the two names. Thus option B is the correct answer.

The next two questions pertain to the following dictionary entry:

Bear *n.* 1. any of a family (Ursidae of the order Carnivora) of large heavy mammals of America and Eurasia that have long shaggy hair, rudimentary tails, and plantigrade feet and feed largely on fruit, plant matter, and insects as well as on flesh. 2. a surly, uncouth, burly, or shambling person <a tall, friendly *bear* of a man> 3. [probably from the proverb about *selling the bearskin before catching the bear*] : one that sells securities or commodities in expectation of a price decline. 4. something difficult to do or deal with <the oven is a *bear* to clean> Middle English *bere,* from Old English *bera;* akin to Old English *brūn* brown—First Known Use: before 12th century.

The following question pertains to the meaning of the word defined here:

Which of the following statements is NOT supported by the definition above?

(A) The word "bear" denotes a kind of mammal.
(B) The word "bear" has positive and negative connotations.
(C) The word "bear" has literal and figurative meanings.
(D) The word "bear" has an old English derivation.
(E) The word "bear" can refer to someone who sells securities.

A small number of questions in the CLEP College Composition/College Composition Modular exams will ask you to choose an option that does "NOT" meet some criterion. For example, in order to answer the question above, you must reject options that *are* supported by the definition. This is tantamount to rejecting all of the options that consist of accurate statements.

Option A is supported by the definition, because denotation refers to the literal meaning of a word, and a bear is described here as a type of large mammal. Thus, option A can be rejected.

In contrast, option B is not fully supported by the definition. While some of the connotations of "bear" are clearly negative, none of them appear to be positive. Hence, B appears to be the correct answer. In order to be sure, you should evaluate the remaining options.

Option C is supported by the definition. The word "bear" refers in a literal way to a type of mammal, and in metaphorical way to people and things. Thus option C can be ruled out.

Option D is supported by the definition, in that an Old English derivation is mentioned near the end of the entry. Thus option D can be ruled out.

Finally, option E is supported by the definition, as reflecting one of the meanings of the word "bear." Thus option E can be ruled out, and we can be sure that option B is the correct answer.

Following is another question that asks you to choose the one inaccurate option out of all options provided:

Information about each of the following is provided in the entry EXCEPT

(A) Etymology
(B) Part of speech
(C) Usage
(D) Denotation
(E) Inflection

Your task here is to reject options that are provided in the entry. Option A can be rejected because etymological information about the origin of the word "bear" is provided at the end of the entry. Option B can be rejected because the word is labeled as a noun by means of the italicized "n." Option C can be rejected as well because phrases such as "a tall, friendly bear of a man" are provided as examples of usage. Option D can be rejected because the denotation is provided. Option E is correct because no information is given as to how the word can be inflected (e.g., by adding an "s" to the end in order to pluralize it).

The next three questions pertain to the following passage:

(1) In 1931, during the Great Depression, the U.S. Congress passed the Davis-Bacon Act. (2) This Act required governmental contractors to pay "prevailing wages" on public works projects. (3) That is, contractors carrying out work for the government were required by the Act to pay workers at least as much as they would ordinarily be paid for comparable work on similar projects in the area. (4) More than 40 states then adopted "prevailing wage" laws. (5) Although later some states repealed these laws, at present many states continue to maintain them (Smith 1998). (6) There continue to be claims that these laws were originally motivated by the desire to exclude African American contractors. (7) Clearly, racism was not the only contributor to the passage of Davis-Bacon Act.

The first two questions below pertain to the one citation given in the passage:

Which of the following is cited in sentence 5?

(A) A website
(B) A newspaper
(C) A journal article
(D) A book
(E) Cannot tell

In the absence of further information, you cannot be sure what "Smith 1998" refers to. For example, in either APA, MLA, or Chicago style it could be a book, an article, or one of many other sources. Thus option E is the correct answer.

What is the purpose of citing Smith in sentence 5?

(A) To provide a source for quoted material
(B) To refer the reader to page 1998 of a work by Smith
(C) To provide a source for the facts given in the sentence
(D) To provide a source for the statement in Sentence 6
(E) To present an overview of a debate

Since no material is quoted in the passage, option A is incorrect. Option B is incorrect because in styles such as APA, MLA, and Chicago, the "1998" would be year of publication rather than page. Option C appears to be correct. However, you should look through all options before choosing an answer. Option D is incorrect, because a citation will refer to the sentence in which it appears, if not also the preceding sentence(s), but it will not refer to a later sentence. Option E is incorrect because there is no reference to a debate in sentence 5. Thus, option C is indeed the correct answer. Smith has apparently published some sort of work in 1998 in which the facts described in sentence 5 are presented.

The next question pertains to the difference between fact and opinion:

Which sentence in the passage expresses an opinion?

(A) Sentence 1
(B) Sentence 3
(C) Sentence 4
(D) Sentence 6
(E) Sentence 7

Option A is incorrect because Sentence 1 consists of a simple statement of fact. Option B is incorrect because Sentence 2 consists of a paraphrase of a previously stated fact. Option C is incorrect because Sentence 3 consists of a simple statement of fact. Option D is incorrect for the same reason. Although an opinion is mentioned in Sentence 6, the sentence itself does not convey an opinion. Rather, it consists of a statement that a certain opinion has been expressed. Option E is correct because sentence 7 presents an assertion about causal contributors to a historical event. Although the writer uses the term "clearly," no evidence for the assertion presented in sentence 7 is given in the passage. As a result, the word "clearly" merely emphasizes the writer's confidence in the accuracy of his or her opinion.

Finally, here is a question about documentation of sources:

Which of the following sentences most needs a citation?

(A) Sentence 1
(B) Sentence 2
(C) Sentence 3
(D) Sentence 4
(E) Sentence 6

Although a citation could be provided for any of these sentences, sentences 1 through 4 present simple facts that can be easily verified, and thus it is not critical that a citation be provided. Sentence 6 also presents a simple fact, but since it refers to a difference of opinion, perhaps among historians, a citation is needed. A citation would support the contention that a controversy exists, and it would provide the reader with information about further reading.

The next set of questions pertain to the following passage:

(1) Nikolai Gogol's story, "The Fair at Sorochintsy," begins with a dramatic and lovely description of the lush countryside in Little Russia. (2) The narrator's tone is reverent and awed; even insects are described as "sparks of emerald, topaz, and ruby." (3) The profound silence and stillness of the region, a magical place adorned with otherworldly flora and fauna, immediately conjures up an image of Eden in the reader's mind. (4) This prefatory section contrasts sharply with the rest of the story, which includes rough provincial humor, the activities of unruly but appealing riffraff at a local fair, and most notably the mysterious and mischievous presence of the devil. (5) Thus the story turns out to be a delightful recounting of devilish pranks in the Garden of Eden, contrary to the less favorable assessment of the story as "facile and unengaging" by a renowned critic (qtd. in Saronoff 334). (6) Moreover, the story can be thought of as a moving religious allegory rather than merely a fanciful account of life in rural Russia.

The following question pertains to the tone of the entire passage:

Which of the following best characterizes the writer's attitudes concerning Gogol's story?

(A) The writer likes the prefatory part of the story more than the remainder of the story.

(B) The writer has a generally negative impression of the story as a whole.

(C) The writer has a generally positive impression of the story as a whole.

(D) The writer describes most details of the story neutrally without conveying an opinion.

(E) The writer approves of Gogol's writing but not of the events of the story.

Option A is not clearly supported by the passage. The word "delightful" in sentence 5 suggests that the writer has a positive view of the remainder of the story after the devil makes an appearance.

Option B can be ruled out quite easily, in light of the writer's use of several positive descriptive terms in sentences 1, 2, and 5. For the same reason, option C appears to be correct. However, you should consider the remaining options.

Option D is not supported by the passage. Most of the factual details about the story provided by the writer are conveyed in a way that implies a positive opinion. For example, in sentence 1 the fact that Gogol describes the countryside of Little Russia in the opening part of the story is not conveyed neutrally. Rather, the writer refers to this description as "dramatic and lovely."

Option E is not supported by the passage either. The writer does not explicitly judge the events in the story. If anything, his or her choice of words in some cases implies approval—as in the reference in sentence 4 to the riffraff as "appealing." Hence option C is clearly the correct answer.

The following question pertains to the quotation in sentence 2:

What information should be given in a parenthetical citation for the quoted material in sentence 2?

(A) Page number
(B) Author and page number
(C) Author, title, and year
(D) Author, year, and page number
(E) Author, translator, and page number

In context, the author and title are clear and need not be provided in the citation. Full bibliographic details will be provided separately in a footnote, endnote, reference list, or works cited list. The only other information the reader needs in order to locate the quote would be the page number, and thus option A is correct.

The next question pertains to the interpretation of sentence 3:

Which of the following best characterizes sentence 3?

(A) The author expresses an opinion without providing supporting evidence.
(B) The author presents a simple statement of fact in a neutral way.
(C) The author qualifies an opinion developed throughout the passage.
(D) The author presents an opinion supported by details given in sentences 2 and 3.
(E) The author presents key facts along with an analysis of those facts.

In sentence 3, the author provides some details about what Gogol describes in the first part of his story. However, the assertion that the reader will think of Eden when reading this part of the story reflects an opinion presented by the writer. This opinion is supported by some of the details that the writer provides, such as the description in of the narrator's tone as "reverent" and the flora and fauna as "otherworldly." Thus, option D is the correct answer. Option A is incorrect because supporting evidence is indeed provided. Option B is incorrect because impressions and interpretation rather than merely facts are presented. Option C is incorrect because the sentence contributes to rather than qualifies an opinion. Finally, option E is incorrect because the sentence does not primarily convey analysis of factual information.

The next question pertains to the citation in sentence 5:

Which of the following is NOT indicated by the citation given at the end of sentence 5?

(A) The quoted material appears in a work by Saronoff.
(B) Saronoff is the author of the source.
(C) Saronoff has written about Gogol's story.
(D) The source is a scholarly article written by Saronoff.
(E) The phrase "facile and unengaging" appears on page 334 of the source.

From the citation, you can tell that the phrase "facile and unengaging" is used on page 334 of a work written by Saronoff, a work that presumably concerns Gogol's story, at least in part. Thus options A, B, C, and E are not correct, because each option describes information that can be gleaned from the citation. Option D is the correct answer because it is not clear that the source is an article, as opposed to a book or some other scholarly work.

Finally, here is a question about the assertion made in sentence 6:

Which of the following best characterizes sentence 6?

(A) It is a simple statement of fact.
(B) It is an opinion that is supported by very strong evidence.
(C) It is an opinion that is undermined by evidence given in the passage.
(D) It is an opinion that is presented without strong evidence.
(E) It is a factual statement asserted by Saranoff.

Option A is incorrect, because the description of the story as "moving" and as something that "can be thought of as" an allegory all indicate that the writer is expressing an opinion.

Option B also seems to be incorrect, because there is not strong evidence or analysis favoring an interpretation of the story as allegorical rather than literal.

Option C is incorrect because even though there is not strong evidence for the assertion that the story is an allegory, the writer provides no evidence that contradicts this assertion.

Option E is incorrect because the statement is not attributed to Saronoff, nor does it appear from context that Saranoff would have made the statement.

Option D appears to be correct. Sentence 6 presents an opinion. The only "evidence" is the writer's own assertion in sentence 3 that the reader would think of Eden when reading the story, along with other details such as the reference in sentence 2 to the author's "reverent" tone.

Chapter 4

Rhetorical Analysis

In the Rhetorical Analysis section, the ability to analyze writing is tested through both passage-based and stand-alone questions. These questions measure critical thinking, as well as an understanding of organization, style, audience, purpose, tone, and rhetoric. Each of these skills is discussed below, followed by guidance on how to approach Rhetorical Analysis questions, and finally some practice questions with answers and explanations.

CRITICAL THINKING

In order to apply critical thinking to the analysis of writing, one must be able to analyze facts and options, evaluate arguments, compare and synthesize details, and make inferences.

Analyzing Facts and Opinions

Rhetorical analysis includes the ability to identify key facts, to distinguish between facts and opinions, and to understand the source and purpose of the opinions that a writer presents.

A fact is typically defined as a statement that is known to be true, and that can be verified or proven by means of evidence. For example, it is a fact that Providence is the capital of Rhode Island, because one can verify the statement by consulting the appropriate sources. In contrast, an opinion is a statement that someone thinks is true, but that has not been—or cannot be—proven through evidence. For example, the statement that Boston is a splendid place to live represents an opinion. One could find evidence in favor of the statement, but it is not the sort of statement that can be proven. One could also find evidence that undermines the statement, along with people who feel that it is wrong.

In some cases, the distinction between fact and opinion is clearly marked by the writer, as in the following example:

"Every year there are more than six million traffic accidents in the United States. I think that number is much too high."

In this example, the first sentence is a statement of fact, while the second sentence expresses an opinion. The statistic reported in the first sentence may or may not be correct, but it is presented as a fact rather than as an opinion. The phrase "I think" at the outset of the second sentence alerts the reader that an opinion will follow. A few of the many phrases that writers use to explicitly signal opinions are used in the following sentences:

"I believe that it rained more than once yesterday morning."

"It seems to me that hard work ultimately pays off."

"Kindness is a virtue, in my view."

"As I see it, special interest groups exert an undue influence on national politics."

"I would say that teachers need to be committed to the well-being of their students."

"My sense is that the knee is sprained rather than fractured."

In some cases, distinctions between fact and opinion are not explicitly marked by the writer and must be identified by the reader. For example, consider the following passage:

"In 2000, 15% of high school students in Sheffield County dropped out of school. By 2010, the dropout rate was 24%. The steady decline in percentage of Sheffield County students who graduate from high school is troubling. It's not easy to find a decent job without a high school degree."

In this passage, the first two sentences present facts, while the last two sentences present opinions. However, the final statement is so widely accepted that many readers will view it as a fact. As discussed below, treating statements such as this as facts can be problematic.

Readers must approach both facts and opinions cautiously. The "facts" that a writer reports may be misleading, incorrect, and/or incomplete. For example, the passage above contains reference to a "steady decline" in Sheffield County graduation rates. If the writer has seen the county's graduation statistics for each year from 2000 to 2010, he or she may be accurate in referring to a steady decline. However, if the writer has not seen those statistics, it may not be accurate to assume that the decline was "steady." Perhaps the dropout rate was consistently around 15% from 2000 through 2009, with an abrupt increase to 24% in 2010.

As for the final sentence of the passage, it does sound like a fact. One could find evidence to support the assertion that it's not easy to find a decent job without a high school degree. However, one could also find evidence that it's not easy to find a decent job even when a person has a degree. How one interprets such evidence depends on how one defines terms like "easy" and "decent." Thus, the final sentence reflects more of a commonly held opinion than a fact.

The distinction between fact and opinion is not always clear-cut. For example, writers will often make a factual assertion but acknowledge some degree of uncertainty or possibility of error, as in the following example.

"It appears that global average temperatures were higher during the first half of 2010 than during any other six-month period in modern history."

In the sentence above, the writer states a fact about global temperatures but acknowledges by means of the phrase "It appears" that the fact could be incorrect. Thus, the writer's statement about global temperatures represents an opinion. Other phrases that acknowledge some degree of uncertainty about factual assertions are used in the following sentences:

"Apparently, the batter felt bad about striking out with the bases loaded, as he ran back to the dugout with his head down."

"It is likely that this new legislation will be unsettling to almost everyone."

"The snow seems to have stopped falling."

"Evidence suggests that the level of radioactivity at Chernobyl has returned to normal levels."

"Surely the two vehicles made contact before the blue car skidded into the ditch."

Critical thinking allows the reader to not only recognize that opinions are expressed in these sentences, but also to evaluate the accuracy and persuasiveness of those opinions. The first sentence, for example, includes evidence for the opinion that the batter felt bad. Given the circumstances, the opinion is plausible. In contrast, the opinion outlined in the second does not seem plausible without further evidence. The opinions in each of the five sentences above may be judged as more or less plausible and persuasive depending on the nature of any additional evidence the writer provides as well as strength of the argument that the writer develops from the evidence. The skills discussed in this chapter help the reader evaluate the argumentation that underlies a writer's opinions.

Notice that in some cases, the writer's insistence on the certainty of a factual assertion actually implies the possibility that the assertion is incorrect, as illustrated by the following example:

"I am convinced that the country's standard of living rose last year."

In the example above, the fact that the writer is convinced indicates that he or she could have arrived at a different conclusion. The possibility that the country's standard of living did not rise during the previous year is implied. The writer is saying, in effect, "I considered whether or not the country's standard of living rose last year, and some evidence convinced me that it did."

Finally, a distinction can be made between the opinion that someone expresses and the fact that they have expressed an opinion. For example, consider the content of the following sentence:

"After the Treaty of Paris was signed on 20 November 1815 and news of the treaty was made public, some French citizens stated pessimistically that France would never again be a dominant power in Europe."

In this sentence, the date of the Treaty of Paris is a fact. It is also a fact that some French citizens responded to the treaty pessimistically. However, their pessimism itself reflects an opinion. Their statement that France would never be a dominant power is an opinion about the future political development of the country.

Evaluating Arguments

Rhetorical analysis includes the ability to understand and evaluate the arguments that a writer presents. To evaluate an argument, you must be able recognize the logic underlying the argument, and to judge the strength of the evidence that the writer offers in support of the argument.

In some cases, it is relatively easy to spot the flaws in an argument. For example, in the following passage, the logical contradiction is clear:

"Newton was a peevish, suspicious, and relatively antisocial person who valued his work above all else. As director of the Royal Mint, he spent a great deal of time enjoying conversation with friends and colleagues."

In the previous passage, there is a direct and readily detected contradiction between the description of Newton as peevish and antisocial and the anecdote of him enjoying interactions with friends and colleagues. In other cases, weaknesses in the logic of an argument and/or the nature of evidence presented are not as readily perceived. For example, consider the following passage:

"I agree with Smith's contention that Hitchcock was a terribly overrated director. Smith was fond of pointing out that although Hitchcock made movies for over half a century, he never won an Oscar."

The information provided in the second sentence of this passage includes details intended to support the opinion outlined in the first sentence. However, the logic of the argument is questionable. In order to claim that an artist's work is overrated, one must demonstrate or at least assert that the work is admired to a certain extent, and one must then argue that the quality of the work does not merit quite so much admiration. In this passage, no statements are made about the extent to which Hitchcock's work is admired. Arguably, this omission is forgivable, because Hitchcock happens a famous director. The writer seems to assume, as most readers would, that Hitchcock's work as a director is rated very highly. A more serious problem is that the passage contains no direct statement about the quality of Hitchcock's work. Rather, the writer simply notes that Hitchcock made movies over a long period of time but never received an Oscar.

One way to strengthen the argument in the preceding passage would be to explicitly state that the true quality of Hitchcock's work is reflected in the fact that he never won an Oscar. For example, consider the following revision of the passage:

"I agree with Smith's contention that Hitchcock was a terribly overrated director. Smith was fond of pointing out that although Hitchcock made critically-acclaimed movies for over half a century, he never won an Oscar. I believe, as Smith does, that regardless of what critics say, a director's work is no good unless he or she has won an Oscar."

In this revised passage, the logic of the argument is clearer. There is a phrase implying that Hitchcock's work is admired (i.e., "critically-acclaimed") and there is a statement that the work is not worthy of such admiration (i.e., "a director's work is no good unless he or she has won an Oscar).

Although the logic of the argument in the revised passage is clearer, one might still question the strength of the evidence that is presented. Smith's argument relies on the assumption that a director's work cannot be good unless he or she has won an Oscar.

This argument seems to imply a simplistic distinction between "good" and "no good," and it presumes that winning an Oscar is the sole criterion for judging the quality of an director's work.

In sum, the argument that the writer develops is not very persuasive, because it depends on at least two questionable assumptions. This is not to say that the writer is wrong. It may be that all works of art can be judged as either good or no good, and it may that winning an Oscar should be the sole criterion for judging a director's work to be good. However, the writer presents no evidence in support of these assumptions. Since it seems likely that very few people would agree with those assumptions, the writer's argument is weak.

There are many types of potential flaws in the logic of an argument. The reader must analyze a writer's assertions carefully, as some of these flaws are more difficult to spot than others, and the writers themselves may not even be aware of the logical fallacies that undermine their arguments. Following are examples of just a few of the many possible fallacies.

Some fallacies pertain to the way evidence is used. For example, the writer may draw stronger links between causes and effects than the evidence warrants, as illustrated in the following passage:

"I've had the flu many times in my life. Last time I had it, I drank jasmine tea three times a day, and I recovered much more quickly than ever before. I'm convinced now that jasmine tea kills the flu virus."

In this passage, the writer asserts that jasmine tea kills the flu virus, because he recovered from the flu more quickly than usual after drinking the tea. One problem with this line of reasoning is that it fails to acknowledge other possible causes of the writer's speedy recovery. Perhaps it was not the tea, but some other factor, that helped him recover. Another problem with the writer's reasoning is that even if the tea was helpful, it does not follow that the tea kills the flu virus. Perhaps the tea merely alleviates flu symptoms. In sum, the causal connection between drinking tea and the demise of flu virus has not been clearly established.

Another kind of misuse of evidence occurs when writers overstate their conclusions. Overstatements can occur when a merely probable outcome is treated as a matter of necessity. For example:

"Computer viruses are prevalent on the Internet. If you use the Internet, it is inevitable that your computer will be infected by one of these viruses someday."

The first sentence of this passage suggests that it is possible, or perhaps even probable, that continued use of the Internet will result in one's computer becoming infected by a virus. However, this outcome is not inevitable. "Prevalent" does not mean "everywhere at all times." Moreover, computer users have access to anti-virus software and other protective strategies which help ensure that even if their computers are exposed to viruses, the computers may not be infected.

Another type of overstatement occurs when the writer is not careful about generalizing from known facts, as in the following passage:

"Pickup trucks require much more gasoline than cars do. Thus, pickup trucks are consuming much more of the world's dwindling fuel supply."

The conclusion expressed in the second sentence may be true, but it does not follow necessarily from the first sentence. There are more cars on the road than pickup trucks. Thus, it may be that cars are consuming much more of the fuel supply.

Still another type of overstatement occurs when the writer assumes a series of gradations and concludes that a relatively extreme   will occur. For example:

"Last week the governor granted a pardon to a man who had been convicted of aggravated assault. Two months ago he pardoned another hardened criminal. At this rate, criminals will continue to be released from jail until the streets are filled with them and ordinary citizens can no longer feel safe in their own homes."

In this passage, the writer concludes without evidence that the governor will continue to issue pardons, and that the rate of pardons will be so great that the streets are "filled" with criminals. The writer predicts an escalation in the rate of pardons without considering whether the earlier pardons represent exceptional cases, nor does the writer acknowledge that pardons are typically granted because the individual is presumed to be innocent or at least to no longer poses a threat.

In some cases, the problem is not that a conclusion is overstated, but rather that the writer distorts his or her argument in such a way that any conclusion would be fallacious, as in the following passage:

"If you're patriotic, you support the current military action. You're either with us or against us."

In this passage, the first sentence implies that all patriots support the current military action—i.e., that it is impossible to be patriotic unless one supports this action. This is a questionable assumption. Conceivably, there is a definition of patriotism according to which some people are patriots yet do not support any military action. The second sentence of the passage is problematic because it reduces all possible attitudes to either "for" or "against" the military action. This dichotomization excludes the possibility of mixed feelings or indifference. It also glosses over differences in degree of support: Some people who are "with us" concerning the military action may possess a much greater degree of commitment and certainty than others who would also describe themselves as supporters.

In the previous example, the problem is that no middle ground is permitted between extreme positions. A different sort of fallacy occurs when extreme positions are presented and it is implied that only some sort of middle ground could be acceptable. For example:

"Some members of Congress are saying that these tariffs should be doubled. Others are saying the tariffs should not be changed. Clearly what would be best for the economy is to raise tariffs moderately."

In this example, the existence of extreme positions is used as evidence that a moderate position would best. However, economic data might conceivably show one that one of the extreme positions is overwhelmingly superior to the middle ground. (To illustrate this point, imagine that two people who have just washed your car disagree on how much to charge you. One person asserts that the going rate is about $10 while the other claims that most people would charge about $190. Here, the middle ground is $100, but that is not reflective of a typical price for a car wash, nor could one make a very persuasive argument that it is an appropriate price.)

The preceding examples illustrate logical fallacies that are reflected in the structure of an argument. Other fallacies arise from the use of evidence or argumentation that is more or less irrelevant to the main thrust of the argument. For example, consider the following six versions of a passage written by someone who disagrees with the tax policies of a commentator named Smith:

1. "Smith actually claims that lowering taxes by as little as 10% per capita would destroy the national economy. That is a ridiculous assertion."

2. "Smith actually claims that lowering taxes by as little as 10% per capita would destroy the national economy. Nothing could be further from the truth. Economists agree that our country has the strongest economy in the world. A change in tax rates would not significantly alter the strength of our economy."

3. "Smith actually claims that lowering taxes by as little as 10% per capita would destroy the national economy. I find Smith's objection to lowering taxes misguided, and somewhat surprising given the fact that he was convicted of tax evasion in 1997 and 2009."

4. "Smith actually claims that lowering taxes by as little as 10% per capita would destroy the national economy. My concern about Smith's argument is not just that he is wrong, but that he is dangerous. What would destroy the national economy is for anyone to take his view's seriously. I would hate to see my children begging on the street corner because of him."

5. "Smith actually claims that lowering taxes by as little as 10% per capita would destroy the national economy. Nobody holds such a view anymore."

6. "Smith actually claims that lowering taxes by as little as 10% per capita would destroy the national economy. Smith is wrong. The flaw in his argument was pointed out very clearly in an influential article written by the internationally renowned economist Jane Doe."

In the first passage, reference to Smith's opinion as ridiculous does not contribute in any substantive way to the assertion that Smith is wrong. Ridicule or praise do not in themselves contribute substantively to an argument. If anything, the fact that the writer refers to Smith's view as ridiculous but does not provide any evidence to that effect undermines the writer's own persuasiveness. That is, the reader of this passage is likely to think more poorly of the writer rather than Smith.

In the second passage, the writer does provide evidence in favor of his or her objection to Smith's view, but the evidence is of questionable relevance. Even if the writer's country does have the strongest economy in the world, it does not follow that a particular change in the country's tax rates could not damage its economy. Also irrelevant to an evaluation of Smith's view is the phrase "Nothing could be further from the truth." This is an example of hyperbole—an exaggerated statement—and like most hyperbolic statements it contributes nothing to the argument.

In the third passage, the writer introduces a personal attack apparently intended to undermine Smith's credibility. The writer gives no evidence that Smith's crime bears on his point of view. Without additional evidence, the fact that Smith was convicted of tax evasion is irrelevant to the question of whether his claim about taxes and national economy is accurate.

In the fourth passage, the writer attempts to frighten the reader. Rather than presenting evidence that Smith is wrong, the writer focuses on describing what would happen if Smith is wrong but people take his views seriously. Thus, the writer attempts to distract the reader. If the writer believes that Smith is in error, the writer should present evidence to that effect. If the writer also wishes to assert that Smith's errors are dangerous, a separate argument, with evidence, would be needed. In this passage the writer presents no evidence for any assertion.

In the fifth passage, the writer's evidence consists solely of an alleged lack of popularity. The assertion seems to be that because nobody holds the view that Smith espouses, Smith must be wrong. Arguably, the popularity of an opinion should play some role in how it is evaluated. However, the fact that an opinion is widely accepted does not guarantee that it is true, any more than lack of popularity for an opinion guarantees that it is false. The writer's argument in this passage is weak because he or she merely states, without evidence, that Smith's view is not widely accepted anymore.

In the final passage, the writer appeals to authority. The evidence that Smith is wrong consists of reference to an "influential" paper written by an "internationally renowned" expert. Certainly, the opinions of experts should be considered when evaluating an argument. But even assuming that an expert did directly refute Smith's view, the fact that she did so does not necessarily constitute strong evidence against Smith. The expert may be wrong. It may be that other experts support Smith's view. Smith himself may be an expert too. (The reader might ask whether an internationally renowned expert would take the trouble to attack Smith if Smith were not somewhat prominent himself.) In short, the weakness of the argument in this passage is not that the writer cites an authority, but that the sole focus is on the authority's conclusions rather than on the evidence that Smith is misguided.

Comparing and Synthesizing Details

Rhetorical analysis includes the ability to compare and synthesize various details that a writer presents.

Synthesis is needed for many purposes. First, a writer's general theme can be determined by synthesizing pertinent information. Consider, for example, the details given in the following passage:

"Ben Franklin, born in Boston in 1706, grew up to become Philadelphia's most famous citizen. He moved to Philadelphia at the age of 17 and quickly became a successful writer, editor, and printer. During his long life he was a prolific inventor as well. Franklin invented the lightning rod, the Franklin stove, bifocals, and a musical instrument that he called the glass armonica. In addition, as one of the Founding Fathers, Franklin was an extraordinarily accomplished politician, holding a variety of political offices including President of the Supreme Executive Council of Pennsylvania, Speaker of the Pennsylvania Assembly, U.S. Postmaster General, U.S. Ambassador to France, and U.S. Ambassador to Sweden."

Many details are provided in the passage, but the writer does not explicitly state his or her theme. Through synthesis, however, the reader can identify the theme. The reader will observe that each detail in the passage consists of one of Franklin's accomplishments. Phrases such as "as well" and "In addition" hint that the writer is presenting a list. This list of accomplishments is relatively long, and when the items on the list are compared, the reader will notice that the items are very different from each other (i.e., they represent very different kinds of accomplishments). Thus, through synthesis the reader can determine that the theme of pertains to the extent and diversity of Franklin's accomplishments. The theme of the passage is that during his life Franklin achieved success in many different kinds of endeavors.

A second use of synthesis is to collate details from different statements in a passage and identify missing information. For example, suppose that the following sentence were added to the end of the preceding passage:

"This concludes my brief introduction to the life of Benjamin Franklin."

By synthesizing the various details of the passage, including the final sentence, the reader can see that certain kinds of information are missing. All we can gather from the passage about Franklin's life other than a sense of the extraordinary breadth of his accomplishments is his birthplace, his age when he relocated to Philadelphia, his longevity, and the fact that success as a writer, editor, and printer predated some of his other achievements. Missing is the chronology of those achievements, as well as details of his personal life, his world view, and many other kinds of information.

Finally, when different points of view are presented, synthesis can help the reader identify key similarities and differences between views. For example, consider the following passage:

"According to a recent study, taking aspirin on a regular basis reduces the risk of certain kinds of cancer. The study followed a large sample of people over a period of 20 years. People who took aspirin regularly had a lower incidence of cancer as compared to those who did not take aspirin. However, doctors caution that regular use of aspirin can increase the risk of gastrointestinal bleeding."

A reasonable synthesis of the information presented in the above passage is that taking aspirin regularly has potential benefits as well as potential risks to one's health. This illustrates the use of synthesis to identify a theme. At the same time, synthesis helps us recognize that whether we wish to understand the benefits or the risks of aspirin consumption, one key piece of information missing from this passage is a definition of "regular."

Making Inferences

Rhetorical analysis includes the ability to make inferences about the meaning, purpose, and impact of what a writer presents. Broadly, there are two kinds of inference: deductive and inductive.

Deductive inferences yield conclusions that necessarily follow from premises. Here is a simple example of deductive reasoning:

1. A person who is alive has a heartbeat. (Premise)
2. John P. has a heartbeat. (Premise)
3. John P. is alive. (Conclusion)

In the preceding example, the conclusion (John P. is alive) follows necessarily from the premises. If you accept the premises, you must accept the conclusion.

To illustrate how deductive inference can be used when analyzing a piece of writing, consider the following sentence:

"The witness said that she saw three men enter the bank."

From this sentence, we can deduce that the witness is female. Our reasoning can be reconstructed as follows:

1. Only females are referred to by the pronoun "she." (Premise)
2. The witness is referred to by the pronoun "she." (Premise)
3. The witness is female. (Conclusion)

Inductive inferences yield conclusions that go beyond their premises. The conclusions are only suggested by the premises. Thus, the conclusions cannot be drawn with total certainty. For example:

1. Everyone I have met in my life has a first and a last name. (Premise)
2. I will meet new people tomorrow. (Premise)
3. Everyone I meet tomorrow will have a first and a last name. (Conclusion)

In the example above, the conclusion (Everyone I meet tomorrow will have a first and a last name) is suggested by the premises, but it does not necessarily follow from those premises. It is possible (though unlikely) that I will meet someone tomorrow who only goes by one name.

To illustrate how inductive inference can be used when analyzing a piece of writing, consider the following sentence:

"The witness said that she saw the three men leave the bank carrying several bags of money."

From this sentence, we can inductively infer that the three men have robbed the bank. But we cannot be sure. Perhaps the three men are actually security guards bringing the money to an armored car, and the witness is being interviewed about what happened when the armored car was subsequently robbed. Thus, the sentence suggests that the three men are robbers, but it does not offer definitive proof for this conclusion.

Now consider some of the deductive and inductive inferences that can be drawn from the following passage:

"Bullying continues to be a major problem in American schools, and now Internet applications such as Facebook are being used by bullies to harass their victims. Online bullying is called "cyberbullying," and it can be every bit as devastating to victims as traditional forms of bullying behavior. Parents and school administrators should be aware of the potential threats posed by cyberbullying activities. As Mary, a 9th-grade cyberbullying victim describes it, "the bullies who kept posting nasty comments about me on their Facebook pages made my life hell."

A number of important deductive inferences can be made from this passage. For example, we can infer from the first sentence that bullying is not a new problem in American schools. This inference is supported by the phrase "continues to be." From the second sentence we can infer that traditional forms of bullying are harmful to victims. The phrase "every bit as" is key to this particular inference.

This passage also sustains some important inductive inferences about the writer's opinions about bullying and his or her purpose in writing this passage. From the third sentence we can infer that the writer considers bullying to be a serious problem. This inference is supported by the recommendation that parents and administrators be aware of the threats posed by cyberbullying. We can also infer that the purpose of the final sentence is to provide a concrete illustration of the writer's theme. The student's reference to life becoming "hell" as a result of cyberbullying is part of an anecdote that is consistent with the theme developed in each sentence of this passage.

One of the specific applications of inductive inference is in identifying logical fallacies of the sort described above in the evaluating arguments section. Another application is in determining the likely meaning of unfamiliar words. Some of the questions in the Rhetorical Analysis section of the CLEP College Composition and College Composition Modular exams will pertain to the meanings of specific terms. At the same time, you may encounter words in any section of these exams that are unfamiliar to you. By looking at how the words are used in context, you may be able to infer something about their likely meaning.

In some cases, the meaning of the word can be inferred from a restatement of its essential meaning, as in the following sentence:

"She gave me a lugubrious look, and her sad eyes filled with tears."

From this sentence, the reader can infer that "lugubrious" and "sad" are most probably synonymous.

In other cases, the meaning of the word is not directly restated, but inferable from an elaboration of the meaning. For example:

"The main character in this book is sometimes described as suffering from dipsomania, which is understandable given that he was never without a bottle of beer in his hand."

Here the reader can infer that dipsomania has something to do with consumption of beer, or perhaps alcohol more generally. Reference to the character "suffering" from dipsomania suggest that the term denotes a problematic condition. Thus, the reader may guess that "dipsomania" refers to alcoholism, or a craving for alcohol. The root "mania," which appears in the word, is also a potential clue as to its meaning.

In still other cases, something about the meaning of a word can be inferred from evidence about what it does *not* mean, as in the following sentence:

"The student was belligerent while the teacher was scolding him, but when the principal appeared, he suddenly became very well-behaved."

In this sentence, the meaning of "belligerent" appears to be something like the opposite of "well-behaved."

In sum, deductive and inductive inference are tools of considerable usefulness in the evaluation of writing. Inference contributes in one way or another to all of the skills described in this chapter.

UNDERSTANDING OF ORGANIZATION

Rhetorical analysis includes the ability to recognize and evaluate the organization of information in a piece of writing. Organization can be thought of in terms of the order in which information is presented. Below is a table showing the six most common types of organization for non-fiction writing.

Organization of Writing	Characteristics
Chronological	Presents information in order of occurrence (i.e., reporting of historical events or an eyewitness account; telling of a fictional story)
Emphatic	Information is presented in order of importance; author chooses to begin with the most important point—or the least important point
General to Specific	Presents information in order of specificity (i.e., starts with a general theme but leads to a specific topic)
Comparison	Information is offered about two or more things, events, or ideas in order to compare/contrast them.
Cause-and-Effect	Presents information about the causes of an outcome. It then discusses the different causes and their contribution to the outcome.
Problem-Solving	A problem is presented followed by a description of one or more solutions.

Chronological Organization

Chronological organization presents information in order of occurrence. The information could consist of a sequence of events, as seen in the reconstruction of a historical event, the telling of a story, or the report of an eyewitness. Chronological organization is also used in scientific reports, in which a series of procedures is described, and in essays in which the writer describes the development over time in his or her own views about a topic. The following passage illustrates chronological organization:

"In order to create this type of transistor, engineers begin with a silicon wafer. A layer of oxide is deposited on the wafer. Next, photolithographic techniques are used to etch the wafer. Etching creates all of the key devices on the wafer's surface. Finally, the functionality of these devices is tested."

Emphatic Organization

Emphatic organization presents information in order of importance. In some cases, the writer begins with the most important point. The writer may wish to capture the reader's attention, or to persuade the reader of some idea before the reader loses interest or gets caught up in details. In other cases, the writer begins with the least important point and builds to a crescendo, in hopes that the impact on the reader will increase as well. The following passage illustrates emphatic organization of the first type (most to least important):

"I have been a vegetarian since I was 18 years old, and I think that others should give up eating meat too. I believe it is unethical to raise and kill animals for food. That is a completely unfair and exploitative practice, and if you eat meat, you should pause for a moment to consider the moral implications. And although vegetarianism should be practiced for ethical reasons, you should also keep in mind that a vegetarian diet, if carefully chosen, is more healthy than one that includes meat. Healthier, and cheaper as well."

Generality Organization

Generality organization presents information in order of specificity. In some cases, the writer begins with a general theme and then focuses in on a specific topic of interest. In other cases, the writer begins with a highly specific point that he or she subsequently broadens. There are also cases in which the level of specificity is manipulated in a more nuanced way, as in the "five-paragraph essay" that many students learn how to write in middle school and high school. The five-paragraph essay consists of three parts: introduction, body, and conclusion. The introduction begins with a general statement that is narrowed down to the writer's main thesis. The body of the essay contains specific discussion of the thesis. The conclusion provides a summary of the specifics and then broadens the discussion.

In the following passage, generality organization is used to proceed from specific to general:

"In 2005 more than 300 people were crushed to death during a pilgrimage to Mecca. In 2010 more than 300 people died during a stampede at the Water Festival along the Tonle Sap River. There are countless other stories of people being injured or killed by crowd crush at concerts, sporting events, and other events. What all of stories have in common, besides the tragic loss of life, is evidence that the relevant authorities failed to provide adequate crowd control. The management of crowds during organized events is becoming increasingly critical across the globe."

Comparison Organization

Comparison organization presents information about two or more things, events, or ideas in order to compare and contrast them. In some cases, the writer's purpose is simply to document similarities and differences. The writer may wish to develop a system of classification, in which categories and sub-categories are identified. Often, the writer's purpose is also evaluative, in that he or she asserts that one thing is more appealing, important, worrisome, or funny than another. The writer may conduct a comparison by discussing concepts simultaneously, or by largely focusing on one concept at a time. In the following passage, comparison organization is used to contrast two concepts in sequence rather than simultaneously.

"The critical importance of hydration is a fairly recent idea in high school athletics. Traditionally, coaches felt that too much water would be harmful to young athletes. Besides slowing the athletes down, coaches believed that ready access to water would reduce athletes' toughness. In some cases, water was even withheld as a form of discipline. During the past two decades, following the high-profile deaths of athletes resulting from dehydration or heat stroke, high school coaches have come to recognize the critical importance of keeping their athletes hydrated. These days, water and sports drinks are mandatory during practice and on game day."

Cause-Effect Organization

Cause-effect organization presents information about the causes of some known or likely outcome. The writer presents a discussion of different causes and how each one contributes to the outcome. The following passage illustrates cause-effect organization.

"One of the contributors to poor performance on standardized tests of math achievement is inadequate instruction. The math classes that many students taken simply do not prepare them to do well on these tests. Exacerbating the problem is the fact that most parents are unaware of the poor quality of instruction, and thus they do not provide their children with additional support for math skills. A further contributor to poor achievement test performance is math anxiety. Some students, regardless of actual mathematical skill, find math to be unpleasant and anxiety-provoking subject, and so the prospect of taking a math test is positively terrifying to them."

Problem-Solution Organization

Problem-solution organization presents information about a problem, followed by a description of one or more solutions. The writer may briefly summarize the solutions, compare and contrast solutions, evaluate the solutions, and/or provide a recommendation as to the preferred solution. Problem-solution organization is illustrated in the following passage:

"Attention Deficit Hyperactivity Disorder (ADHD) poses significant academic challenges to students who suffer from the disorder. During lectures, and when receiving instructions about homework and other assignments, students with ADHD often miss key information because they had been "zoning out" or acting impulsively while the teacher was talking. During tests and other assessments, students with ADHD may not perform well for much the same reasons. In hopes of dealing with these and other challenges, parents of children with ADHD have two general options. The first is for the children to regularly use stimulant medicines. These medications are known by brand names such as Ritalin, Adderall, and Concerta, and they have been shown to be somewhat effective at diminishing ADHD symptoms. The second option is the regular application of behavioral management strategies that involve parents, teachers, and the students themselves. These strategies have also proven to be somewhat effective. Each of these approaches, medical and behavioral, has its strengths and weaknesses, and experts often recommend that they be carefully combined."

The six types of organization discussed here each reflect a different ordering of information. In descriptive writing, the information may not be presented in any particular order. Rather, the characteristics of some person, place, event, or thing may simply be described, as in the following passage:

"With an American father and a Chinese mother, New Year's eve at my house is a startling mix of cultures. We drink eggnog and sing 'Auld Lang Syne.'

We make resolutions. We also make *jiao zi*, which are dumplings filled with pork, cabbage, and other goodies, and when mom serves the chicken for our main course, it still has the head and feet on it. I think that represents togetherness. I'm not sure, because I always close my eyes and ears when her chicken appears."

Framing and Transitions

Each type of organization discussed in the previous section pertains to an entire piece of writing. Rhetorical analysis also includes the ability to recognize and evaluate organizational strategies that are used within and across individual sentences. Two of the most important organizational strategies used at the sentence level are framing and transitions.

Framing refers to the way a writer lets readers know what will be discussed prior to the actual discussion. Framing statements give the reader some sense of what to expect. A framing statement may pertain to the entire piece of writing, to one passage, or to a single sentence. In each of the following sentences, the first several words provide the reader with some information about what will be discussed next.

"In this review I will describe three limitations of Smith's theory, and then describe a plausible alternative."

"Now let me explain why I referred to Faulkner as a 'limited' novelist."

"There are two good reasons to purchase a hybrid vehicle."

"This next section focuses on some of the more specific contributors to Kahlo's distinctive style."

Framing statements are useful because they inform readers about the content as well the organization of what they are about to read. In a similar way, transitions provide information about content and organization. A transition term informs readers that there will be some sort of change in the writing, thereby allowing what was previously expressed to be linked smoothly to what is expressed next. Examples of transition terms include "for example," however," "in contrast," "moreover," "thus," and others. For example, the term "however" typically alerts the reader that the next statement will qualify the previous one. Consider the following examples:

"Lismont was fast; however, Rogers was faster."

"Scientists agree that many factors influence IQ. However, there is no consensus as to which factor has the greatest influence."

"Johnny claimed that he didn't eat the candy. I could tell, however, that he was lying."

In each example, the clause following the word "however" introduces a qualification to the previous clause. The previous clause is not actually denied in these sentences. Rather, the word "however" tells the reader in each case that the previous clause does not convey the whole story. Lismont was indeed fast, but someone else happened to be faster. Scientists agree that many factors influence IQ, but they don't agree about everything. And Johnny did in fact claim that he didn't eat the candy. It just so happens that he was lying, according to the writer.

Transition terms such as "however," "but," "nevertheless," "all the same," and "in contrast" mark some sort of contrast between the previous sentence or clause and what follows, as in the following examples:

"Mary's mother asked her to speak more softly during the service, but the little girl was not old enough to remember to do so."

"Sartre and Camus disagreed on many topics, both philosophical and artistic; nevertheless, they remained friends for quite some time."

"The hiker knew that the path ahead was treacherous. All the same, she chose to forge ahead anyway."

"English plurals are marked by morphological changes such as the addition of an "s" to the end of a word. Chinese, in contrast, does not mark pluralization through morphological changes."

The transition terms in the previous examples indicate a contrast between sentences or clauses. Other transition terms, such as "in the same way," "similarly," and "likewise" highlight similarities, as in the following examples:

"Jini shouted at Lester, in much the same way that Lester had shouted at her earlier that evening."

"By means of camouflage, flounder blend in with the sea floor; similarly, butterflies may be indistinguishable from the leaves on which they rest."

"A man hopes that his future spouse will suit him perfectly. Likewise, women hope to find the perfect spouse."

Transition terms such as "as a result," "consequently," and sometimes "thus," indicate a causal relationship, as in the following examples.

"Almost every evening that year, Jordan practiced basketball with his father. As a result, his skills improved significantly."

"The intern showed up late for work four days in a row; consequently, he was fired."

"Clarissa was standing on a stepstool when she dropped the bowl. Thus, the bowl shattered when it hit the kitchen floor."

In each of the preceding examples, the clause following the transition term describes an outcome caused by the action described in the clause that came right before the transition term.

Transition terms such as "then," "afterwards," and "later" are used to indicate temporal sequence, as in the following examples:

"He dropped his bat, amazed to have hit the ball. Then he scampered to first base."

"On Saturday it rained in Houston from about 6 a.m. to 6 p.m. Afterwards, some of the downtown streets were flooded."

"Garfield was assassinated shortly after taking office; later, McKinley and then Kennedy were assassinated as well."

Some transitional phrases, such as "in other words," "that is to say," and "to reiterate," tell the reader that what follows is essentially a restatement of what preceded the phrase. Other transitional phrases, such as "in short," "in sum," or "to put it briefly" indicate that what follows is a succinct summary of what preceded that phrase. Following are some examples:

"I believe that a lack of caffeine undermines success; in other words, you pretty much have to drink coffee in order to be successful."

"The downfall of many televangelists has been concupiscence; that is to say, lust."

"The next step on the road to economic recovery is more responsible federal spending. To reiterate, greater responsibility in federal spending should be our immediate priority in strengthening the economy."

"It is critical to the health of our society that every adult citizen exercise his or her right to vote; in short, you need to vote."

"First he lost his keys, then his car wouldn't start, and when he finally did the car started he noticed that it was almost out of gas. In sum, he had a very trying morning."

"Picasso had the uncanny ability to anticipate new developments in the visual arts and then modify his work so that it quickly moved to the forefront of those developments. To put it briefly, he was a most talented innovator."

Some transitional phrases, such as "for example," "specifically," and "in general" tell the reader that what follows bears a more specific or more general connection to what preceded the phrase, as in the following examples:

"Most professional athletes are not successful when they attempt to change sports; for example, after his first retirement from professional basketball, Michael Jordan was unable to become a major league baseball player."

"Orcas show great patience when hunting young whales; specifically, they will chase young whales and their mothers for great distances, waiting until the pair grow tired before attempting to separate them prior to the kill."

"The nobility objected to the king's approach to foreign affairs, the merchants detested his tax increases, and the peasants chafed under his onerous penal code. In general, the populace was dissatisfied with the king's leadership."

There are many other kinds of transition phrases. Most of these phrases inform the reader about the nature of the relationship between clauses or sentences. In some cases, the phrases indicate this relationship in a very specific way. For example, the phrase "for example" indicates the a very specific kind of relationship between the previous statement and the information that follows. In other cases, the transition phrases provide the reader with somewhat less specific guidance as to how later details connect with earlier ones, as in the following examples:

"Yolanda was at the party, so Jimmy came too."

"Visitors must be careful when walking around the city at night. And they must be especially careful not to lose their way."

Finally, some transition terms can be used to indicate more than one kind of relationship. Consider, for example, the following uses of the word "thus:"

"The bowl was already cracked when Clarissa dropped it. Thus, it shattered instantly upon hitting the floor."

"Jackson grew up in Paris; thus he speaks French quite fluently."

"After we finished quarreling, she kissed me one last time and left for good. I watched, expressionless. Thus we ended a long and bittersweet relationship."

In the first passage, "thus" indicates a causal relationship and is synonymous with "as a result." In the second passage, "thus" marks a logical relationship and is synonymous with "therefore." In the third passage, "thus" summarizes the previous anecdote and is synonymous with "in this way."

UNDERSTANDING OF STYLE

Style reflects choices made by a writer that affect the way in which information is communicated. Different topics and audiences call for different styles. At the same time, a writer may develop a distinctive style that can be recognized across different pieces of writing. Some of the many contributors to style include diction, syntax, and point of view.

Diction

Diction refers to a writer's choice of words. There are many different ways to convey essentially the same idea. However, the particular words that a writer uses to express an idea will impact the meaning, appeal, and persuasiveness of the idea, as well as the reader's sense of the writer's attitudes. Consider, for example, the following three sentences:

"With respect to alcohol consumption, I suspect that she resembles her father in a tendency to overindulge."

"When it comes to drinking, I think she takes after her dad. They both seem to overdo it."

"She's a drunk, just like her dad."

All three sentences convey essentially the same idea. However, as a result of differences in word choice, each sentence will probably have a different impact on readers.

For example, the first sentence is much more formal than the other two. In fact, it is formal to the point that in most contexts it would seem pretentious, or stilted. The second and third sentences are quite informal.

Another difference in the diction of the three sentences is that the third sentence indicates considerable certainty that the girl and her father have an alcohol problem, while the first two sentences convey an element of uncertainty, or at least open-mindedness. The phrase "I suspect that" in the first sentence, and the phrases "I think" and "seem to" in the second sentence all imply that the writer is open to the possibility of being wrong. In order to see this difference in certainty, notice how the first two sentences would read if these phrases were removed: "With respect to alcohol consumption, she resembles her father in a tendency to overindulge." And: "When it comes to drinking, she takes after her dad. They both overdo it." Notice how the sentences now indicate greater certainty on the writer's part.

A further difference among the three sentences that can be attributed to word choice is in what they imply about the writers' attitudes. The first two sentences are fairly neutral. In each case, the writer is cautious about attributing an alcohol problem to the girl and her father, and no judgment is offered. In contrast, the use of the derogatory term "drunk" in the third sentence conveys a more negative appraisal. The writer clearly disapproves. (Although not strictly a matter of diction, the brevity and definitiveness of the third sentence also contribute to its negative tone.)

Following are some of the dimensions on which a writer's diction can be analyzed.

First, some words and phrases are more formal than others, as illustrated by the following sentences:

"The prince bestowed a fine ring upon his servant."

"The prince gave his servant a fine ring."

Second, some words and phrases are more specific than others, as illustrated by the following references to the same individual:

"He was born in New Haven, Connecticut."

"He was born in New England."

"He was born up north somewhere."

Third, some words and phrases are more direct than others, as illustrated by the following sentences:

"She died last year."

"She passed away last year."

"She left us last year."

Third, in a particular context, the meanings of some words and phrases will be clearer than others, as illustrated by the following sentences (arranged in order of decreasing clarity):

"He spent most of New Year's Day attempting to understand some of the recent events in his life."

"He spent most of New Year's Day attempting to process some of the recent happenings."

"He spent most of New Year's Day attempting to deal with things."

Fourth, in a particular context, some words and phrases will be relatively fresh, while others will sound more clichéd, as illustrated by the following:

"The child is so thin. She's as light as a breath."

"The child is so thin. She's as light as a feather."

"The child is so thin. She's as thin as a rail."

Fifth, some words and phrases are literal, while others are more figurative, as can be seen in the following examples (arranged in order of increasingly figurative usage):

"The boy had a timid look."

"The boy had a mousy look."

"The boy had a frightened rodent look in his eyes."

"The boy had a mousetrap-closing-on-me look in his feral eyes."

Sixth, some words are more or less concrete, while others are abstract, as illustrated by the following:

"Just then, an orange cat padded out from behind the forsythia bush."

"Just then, a creature padded out from behind the bush."

"Just then, something came out from behind the bush."

Seventh, in a particular context, some words will be more or less appropriate in emphasis, while others will be more hyperbolic, as in the following:

"Amidst smoke, flames, and a loud roar, the rocket climbed up into the sky."

"Amidst smoke, flames, and a deafening roar, the rocket blasted up into the sky."

Finally, some words are more conventional, while others represent jargon, colloquialisms or slang.

"Owing to his difficult childhood, he became a criminal."

"Owing to his difficult childhood, he became a crook."

"Owing to his difficult childhood, he became a total thug,"

As you can see from each of the examples in this section, a writer's diction will have an influence on the clarity and persuasiveness of his or her arguments. However, as discussed later in this chapter, the diction that a writer chooses for a particular piece of writing will often be determined by the intended audience and purpose for the writing. Diction that is clear and persuasive in one context may be confusing and unappealing in another.

Syntax

Rhetorical analysis includes attention to **syntax**, or the order of words in a sentence. The sentences that a writer uses will vary in length, complexity, and internal structure. Across sentences there will be a greater or lesser extent of grammatical variety. These differences in syntax contribute to the style and in many cases the meaning of the sentences.

Note that while the ability to recognize and correct syntactic errors is tested in the Conventions of Written English and Revision Skills sections of the CLEP

College Composition and College Composition Modular exams (and the ability to use syntax correctly contributes to how one's essays for each of these exams are graded), the ability to understand how syntax contributes to style and meaning is tested in the Rhetorical Analysis section.

Among the many syntactic rules governing English sentences, an important stylistic distinction can be made between active and passive voice, as illustrated by the following pair of sentences:

"The dog smashed the vase." (Active voice)

"The vase was smashed by the dog." (Passive voice)

These sentences both convey the same meaning and consist of almost the same words. However, the first sentence is written in active voice, while the second sentence reflects passive voice.

Active voice means that the subject *carries out the action* indicated by the verb. **Passive voice** means that the subject *is the recipient of the action* indicated by the verb. In the first sentence, the subject is "The dog," while in the second sentence, the subject is "The vase." Because the dog carries out the action of smashing the vase, the first sentence reflects active voice. Because the vase is the recipient of the action of being smashed, the second sentence reflects passive voice.

Although writers are often encouraged to use active rather than passive voice, some authorities on style hold that passive voice is useful when the recipient of the action is of greater importance than whatever carried out the action. For example, consider the following questions:

"What was that noise?"

"I cannot find my priceless 17th century Ming vase. Do you know where it is?"

The answer to the first question should be expressed in active voice ("The dog smashed the vase.") However, the answer to the second question should be expressed in passive voice ("The vase was smashed by the dog.") because the vase and its destruction are much more important at the moment than the fact that a dog (as opposed to some other creature) was responsible for smashing it.

Writers vary their syntax in order to keep their writing more interesting to the reader. For example, compare the following descriptions of the same event:

"I got into my car this morning. I drove to school. I saw a peacock on the way to school. I saw the peacock standing on the corner of Larchmont Avenue. I pulled over to look at it for a moment. I guess it was someone's pet."

"This morning I got into my car and drove to school. On the way I saw a peacock standing on the corner of Larchmont Avenue. I pulled over to look at it for a moment. It was someone's pet, I guess."

Both passages recount the same event using almost exactly the same words. However, by varying the syntax, the second passage sounds more natural and interesting than the first one, and is more likely to hold the reader's attention.

The contribution of syntax to style is illustrated in this third rendition of the peacock incident:

"Got into the car this morning, drove to school. Saw a peacock on the way. A peacock. Standing on the corner of Larchmont Avenue. Pulled over to look at it for a moment. Someone's pet, I guess. A peacock."

In this passage, the writer suspends some of the rules of syntax that apply in formal writing. As you can see, the result is very different stylistically from the first two versions of the passage.

As syntactic structures become more complex, rhetorical analysis depends increasingly on determining what the writer is saying and how the different parts of a sentence contribute to the overall meaning. For example, consider the following, relatively elaborated sentence:

"Yesterday evening, the tiger that had terrorized the village last year made a reappearance, according to an elderly villager who commented that he had been sitting on his porch when he heard the tiger's distinctive, terrifying growl, prompting him to rush inside and phone the authorities."

From this sentence, the reader can glean several facts: a) The village had been terrorized by a tiger during the previous year. b) An elderly man reported that the tiger had been in the village on the previous evening. c) The man had been sitting on his porch when he heard the tiger. d) The man phoned the authorities to say that he had heard a tiger.

Point of View

Rhetorical analysis includes attention to **point of view**, which refers to the perspective through which information is conveyed. The three main points of view are referred to as first person, second person, and third person.

First person point of view conveys information from the author's or narrator's own perspective. Pronouns such as "I" and "me" are used. In literature, the "I" who tells the story is the narrator, and the narrative voice may be that of the author or a fictional character. In nonfiction writing, the "I" is the author, as illustrated in the following sentence:

"I have found that rugby is more popular in southern France than in the north."

Second person point of view conveys information from the reader's perspective. Pronouns such as "you" are used, as in the following example:

"When you visit France, you find that rugby is more popular in the south than it is in the north."

Third person point of view conveys information without explicitly mentioning author, narrator, or reader. Pronouns such as "he," "she," "it," and "they" are used, and information is conveyed as if by an unseen observer. For example:

"When people visit France, they find that rugby is more popular in the south than it is in the north."

Each of the three points of view allows the writer to present a different extent of detail and topical emphasis. A writer's style is defined in part by the particular point of view, or mix of points of view, that he or she uses. Although mixing is common, one point of view will often predominate in a piece of writing.

Writing from an exclusively or predominately second person point of view is not very common, owing in part to the potential ambiguity in who is being referred to. This ambiguity is illustrated by the following passage:

"True enough, you will quarrel with your spouse once you are married, but you will also appreciate the support of this special person who knows you best and loves you most, and so in the end you will find that the advantages of marriage far outweigh the disadvantages."

The persuasiveness of this passage is limited by uncertainty as to whether "you" refers to the individual reader, all readers, or everyone in society whether or not they read this passage. The writer appears to be addressing everyone, but is it credible that everyone will have the sort of experience described in the passage? Conceivably, the reader is already married and has (a) never quarreled with his or her spouse, or (b) quarreled with the spouse so frequently that he or she has concluded that the disadvantages of marriage far outweigh the advantages. At the very least, the reader may know of others who would consider marriage a primarily disadvantageous arrangement, in which case it is unclear exactly who "you" is intended to be.

When a writer is describing something that he or she has done, thought, or felt, first person point of view may be most appropriate. First person often seems more personal than third person, in that in first-person writing the author or narrator appears to be speaking directly to the reader. However, first person is not preferable to third person in every situation. For one thing, constant use of pronouns such as "I" and "me" may seem intrusive and unnecessary to readers. When describing a tribal culture, for example, an anthropologist who has lived among the tribe need not constantly say "I saw" this and "I heard" that. Rather, the anthropologist can simply describe what he or she saw and heard using third-person point of view, because the reader will understand that in each case it was the anthropologist who had been the observer. In such cases, third-person writing will predominate, and first person may be used sparingly.

In some cases, first person is actually prohibited in scientific writing, under the assumption that science is an objective activity, and that scientific principles and findings exist independently of the scientific enterprise. At the same time, because many scholars agree that the personal biases of scientists cannot be completely expunged from scientific activity, and because it is individual scientists after all who engage in such activities, first person is sometimes accepted or even encouraged in scientific writing. To illustrate the relative merits of third- and first-person writing in science, consider the following procedural descriptions:

"The wafer was immersed in BOE and then rinsed with deionized water."

"I immersed the wafer in BOE and then rinsed it with deionized water."

The third-person phrasing in the first sentence contributes to a sense of "objectivity," but because this sentence reflects passive voice, it is not clear to the reader who immersed and rinsed the wafer (or whether it was even the same person in each case). In the second sentence, first-person phrasing makes it clearer that one person, the writer, carried out both procedures. At the same time, in a scientific report, third person may be used at least some of the time when it is clear that the scientist is reporting his or her own activities.

In the end, the point of view that predominates in a piece of writing is often determined by editorial policy rather than the writer's own preference. The scholarly journal in which a scientific report appears, for example, may have a policy concerning point of view.

UNDERSTANDING OF AUDIENCE, PURPOSE, AND TONE

Audience

Audience refers to the person or people who are likely to read a piece of writing. Writers must consider their audience when making decisions about the style, length, and informativeness of what they write. Both the expertise and the interests of the audience will be relevant. For example, a description of a particular military battle will be very different depending on whether it is written for a group of army officers versus the general public versus the bereaved spouse of a soldier who committed an act of heroism during the battle.

The description of the battle written for army officers is likely to be highly detailed, neutral in tone, and focused on specific military issues. The diction will probably be formal and replete with technical terms. The following passage might be part of such a description:

"Armed with handguns and a stolen M14, 8 hostiles then proceeded north toward a disabled AMX-30 approximately one half klick from 3rd Platoon flank. Hostiles approached 3rd Platoon with weapons drawn. SFC Jones initially detected their advance and opened fire at once while simultaneously ordering nearby subordinates to take cover."

The description of the battle written for the general public (e.g., in the form of a magazine or newspaper article) will be less formal and technical than the description written for army officers. The syntax will not be overly complicated, and the choice of details as well as the diction will probably be intended to evoke some sort of emotional response among readers. Following is a passage that might be found in such a description:

"The insurgents were a rag-tag bunch, armed with nothing more than handguns and a rifle scavenged from a dead soldier. Moving quietly, they crept toward a burned-out tank only 300 yards from one side of the platoon where Sergeant Ron Jones was chatting with subordinates. Sergeant Jones was the first to spot the enemy. As the insurgents advanced on the platoon, brandishing their weapons, Jones wheeled and opened fire while shouting orders to the other men."

The description of the battle written for a bereaved spouse will formal but not at all technical. The diction will be very carefully managed. The description will be vague on some points but more specific about details that convey the fallen soldier's heroism and service to his country.

"Sergeant First Class Jones was engaged in conversation with several of his men when eight insurgents approached them with the intention of attacking the platoon. Sergeant Jones was the first to detect their approach and opened fire while instructing his men to take cover. Sergeant Jones displayed quick thinking and admirable courage by opening fire immediately rather than taking cover himself. Moreover, Sergeant Jones' leadership skills and great concern for his men were evident in the fact that he was able to request that they seek cover while he simultaneously acted to protect them as well as the rest of the platoon."

In sum, these three different descriptions of the same event vary greatly in diction, level of detail, and other characteristics in light of the audience who will be reading each description.

Purpose

An author's **purpose for writing** is inextricably linked to his or her intended audience. The description of a military battle written for army officers is most likely to be created for the purpose of providing information, presenting an analysis, or advocating a theory, if not some combination of the three. A description of the battle written for the general public might also be written in order to inform or analyze, but it may serve some other purpose as well. Articles, blogs, essays, and works of fiction written for the general public are also meant to entertain, to stimulate public debate about important issues, to spark moral outrage, and so on. In contrast, a description of the battle presented to the bereaved spouse of a heroic soldier will have been written solely to inform the spouse of the soldier's heroism and subsequent demise.

Different types of writing can be defined according to their purpose. For example, **expository writing** can be defined as writing intended to describe or explain a topic. In brief, the purpose of expository writing is to inform the reader about something.

Various kinds of expository writing can be further distinguished based on their specific purposes. For example, the writer may wish to teach the reader how to do something (e.g., cook, do algebra, play guitar). The writer may wish to describe a phenomenon (e.g., photosynthesis, road rage, the most recent presidential election), compare different entities (e.g., sports teams, cities, nocturnal predators), or describe cause-effect relationships.

Expository writing can be evaluated in terms of its accuracy, completeness, and often persuasiveness (even if the purpose of the writing is not to persuade the reader to act or think in a certain way). Other types of writing that are sometimes distinguished from expository forms include narrative and persuasive writing, each of which tend to reflect a somewhat different purpose.

The purpose of **narrative writing** is to relate a story. Rhetorical analysis of narratives focus on how writers create various kinds of effects on readers. In such analyses, the accuracy or truthfulness of the writing will not usually be evaluated (although the accuracy with which a narrative writer presents a technical description may be praised, just as inaccuracies that are unintended might be criticized as distractions to the effects that the writer intends to create). Typically, the persuasiveness of narrative writing is only evaluated in terms of how much the reader has been caught up in the story and is influenced by its rhetorical devices.

The purpose of **persuasive writing** is to convince the reader of something. In practice, the distinction between expository and persuasive writing is not always clear cut. For example, the scientist who is describing a new species is not just attempting to inform readers but also persuade them of the accuracy of his or her distinctions. At the same time, the essayist who is advocating education reform may not just be attempting to persuade readers but also to provide them with details necessary for making an informed judgment. In each case, both the accuracy and the persuasiveness of the writer can be evaluated.

Tone

A writer's attitude is referred to as his or her **tone**. Tone can be inferred from the writer's diction, phrasing, choice of content, and stated opinions. For example, compare the following two passages:

"Smith's book is a highly appealing introduction to the art of baking bread. It contains some tidbits about the history of bread and the chemistry of baking, as well as numerous recipes for the breads that most people—including yours truly—dearly love. I tried out several of these recipes myself, and each time the results were fantastic!"

"Smith's book is an interesting introduction to the art of baking bread. It contains information about the history of bread and the chemistry of baking, as well as numerous recipes for the breads that most people love. I tried out several of these recipes myself and found them easy to understand."

The tone of the first passage is positive and enthusiastic. This is evident from word choice (e.g., "highly appealing") as well as from overt statements of praise (e.g., "the results were fantastic"). In contrast, the tone of the second passage is considerably less enthusiastic. Although some praise is offered, it is much fainter than that of the first passage (e.g., the book is described "interesting" rather than "highly appealing"). The absence of certain information in the second passage is also telling. The writer of the second passage refers to breads that most people love, without indicating whether he or she is one of those people. And, the writer refers to how easy it is to understand the recipes, without noting whether the results were appealing. There are some hints here—not proof, but just some hints—that the writer of the second passage does not particularly like the book or its recipes. Clearly, whatever the writer of the second passage thinks, he or she is less enthusiastic than the writer of the first passage.

In some cases, the tone of a passage will be at odds with its literal meaning. For example, irony can be detected when the literal meaning of a passage contradicts what must be the intended meaning. Consider the father's terse comment in the following passage:

"Dad," said the little girl, "I accidentally spilled a whole glass of milk on your keyboard."

"Great," he replied.

The fact that the father's reply was ironic is suggested by the obvious discrepancy between the situation (a possibly ruined keyboard) and the literal meaning of the father's comment. In the absence of any other information about the father, we can assume that he probably does not think it is great to have a whole glass of milk spilled on his keyboard. Thus, we infer that his comment was ironic. What he intended to say is that the situation is *not* great.

Among the many uses of irony is satire, a form of criticism in which people or practices are held up to ridicule. For example, in order to criticize the British treatment of the Irish poor during the 18th century, Jonathan Swift wrote an essay known as *A Modest Proposal* in which he suggested that the Irish would improve their economic situation by selling their children as food to the upper class British. Swift did not actually believe that the Irish should do so. Rather, as Swift's essay progresses, one realizes that he wished to call attention to the mistreatment of the Irish. After describing the plight of the Irish poor in serious and poignant terms, Swift suddenly launches into a startlingly cheerful description of this proposal:

"I have been assured by a very knowing American of my acquaintance in London, that a young healthy child well nursed is at a year old a most delicious, nourishing, and wholesome food, whether stewed, roasted, baked, or boiled; and I make no doubt that it will equally serve in a fricasie, or a ragout."

The outrageousness of the suggestion, combined with the level of detail concerning preparation ("stewed, roasted...") are among the clues that Swift's tone was satirical rather than literal.

Tone is related to purpose and audience. In *A Modest Proposal*, Swift was speaking to British citizens of his day, including the wealthy and powerful, in order to effect a change in their attitudes. Now consider again the description of a particular military battle written for different audiences. The tone of the description written for army officers is likely to be serious. In addition, the writer will either be neutral or openly favor some analytical perspective. The tone of the description written for a bereaved spouse will be equally serious, and admiration and gratitude for the soldier's heroism will be clearly conveyed. As for descriptions written for the general public, many kinds of tone are possible. The writer may be neutral, or the writer may choose to take a stand for or against some aspect of the military situation, if not military action more generally. The writer may be primarily concerned with expressing a particular moral perspective or emotional state (e.g., outrage) or the writer's concern may be more intellectual and focus on developing an idea.

UNDERSTANDING OF RHETORIC

Rhetoric refers to the use of language in an effective and persuasive way. Writers always hope to make an impact on their readers, and in many cases a writer's purpose will be to persuade. Generally speaking, the goal of persuasion is to effect some sort of change in the reader.

Writers seek to change their readers in many different ways. In some cases, the writer wishes to change the reader's present or future behavior, as illustrated by the following sentence:

"In light of the many adverse health effects of smoking, not to mention the actual cost of cigarettes and other nicotine-delivery products, you owe it to yourself not to smoke—or if you do smoke, to give up the habit as soon as possible."

In some cases, the writer may wish to change the reader's attitudes about an issue of present or future importance. For example:

"John Doe may have won the last election by a landslide, but he has yet to fulfill any of his campaign promises, and his public statements on domestic spending, tax reform, and environmental conservation reveal a politician who will say anything to please the audience before him. Think carefully before deciding who to vote for in the next election."

In some cases, the writer may wish to change the reader's views about an event from the past, as in the example of an "exposé" of a widely-respected historical figure in which the writer places great emphasis on personal and professional flaws, or the example of a critic who argues that a particular work of art from the past deserves greater or lesser admiration than it currently receives.

In still other cases, the writer may simply wish to persuade the reader to feel a certain way for a moment—to remember, to honor, or perhaps even to scorn.

Traditionally, rhetorical effects were said to be produced by appealing to the reader's intellect, emotions, and/or beliefs about the writer's motives and character. The distinction between these three sources of rhetorical effects emphasizes the fact that writers have many tools for creating such effects. These tools include each of the skills discussed in this chapter and more.

Rhetorical Devices

A rhetorical device consists of anything that a writer does to increase the persuasiveness of a statement or passage. As noted, all of the skills discussed in this chapter can be used in the service of creating rhetorical devices. Scholars have distinguished among dozens of different rhetorical devices, many of which are ultimately a matter of diction (i.e., word choice).

Among the rhetorical devices that have not yet been discussed here, one of the most powerful and frequently used is a manipulation of syntax known as parallelism. **Parallelism** refers to any grammatical structure that balances similar elements. These elements could be virtually any part of speech, component of a sentence, or section of a passage.

One of the simplest yet most effective examples of parallelism is G. K. Chesterton's pithy remark about change:

"New roads; new ruts."

Here the close similarity of the two nouns ("roads" and "ruts") increases the impact of the remark, which seems to mean that as we embark on new activities in our lives (thereby breaking out of old ruts), we have a tendency to slip once again into routines (i.e., new ruts).

Several kinds of parallelism are illustrated by the following well-known passage from the U.S. Declaration of Independence:

"We hold these Truths to be self-evident, that all Men are created equal, that they are endowed by their Creator with certain unalienable Rights, that among these are Life, Liberty and the pursuit of Happiness."

Here there is a parallelism across three of the clauses (each marked by the word "that"), and in the final clause, there is a rough parallelism across the three abstract nouns ("Life, Liberty and the pursuit of Happiness.")

This excerpt from the Declaration of Independence also illustrates another rhetorical device, called tricolon or "the rule of three," which holds that lists tend to be most effective when they contain three items. Not all lists of three are persuasive, however, and in some cases shorter or longer or lists can be quite powerful, as in the following excerpt from John F. Kennedy's Inaugural Address:

"Let every nation know, whether it wishes us well or ill, that we shall pay any price, bear any burden, meet any hardship, support any friend, oppose any foe to assure the survival and the success of liberty."

In Kennedy's statement, the underlying message of American determination is conveyed in part by the repeated parallelism across clauses that are very similar in rhythm. The same message of strength is conveyed by the unadorned repetition of Julius Caesar's famous "I came, I saw, I conquered."

Parallelism can be carried out by directly balancing elements or by inverting them, as in this famous appeal that Kennedy made later in his address:

"Ask not what your country can do for you—ask what you can do for your country."

The sudden inversion in this statement is surprising the first time it is encountered, and the grammatical twist mirrors Kennedy's appeal for citizens to change the way they think about their relationship to their country.

Parallelism is used sometimes across rather than within sentences. Kennedy makes use of this device several times in his Inaugural Address, as does Martin Luther King in his famous "I have a dream" speech at the Lincoln Memorial. In this speech, which is quite powerful even in written form, King use the refrain "I have a dream" to create these and other parallel sentences:

"I have a dream that one day this nation will rise up and live out the true meaning of its creed: 'We hold these truths to be self-evident, that all men are created equal.'

"I have a dream that one day on the red hills of Georgia, the sons of former slaves and the sons of former slave owners will be able to sit down together at the table of brotherhood.

"I have a dream that one day even the state of Mississippi, a state sweltering with the heat of injustice, sweltering with the heat of oppression, will be transformed into an oasis of freedom and justice...."

Notice that several of King's individual sentences in this excerpt contain parallelisms. For example, the close similarity of elements in "the sons of former slaves and the sons of former slave owners" subtly reinforces King's message that these groups of individuals are brothers. The repetition of the "sweltering with the heat" phrases mirrors the heaviness of the injustice and oppression King is referring to. Within the same sentence, a further parallelism is introduced between the reference to sweltering and the image of an oasis.

This excerpt from King's speech illustrates two important points about parallelism. First, many instances of parallelism incorporate other rhetorical devices. One example discussed already is repetition. Another example is illustrated by the next line in King's speech:

"I have a dream that my four little children will one day live in a nation where they will not be judged by the color of their skin but by the content of their character."

If you read this sentence out loud or listen to a recording of Dr. King, you can hear the impact of the repeated hard "c" sounds in the parallelism at the end of the line. Repetition of a sounds in this way is referred to as **alliteration**. Although alliteration is a rhetorical device of great importance in spoken language, it creates rhetorical effects in written text as well when we can "hear" the sounds as we read.

The excerpt from King's speech also illustrates the fact that parallelism, even when relied on heavily, is not the only rhetorical device that will be used by a skilled communicator. For example, his quotation from the U.S. Declaration of Independence ("We hold these truths to be self-evident . . .) represents an appeal to authority, a common rhetorical device. Although in some cases it will be undesirable to appeal to authority rather than providing evidence, here the practice is effective given that the Declaration of Independence is familiar to Americans and embodies what most citizens consider to be the country's most cherished ideals. Here, King exhorts the audience to live up to the particular ideals reflected in the quotation.

Another set of widely used rhetorical devices that King makes effective use of in this excerpt is figurative language. The "red hills" of Georgia is not just a physical description and reference to a particular region of Georgia, but also a subtle allusion to blood that has been spilled. Metaphorical images such as a table of brotherhood or an oasis of freedom and justice contribute to the persuasiveness of King's message by capturing audience interest through their profound appeal.

Rhetorical Analysis

Rhetorical analysis includes the ability to recognize and evaluate rhetorical effects in a piece of writing. For example, consider the organization and diction of the following two passages:

"Reverend King was an eloquent and riveting speaker. Whether delivering a sermon to a small congregation or a speech to the entire nation, his words touched every heart with their passionate commitment to the possibility of human progress and the eventual brotherhood and sisterhood of all. These words continue to inspire people around the world with their powerful message of hope."

"Reverend King's speeches were eloquent and smooth. These words continue to inspire people with their message. Whether giving a sermon or some other public address, his speeches impacted listeners and hung the moon in terms of their commitment to human progress and equality."

The purpose of each passage is the same—to praise King's oratorical prowess—but the diction is more effective in the first passage than in the second one. For example, consider the word "riveting." To "rivet" something means to drive a mechanical fastening device into it in order to hold it firmly in place. Thus, the word "riveting" in the first passage connotes an audience that has been rendered motionless, held in place by the power of King's words. Another example of an effective rhetorical device that distinguishes the first passage is the parallelism of "delivering a sermon to a small congregation or a speech to the entire nation." The contrast here is more specific and interesting than the corresponding parallelism in the second passage.

In contrast, the second passage exhibits a number of rhetorical weaknesses. In terms of organization, the second sentence would be more effective if it were located at the end of the passage (as in the first passage). There are also at least four problems with the diction of the second passage.

First, the combination of "eloquent and smooth" in the second passage seems redundant, as eloquence would seem to include an element of smoothness. Second, the phrase "Whether giving a sermon or a major speech" is flat. Compare this phrase to the more vivid diction of the first passage ("Whether delivering a sermon to a small congregation or a speech to the entire nation..."). Third, the phrase "impacted listeners" is awkward and vague. Fourth, the phrase "hung the moon" is clichéd, and its informality clashes with the more abstract and formal phrase that follows.

HOW TO APPROACH RHETORICAL ANALYSIS QUESTIONS ON THE CLEP EXAMS

Most of the questions in the Rhetorical Analysis section will be organized around passages. Usually there will be three to five questions per passage. These passages may concern virtually any topic. Each passage may represent an introduction or a conclusion, or it may represent the body of a piece of writing. Some of the passages will be factual, while others will be theoretical or speculative. Many of the passages will be expository, while others will primarily attempt to persuade the reader to adopt a particular point of view.

Each question in the Rhetorical Analysis section will ask you to do one of the following:

- Choose the best synonym for a word in a sentence

- Choose the best description of a word's purpose in a sentence

- Choose the best description of a sentence's purpose in the passage

- Choose the best summary of a sentence's meaning in the passage

- Choose the reordering of sentences that most improves the passage's coherence

- Choose the best description of the author's primary purpose in writing the passage

- Choose the best summary of the passage

- Choose the best summary of the organization of the passage

The directions you can expect to see for the Rhetorical Analysis section are reproduced here from the CLEP College Composition/College Composition Modular Examination Guide:

"The following questions test your ability to analyze writing. Some questions refer to passages, while other questions are self-contained. For each question, choose the best answer."

Sample CLEP Questions

The questions provided in this section draw upon the skills discussed throughout this chapter. The format of the questions closely matches what you will find in the Rhetorical Analysis section of the CLEP College Composition and College Composition Modular exams. That is, the questions pertaining to passages are organized into sets of roughly three to five questions each. The sentences within each passage are numbered, in order to make it easier to refer to them in the questions. Five answer options are given for each question. You are asked to choose the best option.

We will work through the first set of questions together, once you have read the following passage.

(1) Michelangelo di Lodovico Buonarroti Simoni, commonly known as Michelangelo, was born in March of 1475 in the small village of Caprese, roughly 100 kilometers east of Florence. (2) Michelangelo's father was a important official with ties to the ruling Medici family, but the fame that Michelangelo achieved in his lifetime outstripped that of his father. (3) Centuries after Michelangelo's death, many still consider him to be the greatest painter and sculptor who ever lived. (4) By the age of 15, Michelangelo was already an accomplished artist and a favorite of Florence's leading citizens; by 30 he was the most prominent and sought-after artist in Europe. (5) At the time of his death in 1564, his most famous works, including the Pietá, the statue of David, and the ceiling of the Sistine Chapel, had already achieved their enduring and highly influential position in the canon of Western art.

Now consider the following question, which pertains to the purpose of one part of a sentence:

Which of the following best describes the main purpose of the underlined portion of Sentence 1 (reproduced below)?

Michelangelo di Lodovico Buonarroti Simoni, <u>commonly known as Michelangelo</u>, was born in March of 1475 in the small village of Caprese.

(A)   To show that people born in the 15th century often went by one name

(B)   To make sure that the reader knows to whom the full name refers

(C)   To create a short version of Michelangelo's full name for use in the passage

(D)   To emphasize that Michelangelo can be referred to by more than one name

(E)   To draw a contrast between formal and informal modes of address.

As you read through the five options, you should notice that Option A can be ruled out right away, because the passage does not state anything about how people born in the 15th century were named.

Option B may seem like the best answer, but for any question you should be sure to read through each of the options before making a decision.

Although option C is not entirely inaccurate, it is not the best answer. The writer did not "create" a short version of Michelangelo's name. Rather, the writer simply used the conventional name for the artist. Thus, you can rule out option C.

Regarding option D, although it is true that Michelangelo can be referred to by more than one name, the first sentence of the passage does not seem to emphasize this point. In fact, most people can be referred to by more than one name. Thus, you can rule out option D.

Finally, option E can be ruled out because the sentence does not concern the contrast between formal and informal modes of address.

It should be clear now that option B is the best answer. Sentence 1 serves an introductory function in the passage. By alerting the reader to the fact that the long name at the outset refers to Michelangelo, the writer helps ensure that the reader knows who the passage is about. This illustrates how a writer considers his or her audience when deciding on level of informativeness.

Now consider a question about word meaning:

In context, the word "outstripped" in Sentence 2 most nearly means

(A) matched

(B) enhanced

(C) exceeded

(D) contradicted

(E) fell short of

Option A can be ruled out because Michelangelo's father is not mentioned elsewhere in the passage, but the fame of Michelangelo himself is described in the next sentence. Option B is incorrect too, for essentially the same reason. Option D can be ruled out on the grounds of incoherence—one person's fame cannot be said to "contradict" someone else's. Option E is clearly incorrect because Michelangelo is depicted as more famous than his father. Option C is clearly the best answer. In this sentence, the transition word "but" indicates that something is about to be said that contrasts with the first part of the sentence, which includes reference to the importance of Michelangelo's father. The next sentence confirms that the contrast pertains to extent of fame.

The next question pertains to the purpose of a particular word:

What is the purpose of the word "still" in Sentence 3?

(A) To emphasize that the fame Michelangelo achieved in his lifetime endured over time

(B) To indicate that Michelangelo remains famous in spite of questions about his skill

(C) To illustrate the fact that for geniuses like Michelangelo fame will be enduring

(D) To question whether Michelangelo deserves the extent of fame he has achieved

(E) To highlight the fact that opinions about Michelangelo have never changed.

Given that the preceding sentence made reference to the fame that Michelangelo achieved in his lifetime, option A appears to be the best answer. Option B can certainly be ruled out, because the passage contains no references to questions about Michelangelo's skill. Likewise, options C, D, and E can be ruled out, because each one pertains to themes that are not mentioned in the passage. It may be true that Michelangelo's biography illustrates that the fame of geniuses is enduring, but this is not a theme that the writer explores, and thus it does not reflect the purpose of the word "still" in Sentence 3.

The next question pertains to organization:

Which is best to do with Sentence 4?

(A) Leave it where it is.

(B) Relocate it after sentence 5.

(C) Relocate it before sentence 2.

(D) Relocate it before sentence 3.

(E) Relocate it before sentence 1.

Because the organization of this passage is roughly chronological, Sentence 4 seems out of place, and thus option A is incorrect. The chronology of the passage would not be improved through implementing either options B, C, or E. Option D is the best answer. By switching the order of sentences 3 and 4, the chronology of the passage becomes clearer.

Finally, here is a question about the writer's purpose:

Which of the following best summarizes the author's likely purpose in writing this passage?

(A) To illustrate how Michelangelo's father influenced his art

(B) To describe the influence of Michelangelo on society

(C) To provide a brief introduction to the life of Michelangelo

(D) To show why Michelangelo is held in such great esteem

(E) To argue that Michelangelo's reputation is well-deserved

Here, Option C is the best answer, because throughout the chronology of the passage the writer introduces some of the details of Michelangelo's biography. Options A, C, D, and E represent themes that are at most barely alluded to in the passage.

Now have a look at the following passage:

(1) Fishermen love a challenge. (2) The northern pike, a popular species that even professional fishermen call a "prize fish," is one of those more challenging fish that makes a fly-fishing experience worthwhile. (3) Northern pike are rough fighters once they are hooked, often taking refuge in deep water and escaping inexperienced anglers. (4) Experienced fishermen usually catch them.

First, here is an organizational question:

Which of the following best describes the organization of the passage?

(A) A cause-effect relationship is explored with great specificity.

(B) Information is presented in order of decreasing importance.

(C) Different approaches are compared and contrasted.

(D) A general theme is illustrated by increasingly specific details.

(E) A chronological sequence of events is described.

Options A, B, C, and E do not reflect the organization of the passage. Option D is best, because the general theme of Sentence 1 is illustrated by specific details concerning the popularity of northern pike among fishermen, and then the specific challenges that these fish pose.

The next question pertains to the purpose of one particular word:

What purpose is served by the word "even" in Sentence 2?

(A) It contributes to the evidence of how challenging northern pike are.

(B) It maximizes the importance of attempting to fish for northern pike.

(C) It helps emphasize the widespread popularity of the northern pike.

(D) It stresses the differences between northern pike and other fish.

(E) It calls attention to the discernment of professional fishermen.

Since the popularity of northern pike is already mentioned in this passage, the word "even" serves to mark the importance of their popularity among an especially expert or discriminating group—fishermen. Thus, option C is the correct answer. The other options do not reflect a purpose that is directly served by use of "even" in this context.

Here is a question about word meaning:

The word "anglers" in Sentence 3 seems to refer to

(A) northern pike

(B) fishermen

(C) fly-fishing rods

(D) observers

(E) fishing gear

The preceding context, and the reference to fishermen in Sentence 4, make it clear that "anglers" is roughly synonymous with "fishermen," and thus option B is the correct answer.

The next question tests your transitional word skills:

If Sentences 3 and 4 were combined, which of the following transition words or phrases would be most suitable to use at the beginning of what is now Sentence 4?

(A) In spite of

(B) It goes without saying that

(C) Although

(D) And

(E) In contrast

Option A is incorrect because it the result would be ungrammatical. Although option B could be used to create a grammatically well-formed sentence, the meaning of the sentence would be problematic. The fact that experienced fishermen would usually catch the northern pike is not so obvious from the passage that it goes without saying. Option D is incorrect because it does not support the intended contrast. Option E would create a sentence that does not make sense. Thus, option C is the best answer.

Finally, a question about what can be inferred from the author's tone:

Which of the following best characterizes the author's attitude toward northern pike?

(A) indifferent

(B) alarmed

(C) dismissive

(D) enthusiastic

(E) ambiguous

Option D is the best answer, in light of the author's diction in several places.

Part III

THE ESSAYS: COLLEGE COMPOSITION AND COLLEGE COMPOSITION MODULAR ESSAYS

Chapter 5

The Essays

OVERVIEW OF THE CLEP COLLEGE COMPOSITION EXAMINATION, INCLUDING MODULAR OPTION

Purpose of the CLEP College Composition Examination and the College Composition Modular Examination

The College Board developed the new CLEP College Composition Examination, with a so-called Modular option, so that people could receive college credit for freshman composition. The new exams replace three discontinued exams: English Composition, English Composition with Essay, and Freshman College Composition. The new College Composition examinations have two parts: a multiple-choice section and an essay section. The multiple choice section tests general writing skills, including rhetorical analysis (25%), use of sources (25%), revision (40%), and the conventions of standard written English (10%). The essay section asks candidates taking the test to apply these writing skills by producing two essays. The first essay asks candidates to take a position in regard to a specific topic. The second essay also asks candidates to take a position in regard to a specific topic, but includes excerpts (with bibliographic information) from two sources. In the second essay, candidates are asked to use the sources in their composition. The essays are then each scored by college faculty from across the nation using a scoring guide provided by The College Board. The two essay scores are combined into one, which is then weighted equally with the multiple-choice section, to produce one weighted score between 20 and 80 (The College Board does not report the individual scores on the two sections, only the one weighted score).

In the CLEP College Composition Modular examination, individual colleges have more control over the essay portion of the exam. Colleges can design their own essay portion of the exam, as well as administer and/or score the essay portion themselves. This allows colleges to tailor the essay portion of the exam better to suit the needs of their program. The multiple-choice section, which CLEP scores, remains the same, as well as the percentages each skill is weighted.

If you are taking the CLEP College Composition examination to receive college credit at a particular college, make sure you check with the college to see if they have chosen the Modular option. If so, the college itself is the best source for how to prepare for the essay portion of the exam. Access the college's website for contact information for the director of the freshman composition program, or simply call the college's main number and ask to be directed to someone who can speak about CLEP exams accepted by the college for credit.

Structure and Scoring of the Essay Portion of the College Composition Examination

The College Board employs experienced college faculty from all across the nation to score the essay portion of the CLEP exam. Each of the two timed essays has its own scoring guide which scorers use to assess the quality of each essay. Each essay is scored by two people to provide one combined score between 0 and 6, with 6 being the highest. The scoring guide for the first essay is similar to the scoring guide for the second essay. The main difference between the two is that the second scoring guide takes into account the use of sources in the composition of the essay.

A careful analysis of the two scoring guides allows candidates to recognize what constitutes a good essay, as well as what writing skills they need to brush up on in order to write a successful response. The scoring guide for the first essay places great emphasis on development of the ideas, or arguments, in the essay, specifically in regard to reasons, examples, and/or details. The scoring guide for the second essay also places great emphasis on the development of a position using reasons, examples and/or details for support, but adds the use of the sources. The differences between a score of 6 and a score of 4 in terms of these criteria is only one of degree, as indicated by the terms "effectively" and "insightfully" for a score of 6, "consistently" and "appropriately" for a score of 5, and "competently" and "adequately" for a score of 4. The last three bullet points for each scoring guide are the same from a score of 2 to 6, again varying only by degree. These three points address focus and organization, vocabulary and sentence variety, and grammar and usage. **It is important to note that even the highest score, 6, allows for some errors in grammar and usage**.

According to the CLEP scoring guide for the first essay, the highest score possible is a "6." Typically, a "6" essay addresses the topic with a clear and thought-provoking position, or thesis statement, as well as good supporting evidence in the form or examples and reasons that fit the position. In addition to this basic argument structure, a "6" essay depicts writing that is focused, organized, and contains a good vocabulary and sentence variety. While the essay may have a few minor errors, overall a "6" essay demonstrates a good command of grammar and usage. Essays that score a "5" and "4" all contain the same criteria, but with less and less skill in each area. With a score of "3," essays begin to show a lack of skill in the above areas, with essays scoring a "2" and "1" showing a serious lack of ability in one or more areas. A "0" score is reserved for responses that do not even attempt to address the writing task.

The CLEP scoring guide for the second essay is identical to the one for the first essay, except that it includes criteria relating to the use of sources. Typically, a "6" essay does everything a "6" essay does in the first scoring guide, but also cites the sources CLEP provides in such a way as to support the position. In effect, the author uses the sources as supporting evidence and/or examples for his or her thesis, or position statement. Again, scores of "5" and "4" all contain the above features, but with diminishing skill level. Also, as in the first scoring guide, it is with a score of "3" that essays begin to show a serious lack of ability in one or more areas, especially in terms of sources. For example, essays that incorporate only one of the two sources CLEP provides will only score a "3," no matter how good the essay is otherwise. Essay with a score of "2" or "1" show a serious lack of skill in one or more area, with a score of "0" reserved for essays that do not attempt to address the writing task.

Based upon these two scoring guides, candidates should focus most of their efforts in improving the area of their writing most highly valued according to the criteria: the basic structure of an argument. For both scoring guides, scores from "6" to "4" must contain these elements. All arguments include a clearly stated position, supported by evidence in the form of reasons and examples. Without having something insightful to say, even the most grammatically correct essay will fail. The advice that follows, therefore, pays scant attention to the standards of written English (10%), while placing a great emphasis on rhetorical analysis (25%), use of sources (25%), and revision (40%).

BASIC WRITING STRATEGIES FOR PRODUCING HIGH-SCORING CLEP ESSAYS

The Basic Structure of a Written Argument Made Simple

All argumentative essays include, in their simplest form, the same basic features: a claim, reasons supporting the claim, evidence supporting the reasons, and refutation of counterarguments. The sample essay below is a good example of an argumentative essay that contains this basic structure.

The lack of available, affordable parking is a complaint heard on many college campuses. Let's suppose a group of students meet to construct a formal request for the school to do something about the problem. Their document might sound something like this:

The parking situation on our campus is deplorable and needs to be improved. There are so few parking spaces near the dorms, many students are forced to park blocks away, on the other side of campus. This is very inconvenient, forcing students to lug books and any other heavy packages they may have long distances, often in the rain and snow. In addition to being inconvenient, it also poses a safety risk for students who have night class, or are returning late from a job or party. With the cost of campus room and board rising each year, students have the right to expect a parking space near where they reside, just like students who rent apartments off campus. While it's true that space on campus is very limited, the school should immediately investigate options to solve the problem, such as building a parking garage, or supplying students with transportation to and from distant parking lots.

The above example contains the basic structure of an argument. The **claim**, or position the author is taking, is found in the first sentence: *The parking situation on our campus is deplorable and needs to be improved.* The claim clearly tells the reader what the topic is, as well as what stand the author is taking in regard to it.

The above example also contains three specific **reasons** that support the claim: (1) the parking situation is inconvenient, (2) it is a safety risk, and (3) students pay for the right to park close to where they reside. These three reasons are each followed by **evidence**, or specific examples, facts, or statistics that support the reasons. Here, the evidence supplied consists of the following specific examples:

Reason 1: Inconvenience

- walking long distances
- carrying heavy books and packages
- walking in rain and snow

Reason 2: Safety

- walking late after night classes
- after a job
- after a party

Reason 3: Already pay for close parking

- rising cost of room and board
- off-campus students have close parking

The more specific evidence provided, the stronger the reasons, and therefore the stronger the argument.

The **counterargument**, or argument someone might make in response to the claim, is found in the phrase *"while it's true that space on campus is very limited,"* followed by the **refutation of the counterargument** in the rest of the sentence: *"the school should immediately investigate options to solve the problem, such as building a parking garage, or supplying students with transportation to and from distant parking lots."* Good writers include counterarguments as a way to anticipate what objections a reader might have upon reading the claim, evidence, and reasons, while immediately satisfying that objection by refuting the counterargument. High-scoring CLEP essays include this basic argument structure.

How to Use Your Imagination to Find Claims, Reasons, Evidence, and Counterarguments

Recognizing the basic features of any argument is a great help when preparing to take the essay portion of the CLEP College Composition examination, but it also takes practice using these features to write effective CLEP essays. Most candidates could identify with the above example, even if they don't live on a college campus. There's no guarantee, however, that the essay prompts on the CLEP exam you take will include such familiar topics. No one can expect to be an expert on all the potential topics possible for inclusion on any specific exam. How then does one prepare? Through the use of imagination!

Take the following essay prompt as an example. Suppose an unmarried seventeen-year-old high school girl discovers she is pregnant. What should be done? You are asked to write an essay where you discuss, in specific, what should be done about the situation, and give reasons to support your position. The only other information you are provided is that she has been dating the father for two years, that they plan to eventually marry, and that they both come from stable families.

It may be easy to imagine what you would do in this situation, but would that yield the best reasons, evidence, and counterarguments? How might you expand upon the range of possible answers? One way is to use your imagination to shift subject positions. What if you thought about the situation not from your own perspective, but from the viewpoint of the girl's father, or the boy's mother? What about the girl's pastor, or the couple's high school counselor? Both sets of grandparents? The boy's college football recruiter? The girl's supervisor at work? By imaginatively placing yourself in another's position, you can come up with more reasons and evidence than you can by simply approaching the issue from your own knowledge and experience.

One claim that could be made from this scenario is that the couple should get married now. What reasons, evidence, and counterarguments refuted could be presented to support this claim? The girl's pastor might argue that this is the best choice from a religious perspective. The school counselor might suggest programs that support high school students who have children, yet wish to finish their degree. A grandparent might provide examples of how couples married young in earlier times, yet had successful marriages. The boy's father might worry about his college future should he marry now; the college football recruiter might reassure everyone with the information that married players are still eligible to play. We don't have to be all of these people in order to imagine how they might feel in this situation. From such speculations, many more ideas can be identified and used than simply those we consider from our own perspective.

How to Organize Your Essay

An additional advantage to knowing and using the basic features of an argument is that it provides a ready-made structure to organize your essay. Most high-scoring CLEP essays contain these features. A good strategy is to plan your essay in terms of a five-paragraph response where the first paragraph states your position, the second paragraph contains reason #1, supported by evidence, the third paragraph contains reason #2 with its supporting evidence, and the fourth paragraph contains reason #3, also supported by evidence. The fifth and final paragraph contains the counterargument and its refutation. This strategy would not work for most writing situations, not even if you were writing for an actual college freshman class. Most writing tasks require much more extensive development than a five-paragraph template can provide. In many testing situations, however, this five-paragraph strategy is both effective and easy to remember. The CLEP College Composition examination is one of them.

Using Signal Verbs and Phrases to Help Integrate Sources

So far, all of the advice provided here has applied to both the first and second CLEP essays. Signal verbs and phrases, however, are designed specifically to help integrate source material within your own writing. The first CLEP essay asks candidates to construct arguments from their own knowledge and experience. The second CLEP essay, however, provides candidates with two sources from which they are expected to take information and use it to compose their essays. How well you integrate this source material is a big factor in how high your essay is scored.

Good writers use a **signal verb** and **signal phrases** to indicate to readers that a quotation is about to be introduced.

In her article on teenage nutrition, **Sally Jones argues** "pizza is a good nutritional choice" (14).

Charles Black claims school lunch programs are responsible for the rise of childhood obesity: "Most school cafeterias serve children food that is high in fat and sugar" (247).

No doubt the most common signal phrase is "the author says." There is nothing wrong with the use of this phrase. The problem comes when the writer must introduce the next quotation and again uses "the author says." Pretty soon his or her essay is peppered with the same repetitious phrase, much to the annoyance of readers. Worse, in test situations like the CLEP essay exam, scorers might see this as a sign of a novice writer, someone whose vocabulary and skills are not at the college level.

Introducing a quotation by using the author's name, as in the example above, is both clear and simple. Furthermore, by choosing a signal verb other than "says," writers can also communicate their interpretation of the source, which enhances the scorer's view of the writer's ability. Remember that when using a signal verb, always refer to a source in the present tense—"Jones argues," not "Jones argued."

Commonly Used Signal Verbs:

advises	agrees	asserts	believes	charges	claims
comments	concludes	considers	criticizes	declares	describes
disagrees	discusses	explains	finds	illustrates	interprets
lists	objects	observes	opposes	proposes	remarks
reports	reveals	states	suggests	thinks	writes

How to Avoid the 10 Most Common Errors Made by College Freshmen

Since grammar and usage accounts for only 10% of the CLEP scoring guide, the preparation you have already done for the multiple-choice section of the exam is sufficient for the essay portion. When writing essays, however, there are a few common errors that can significantly detract from your essays. It's not that these errors are inherently worse than other errors; it's just that they are so common that scorers are immediately aware of their presence in an essay.

Here are the 10 most common errors college freshmen make when writing, along with advice on how to avoid them.

1. **alot**

   a lot is two words, not one.

2. **it's, its**

   it's is a contraction of it is, as in **"It's** a great book."

   its is a possessive pronoun, as in "The dog wagged **its** tail."

3. **your, you're**

   you're is a contraction of **"you are,"** as in **"You're a nice person."**

   your indicates possession, as in **"Your** car is new."

4. **there, their, they're**

   there indicates place, as in **"There** is your hat."

   their indicates possession, as in **"Their** house is green."

   there is a contraction of "there are," as in **"They're** going home."

5. **comma splice**

   Never join two independent clauses together with just a comma. Correct the error by linking the clauses with a semicolon, or with a comma and a coordinating conjunction (*and, but, or, nor, for, so,* or *yet*), or by making them into two separate sentences.

   Incorrect: The author claims the information is correct, it is from a reliable study.

   Correct: The author claims the information is correct; it is from a reliable study.

   Correct: The author claims the information is correct, for it is from a reliable study.

   Correct: The author claims the information is correct. It is from a reliable study.

6. **misuse of quotation marks**

   Never place the concluding quotation mark before the period.

   Incorrect: The author argues that the study "is unreliable".

   Correct: The author argues that the study "is unreliable."

7. **compound subject/verb agreement**

   Make sure compound subjects (connected by "and") have plural verbs

   Incorrect: A pencil, an answer sheet, and a test booklet was issued to each student.

   Correct: A pencil, an answer sheet, and a test booklet were issued to each student.

8. **using commas after introductory elements**

   Make sure you use a comma after introductory elements in a sentence.

   Incorrect: Unfortunately the student lost his textbook.

   Correct: Unfortunately, the student lost his textbook.

   Incorrect: In one of her best games Jane scored three home runs.

   Correct: In one of her best games, Jane scored three home runs.

9. **using commas to separate items in a series**

   Make sure you use commas after items in a series

   Incorrect: The long boring confusing speech left us feeling sleepy.

   Correct: The long, boring, confusing speech left us feeling sleepy.

10. **capitalizing correctly**

    Make sure you capitalize all proper names, ethnic groups, languages, religions, and religious terms

Marilyn Monroe	Chinese
African Americans	Iraqi
Islam	an Islamic

50 Words First-Year Writers Frequently Misspell

Most of the writing done by college freshmen is argumentative, just like the kind of writing the CLEP exam requires. Below is a list of words commonly misspelled by college freshmen as they compose essays similar to the CLEP first and second essay. If you know the meaning of the words below, as well as how to spell them, you will be prepared to use them to your advantage when writing argumentative essays.

50 Frequently Misspelled Words

1. accept	14. conceive	27. manageable	39. sufficient
2. accomplish	15. consistent	28. necessary	40. suppress
3. achievement	16. criticize	29. noticeable	41. tangible
4. against	17. decide	30. occasion	42. tendency
5. alleged	18. definitely	31. occurred	43. therefore
6. apparent	19. dependent	32. perceive	44. thorough
7. argument	20. develop	33. preferred	45. though
8. basically	21. environment	34. realize	46. through
9. beginning	22. explanation	35. relevant	47. truly
10. believe	23. financially	36. sense	48. until
11. business	24. fulfill	37. separate	49. whether
12. cannot	25. guarantee	38. successfully	50. wherever
13. category	26. immediately		

PRACTICE WRITING THE CLEP ARGUMENTATIVE ESSAYS

Sample Writing Prompts for the CLEP First Essay

Writing Prompt #1:

Reality television shows, like MTV's "Jersey Shore" or Bravo's "Real House-wives of New York" do not simply entertain, but in fact pose a threat to our cultural values.

Write an essay where you agree or disagree with the statement above. Support your position with specific reasons and evidence from your reading, experience, and/or observations.

The above statement and directions are very similar to the kind of essay prompts you will encounter for the CLEP First Essay. Note that there are no sources included that you must integrate within your essay. How then does one begin to compose an essay in response?

Remember the basic parts of an argument? Take a few minutes to plan your response by composing a scratch outline of your argument using these basic features. For the claim, pick the side for which you can supply the most reasons and evidence in support. It doesn't matter if this represents your true feelings or not; what matters is that you can come up with a good argument. Now, pick a good counterargument that you can refute.

For example, say you choose to disagree with the above statement and you come up with several reasons that support your position. Choose the best three and support them with specific examples:

Reason #1

1. Reality television shows promote positive behavior

   Evidence/examples, etc.

   - the show *The Biggest Loser* depicts real overweight people learning how to exercise, diet, and deal with the emotional issues connected with losing weight

   - the show *The Nanny* teaches parents with even the most difficult children effective discipline

   - A&E's *Intervention* profiles real addicts, providing them and their families with expert advice on how to treat drug and alcohol addiction

Reason #2

2. Reality television shows help combat stereotypes and social bias

   Evidence/examples, etc.

   - HGTV often profiles homosexual couples in their reality series that focus on house hunting and remodeling

   - shows like *Little Couple* shatter preconceived notions of what those who are physically challenged can do

   - shows like *Extreme Makeover: Home Edition* prove that many poor families in need are deserving of help

Reason #3

3. Reality television shows are inexpensive to produce, compared with scripted shows, and therefore allow for more variety

   Evidence/examples, etc.

   - a wide variety of reality shows today focused on food, such as *Top Chef*, *Chopped*, and *Cake Wars*

- entertainment shows, such as *American Idol*, *Dancing with the Stars*, and *You've Got Talent*
- dramatic shows, such as *First 48*, *Cops*, and *Ice Road Truckers*

Now raise a counterargument, and refute it.

Counterargument

Many people argue that reality television shows promote anti-social behavior, and it is certainly true that some—like MTV's Snooki on the show *Jersey Shore*—seem to glamorize such things as casual sex and drunkenness.

Counterargument refuted

But given the huge number and variety of reality television shows, the bad ones are in the minority.

Once you have an outline of the argument, it's not too hard to construct five paragraphs.

Sample Essay in Response to Writing Prompt #1 Earning a Score of "6"

Using the same prompt and outline from above, below is a typical five-para-graph essay earning a score of "6."

Writing Prompt #1:

Reality television shows, like MTV's "Jersey Shore" or "Real Housewives of New York" do not simply entertain, but in fact pose a threat to our cultural values.

Write an essay where you agree or disagree with the statement above. Support your position with specific reasons and evidence from your reading, experience, and/or observations.

Reality television shows do seem to emphasize the most outrageous behavior, especially where the media is concerned. Of course the drunken antics of Snooki from *Jersey Shore*, or the White House gate-crashers, Michaele and Tareq Salahi, from *The Real Housewives of D.C.* make the news. It is an exaggeration, however, to claim that all these unscripted programs profiling real people, rather than actors, are somehow posing a threat to our culture. Taken as a whole, these shows depict as many people doing positive things as they *do* people doing negative ones. In fact, reality television shows often help society by educating the viewing population.

For every reality show profiling socially deviant behavior, there are several promoting positive behavior. Take, for example, the show *The Biggest Loser* where real overweight people learn how to exercise, diet, and deal with the emotional issues connected with losing weight. This reality television show addresses the number one health concern today in America—obesity. Another show, *The Nanny*, teaches parents with even the most difficult children effective discipline. Perhaps the best example, however, is A&E's award-winning *Intervention*, which profiles real addicts, providing them and their families with expert advice on how to treat drug and alcohol addiction.

In addition to shows that promote positive social behavior, a number of reality television programs help combat negative social stereotypes and prejudice. HGTV often profiles homosexual couples in reality shows that focus on house hunting and remodeling. Programs like *Little Couple* shatter preconceived notions of what those who are physically challenged can accomplish. Shows like *Extreme Makeover: Home Edition* prove that many poor families aren't just slackers, but are deserving of help.

Those who worry about reality television need only remember that as unscripted programming, reality TV shows are inexpensive to produce. This allows for a wide variety of shows that not only shock, but also educate and entertain. Reality television shows like *American Idol*, *Dancing with the Stars*, and *You've Got Talent* provide audiences with wholesome enjoyment. Many shows, like *Top Chef* and *Ice Road Truckers*, promote new professions and/or hobbies.

It is certainly true that some reality television show promote dangerous, anti-social behavior, such as the drunkenness and casual sex depicted on *Jersey Shore*. But given the huge number and variety of reality television shows, the good outweighs the bad.

The sample essay above achieves a score of "6" because it has a clear and thoughtful thesis or position statement that includes reasons and examples that are both specific and relevant. It is focused and organized, and uses a good command of grammar and usage. The above contains paragraphs with short, declarative sentences, as well as compound sentences. The vocabulary is both clear and specific.

Sample Writing Prompts for the CLEP Second Essay

Writing Prompt #2:

Carefully read the two sources found below. Using both sources, write an essay where you agree or disagree that cyber bullying poses a greater threat to children than traditional bullying. Make sure you use and cite both sources in your essay.

Kowalski, Robin M. "Cyber Bullying: Recognizing and Treating Victim and Aggressor." *Psychiatric Times* 25.11 (2008): 45-56. Print.

The following is an excerpt from the above publication:

More individuals are potential cyber bullies than potential schoolyard bullies. People will say and do more things anonymously that they would not say and do directly or in front of someone. This disinhibition effect increases not only the number of potential perpetrators of cyber bullying but also the magnitude of threats, taunts, and so on, that they are willing to deliver. This effect is further compounded by that, in the virtual world, interactants are not privy to one another's emotions. When people tease or bully face-to-face, they use off-record markers (winks, smiles, etc) to indicate the intent behind their behavior. With the exception of emoticons (smiley faces to convey positive affect), such nonverbal accompaniments are not available in the virtual world. Thus, perpetrators cannot see the emotional toll that their cyber bullying may be taking on the target; similarly, targets cannot read the off-record markers accompanying the perpetrator's behavior. Thus, targets cannot know if the perpetrator really is "just kidding."

Bennett, Jessica. "From Lockers to Lockup." *Newsweek* 11 Oct. 2010: 38. Print.

The following is an excerpt from the above publication:

But forget, for the moment, the dozens of articles that have called bullying a "pandemic"—because the opposite is true. School bullying can be devastating, but social scientists say it is no more extreme, nor more prevalent, than it was half a century ago. In fact, says Dan Olweus, a leading bullying expert, new data shows rates of school bullying may even have gone down over the past decade. Today's world of cyberbullying is different, yes—far-reaching, more visually potent, and harder to wash away than comments scrawled on a bathroom wall. All of which can make it harder to combat. But it still happens a third less than traditional bullying, says Olweus.

The reality may be that while the incidence of bullying has remained relatively the same, it's our reaction to it that has changed: the helicopter parents who want to protect their kids from every stick and stone, the cable-news commentators who whip them into a frenzy, the insta-vigilantism of the Internet. When it comes down to it, bullying is not just a social ill; it's a "cottage-industry," says Suffolk Law School's David Yamada—complete with commentators and prevention experts and a new breed of legal scholars, all preparing to take on an enemy that's always been there. None of this is to say that bullying is not a serious problem, or that tackling it is not important. But like a stereo with the volume tuned too high, all the noise distorts the facts, making it nearly impossible to judge when a case is somehow criminal, or merely cruel.

The above directions and excerpted sources are similar to the kind of essay prompts you will encounter for the CLEP Second Essay. Note that there are two sources included that you must integrate within your essay. How then does one begin to compose an essay in response?

Again, recall the basic parts of an argument from Part II. Take a few minutes to plan your response by composing a scratch outline of your argument using these basic features and the information found in the sources above. For the claim, pick the side for which you can supply the most reasons and evidence in support. It doesn't matter if this represents your true feelings or not; what matters is that you can come up with a good argument. Now, pick a good counterargument that you can refute.

For example, you may choose to agree with the above statement and you come up with several reasons that support your position. Choose the best three and support them with specific examples both from the sources provided and from your own knowledge and experience:

Reason #1

1. There are, potentially, more cyber bullies than traditional bullies with more victims

   ### Evidence/examples, etc.

   - according to Kowalski, because technology allows cyber bullies to be anonymous, called the "disinhibition effect," more students will bully another than in traditional public bullying

   - cyber bullies can increase the number of their victims more easily than traditional bullies

   - cyber bullies generally have no witnesses to their actions and therefore run less risk of punishment

Reason #2

2. Cyber bullying causes more harm to victims than traditional bullying

Evidence/examples, etc.

- according to Kowalski, the "disinhibition effect" increases the "magnitude of threats, taunts, and so on, that they are willing to deliver"
- cyber bullying provides a greater variety of ways, thanks to existing technology, to hurt a victim—for example the case of the gay teen who committed suicide after exposure by webcam
- cyber bullying allows the effects of the cruelty to last far longer than traditional bullying

Reason #3

3. Cyber bullying extends beyond classmates and the school grounds

Evidence/examples, etc.

- older siblings and even adults can join in with a cyber bully—for example, the case of the Missouri mom
- cyber bullies have a greater audience than traditional bullies
- cyber bullies can expose their victims to more dangerous, adult predators

Now raise a counterargument, and refute it.

Counterargument

According to Bennett, cyber bullying is just a new form of the same thing schools have always had to deal with, and therefore is nothing to be alarmed about. What is new, she argues, is the way the media is blowing the issue out of proportion thanks to the "frenzy" generated by "helicopter parents" and "cable-news commentators."

Counterargument refuted

It's true that kids have always bullied one another, but to say that the kind of behavior seen in recent years thanks to the advent of technology just a more advanced form of the same thing is patently foolish.

Adults are obliged to protect children from situations where they can endanger themselves and others.

Once you have an outline of the argument, it's not too hard to construct five paragraphs.

Sample Essay in Response to Writing Prompt #2
Earning a Score of "6"

Using the same prompt and outline from above, below is a typical five-paragraph essay earning a score of "6."

Cyber bullying may be prompted, psychologically speaking, by the same childhood impulses as the traditional style of bullying we are so familiar with from our own childhoods, but that's where the similarity ends. The technology which allows the kind of behavior we have seen depicted by the media in recent years is much more complex and dangerous in scope than a typical schoolyard fight.

Thanks to recent technological advances, today we have, potentially, more cyber bullies than traditional bullies—and with more victims. According to Kowalski, because technology allows cyber bullies to be anonymous, called the "disinhibition effect," more students will bully others than would have with traditional public bullying. Cyber bullies find opportunities to taunt, insult, or threaten others through email, instant messaging, via web pages, or through sending texts and/or images via cell phones. Perpetrators can also increase the number of their victims more easily than traditional bullies, given the ease of new technology. With a simple click, a cyber bully can literally reach hundreds of people via the internet. Since cyber bullies generally have no witnesses to their actions, they therefore run less risk of punishment.

Cyber bullying should be a concern for all since it can cause more harm to victims than traditional bullying. The "disinhibition effect" also increases the "magnitude of threats, taunts, and so on" that cyber bullies "are willing to deliver," Kowalski argues. As with traditional bullying, cyber bullying can cause victims to suffer both physical and psychological harm. But the recent spate of teenage suicides has many concerned that cyber bullying is more dangerous than traditional bullying. In the case of Phoebe Prince, cyber bullying allegedly spilled over into actual sexual assault. Cyber bullying also provides a greater variety of ways to hurt a victim than does traditional bullying. On September 22, 2010, Tyler Clementi threw himself off a bridge when his roommate filmed him having sex with another male via webcam and streamed it live to other students in their dorm.

Cyber bullying allows the effects of the cruelty to last far longer than traditional bullying. Calling a victim "gay" in the hall in front of one's peers is nothing compared to having an actual sex tape widely distributed on the internet where it could crop up again and again for years.

The most frightening thing about cyber bullying, however, is that it extends beyond classmates and the school grounds. With the anonymity of the internet, older siblings and even adults can join in with a cyber bully in targeting a victim. For example, Megan Meier committed suicide after cyber bullying by one of her classmate's mother. Cyber bullies have a greater audience than traditional bullies, enlisting a huge number of virtual bystanders that can make victims feel even more threatened and humiliated. Worse such practices by cyber bullies can expose their victims to more dangerous, adult predators.

According to Bennett, cyber bullying is just a new form of the same thing schools have always had to deal with, and therefore is nothing to be alarmed about. What is new, she argues, is the way the media is blowing the issue out of proportion thanks to the "frenzy" generated by "helicopter parents" and "cable-news commentators." It's true that kids have always bullied one another, and it's certainly true that the media have made much of recent cases of cyber bullying. But to say that the kind of behavior seen in recent years, thanks to the advent of technology, is just a more advanced form of the same thing is foolish. Adults are obliged to protect children from situations where they can endanger them-selves and others. Cyber bullying is different from traditional bullying and should be taken seriously by everyone involved.

The sample essay above achieves a score of "6" because it has a clear and thoughtful thesis or position statement that includes reasons and examples that are both specific and relevant. It includes references to both sources, is focused and organized, and uses a good command of grammar and usage. The above contains paragraphs with short, declarative sentences, as well as compound sentences. The vocabulary is both clear and specific.

Part IV
PRACTICE EXAMS

CLEP College Composition

Practice Test 1

TIME: 50 Minutes

Conventions of Standard Written English (10%)

> **DIRECTIONS:** The following sentences test your knowledge of grammar, usage, diction (choice of words), and idioms. Note that some sentences are correct, and no sentence contains more than one error. Read each sentence carefully, paying particular attention to the underlined portions. You will find that the error, if there is one, is underlined. Assume that elements of the sentence that are not underlined are correct and cannot be changed. In choosing answers, follow the requirements of standard written English. If there is an error, select the one underlined part that must be changed to make the sentence correct. If there is no error, select "No error."

1. Violence, corruption, and pollution <u>are among</u> the problems <u>that undermine</u>
                              A   B
    quality of life in industrialized societies, <u>particularly</u> those <u>having</u> autocratic
                                                C   D
    forms of government. <u>No error</u>
                             E

2. <u>Although</u> many people consider Richard Burton <u>to be</u> a fine actor, he never
      A   B
    won <u>no</u> Oscar for <u>his</u> work. <u>No error</u>
         C   D   E

3. <u>Since</u> the early 20th <u>century, significant</u> changes <u>have taken</u> place in
      A   B   C
    educational practice <u>as well as in</u> the field of educational research. <u>No error</u>
                          D   E

4. An <u>astute and powerful</u> woman, Frances Smith <u>had been</u> a beauty-contest
                 A   B
    winner <u>before</u> she became president of Smith Corporation <u>on the</u> death of
            C   D
    her husband. <u>No error</u>
                  E

5. For years, citizens <u>concerned about</u> the environment have compiled statistics
                        A
    which <u>shows</u> that <u>many</u> species <u>are endangered</u>. <u>No error</u>
         B   C   D   E

Revision Skills (40%)

DIRECTIONS: The following passages are early drafts of essays. Read each passage and then answer the questions that follow. Some questions refer to particular sentences or parts of sentences and ask you to improve sentence structure or diction. Other questions refer to the entire essay or parts of the essay and ask you to consider the essay's organization, development, or effectiveness of language. In selecting your answers, follow the conventions of standard written English.

<u>Questions 1–5</u> are based on the following draft of an essay.

(1) The phrase "reading wars" refers to heated debates among educators about the most suitable method for teaching children how to read. (2) Some people argue that phonics-based methods are best for reading instruction. (3) In phonics-based methods, children are taught letter sounds as well as rules for sounding out words. (4) Phonics-based methods are widely used. (5) Phonics-based methods direct children's attention to the constituents of words like their letters and groups of letters. (6) Other educators argue that whole-word methods are preferable for reading instruction. (7) In whole-word methods, teachers involve children in meaningful reading and writing activities even before they can sound out words. (8) So phonics is different from whole-word. (9) However, most whole-word advocates agree that teachers should spend at least some time on phonics instruction. (10) These educators acknowledge that reading instruction should include phonics-based methods, but only in the context of meaningful reading activities. (11) At the same time, advocates of phonics-based methods do not deny the importance of meaningful reading and writing activities.

1. In context, which is the best replacement for "people" in sentence 2?

   (A) citizens

   (B) educators

   (C) researchers

   (D) individuals

   (E) children

2. Which of the following versions of the underlined portion of sentence 5 (reproduced below) is best?

   Phonics-based methods direct children's attention to the constituents of <u>words like their letters</u> and groups of letters.

   (A) words, such as letters

   (B) words, like letters

   (C) words and their letters

   (D) words, with letters

   (E) words, as their letters

3. Which of the following would be the best revision for sentence 8?

    (A) Thus, phonics-based methods are different from whole word.

    (B) Thus, phonics is different from whole word.

    (C) Thus, phonics differs from the whole word.

    (D) Thus, phonics-based methods and whole-word methods are very different.

    (E) Thus, there are differences between the methods of phonics and the whole word.

4. Deleting which of the following sentences would most improve the coherence of the passage?

    (A) Sentence 2   (D) Sentence 7

    (B) Sentence 4   (E) Sentence 9

    (C) Sentence 6

5. Which of the following would be the best sentence with which to end the passage?

    (A) Thus, the "reading wars" are not really wars at all and should be completely abolished.

    (B) Thus, the "reading wars" reflect two distinct positions regarding the most suitable methods for reading instruction.

    (C) Thus, the "reading wars" reflect disagreements about which method of reading instruction should be emphasized rather than disagreements about which method to use.

    (D) Thus, the "reading wars" are based on the mistaken assumption that phonics-based and whole-word methods of reading instruction are actually separate methods.

    (E) Thus, the "reading wars" are based in subtle differences between methods that have escaped the notice of educators.

Questions 6–12 are based on the following draft of an essay.

(1) Santiago, the main character in Ernest Hemingway's novel *The Old Man and the Sea,* displays admirable courage and strength in his fight with a great marlin, which is very symbolic. (2) The old fisherman then suffers a painful loss when sharks devour his marlin, and they left him little more than a skeleton

to lug home. (3) But the novel rises above suffering and loss to express and deliver an inspiring message about the greatness of the human spirit. (4) The nobility of Santiago's character is revealed not only in his remarkable battle with the marlin, but also in his patience during the days and hours leading to it. (5) After 84 days without catching a fish, Santiago remains optimistic. (6) On the day of the battle, he ventures out into deeper water, and when he hooks the marlin, he shows infinite patience in spite of his desperate situation. (7) He is rewarded with the capture of the great fish. (8) But the price of his success is great.

6. Which of the following is the best revision for the underlined portion of sentence 1 (reproduced below)?

    Santiago, in Ernest Hemingway's novel The Old Man and the Sea, *displays admirable courage and strength in his fight with a great marlin, which is very symbolic.*

    (A) when fighting symbolically with a great marlin.

    (B) in his fight with a great marlin, a symbolic fight.

    (C) when he has his fight with a great marlin, which is symbolic.

    (D) in his fight with a symbolic marlin.

    (E) in his symbolic fight with a great marlin.

7. Which of the following is the best revision for the underlined portion of sentence 2 (reproduced below)?

    The old fisherman then suffers a painful loss when sharks devour his marlin, and they left him little more than a skeleton to lug home.

    (A) and little more than a skeleton to lug home.

    (B) they left him little more than a marlin to lug home.

    (C) and it was little more than a skeleton he could lug home.

    (D) leaving him little more than a skeleton to lug home.

    (E) it left him little more than a skeleton to lug home.

8. Which of the following sentences, if inserted between sentences 1 and 2, would make the passage more coherent?

(A) At first, after he hooks the marlin, Santiago is not completely sure what kind of fish he has caught.

(B) As he prepares to go fishing that morning, Santiago is hopeful that maybe today he will catch a great fish.

(C) Although he tries not to be disturbed by the thought, Santiago knows it has been 84 days since he last caught a fish.

(D) After a prolonged and intense struggle, Santiago finally lands the marlin and ties it to the side of his boat.

(E) Slowly and carefully, Santiago guides his boat out into the deep ocean in search of a large fish, such as a marlin.

9. Which is best to do with sentence 3 (reproduced below)?

But the novel rises above suffering and loss to express and deliver an inspiring message about the greatness of the human spirit.

(A) Leave it as is.

(B) Delete "express and."

(C) Place a comma after "message."

(D) Replace "inspiring" with "major."

(E) Replace "rises" with "raises."

10. Which of the following is the best replacement for "leading to it" at the end of sentence 4 (reproduced below)?

The nobility of Santiago's character is revealed not only in his remarkable battle with the marlin, but also in his patience during the days and hours leading to it.

(A) leading up to the battle.

(B) leading him to this.

(C) leading there.

(D) leading to that remarkable battle.

(E) leading that way.

11. Which of the following phrases, added immediately after "deeper water" in sentence 6 (reproduced below), would make the sentence more coherent?

   On the day of the battle, he ventures out into deeper water, and when he hooks the marlin, he shows infinite patience in spite of his desperate situation.

   (A) in order to fish

   (B) with his little boat

   (C) as optimistically as he can

   (D) than he ever had before

   (E) with determination and skill

12. Which of the following is the best way to combine sentences 7 and 8 (reproduced below)?

   He is rewarded with the capture of the great fish. But the price of his success was great.

   (A) He is rewarded with the capture of the great fish, the price of his success was great.

   (B) He is rewarded with the capture of the great fish, if the price of his success was great.

   (C) He is rewarded with the capture of the great fish, as the price of his success was great.

   (D) He is rewarded with the capture of the great fish, thus the price of his success was great.

   (E) He is rewarded with the capture of the great fish, but the price of his success was great.

Questions 13–20 are based on the following draft of an essay.

   (1) Many people consider the motorcyclist a highway nuisance who makes other motorists nervous and he takes the joy out of driving. (2) It cannot be denied that some motorcyclists are egotists who assert the roadways were created for their exclusive use. (3) Admittedly, others are riders who take unnecessary risks. (4) Yet many motorcyclists are responsible drivers. (5) Motorcyclists should always drive with caution. (6) Moreover, any truly honest driver will admit that at times he has envied the freedom of the motorcycle rider. (7) Motorcycles are much less expensive than other vehicles.

(8) Motorcycles are easier to park. (9) And motorcyclists usually enjoy the luxury of low insurance premiums. (10) The main disadvantage of motorcycle riding are the accidents; they are often caused by the motorcyclists themselves. (11) In my opinion the risk of accidents is a little price for the many advantages of riding a motorcycle.

13. Which of the following is the best replacement for the underlined portion of sentence 1 (reproduced below)?

    Many people consider the motorcyclist a highway nuisance who makes other motorists nervous <u>and he takes</u> the joy out of driving.

    (A) and then takes

    (B) and so takes

    (C) and takes

    (D) and soon takes

    (E) and it takes

14. Which is best to do with "assert" in sentence 2 (reproduced below)?

    It cannot be denied that some motorcyclists are egotists who assert the roadways were created for their exclusive use.

    (A) Leave it as is.

    (B) Replace it with "assess."

    (C) Replace it with "believe."

    (D) Replace it with "explain."

    (E) Replace it with "doubt."

15. Which of the following revisions would contribute most strongly to the purpose of sentence 3 (reproduced below)?

    Admittedly, others are riders who take unnecessary risks.

    (A) Admittedly, others are individuals who take unnecessary risks.

    (B) Admittedly, others are skilled riders who take unnecessary risks.

    (C) Admittedly, others are the ones who take unnecessary risks.

    (D) Admittedly, others are cyclists who take unnecessary risks.

    (E) Admittedly, others are daredevils who take unnecessary risks.

16. Which of the following represents the best combination of sentences 2 and 3 (reproduced below)?

It cannot be denied that some motorcyclists are riders who assert the roadways were created for their exclusive use. Admittedly, others are riders who take unnecessary risks.

(A) It cannot be denied that some motorcyclists are egotists who assert the roadways were created for their exclusive use; in addition, others are riders who take unnecessary risks.

(B) It cannot be denied that some motorcyclists are egotists who assert the roadways were created for their exclusive use, while others are riders who take unnecessary risks.

(C) It cannot be denied that some motorcyclists are egotists who assert the roadways were created for their exclusive use, but others are riders who take unnecessary risks.

(D) It cannot be denied that some motorcyclists are egotists who assert the roadways were created for their exclusive use, although others are riders who take unnecessary risks.

(E) It cannot be denied that some motorcyclists are egotists who assert the roadways were created for their exclusive use; however, others are riders who take unnecessary risks.

17. Deleting which of the following sentences would increase the coherence of the passage?

(A) Sentence 2

(B) Sentence 4

(C) Sentence 5

(D) Sentence 6

(E) Sentence 7

18. Which of the following would be the best sentence with which to begin the second paragraph?

    (A) There are many advantages to driving a motorcycle as opposed to some other type of vehicle.

    (B) Motorcycles are quite beneficial to their owners if maintained appropriately.

    (C) All things considered, motorcycles are far from an ideal form of transportation.

    (D) Motorcycles are the preferred mode of transportation among a wide variety of people.

    (E) Motorcycles have a number of disadvantages that offset their obvious strengths.

19. Which of the following is the best revision of sentence 10 (reproduced below)?

    The main disadvantage of motorcycle riding are the accidents; they are often caused by the motorcyclists themselves.

    (A) The main disadvantage of motorcycle riding is the accidents; caused often by the motorcyclists themselves.

    (B) The main disadvantage of motorcycle riding are the accidents, as often caused by the motorcyclists themselves.

    (C) The main disadvantage of motorcycle riding is the accidents that are often caused by the motorcyclists themselves.

    (D) The main disadvantage of motorcycle riding are the accidents, but they are often caused by the motorcyclists themselves.

    (E) The main disadvantage of motorcycle riding is the accidents, which are often caused by the motorcyclists themselves.

20. Which of the following is the best revision of the underlined portion of sentence 10 (reproduced below)?

    In my opinion the risk of accidents is a <u>little price</u> for the many advantages of riding a motorcycle.

    (A) tiny price

    (B) very low price

    (C) minimum cost

    (D) small price to pay

    (E) cheap substitute

Ability to Use Source Materials (25%)

Questions 1–7 refer to the following passage.

(1) Among the influences on both the quantity and importance of educational research in recent years are growing concerns about the academic achievement of American students (Springer, 2010, 3). (2) Since the beginning of public education, concerns about achievement have been voiced by parents, educators, researchers, and policymakers. (3) Fueling these concerns have been studies indicating that the American educational system is in trouble and, in the words of an influential report, *A Nation at Risk*, is threatened by a "rising tide of mediocrity." (4) The most recent responses to concerns about student achievement include federal legislation passed during the first few years of the new millennium. (5) Prominent among this new legislation is the No Child Left Behind Act, signed into law in 2002. (6) No Child Left Behind (NCLB) was designed to "improve student achievement and change the culture of America's schools" (U.S. Department of Education, 2002, 9). (7) NCLB requires that states conduct annual testing of student progress in grades 3–8, and at least once in grades 10–12. (8) Through NCLB, federal spending on schools is linked to the results of these new tests. (9) Federal spending is also linked to attempts to improve student progress through instructional and curricular changes that are scientifically based. (10) Through NCLB, federal support is targeted to educational programs that are informed by rigorous scientific research. (11) In this way, federal support targets educational programs that have a rigorous scientific basis.

References

Springer, K. 2010. *Educational Research: A Contextual Approach*. Hoboken, NJ: Wiley.

U.S. Department of Education. 2002. *No Child Left Behind: A Desktop Reference*, Washington, D.C. 20202.

1. Which of the following is cited in sentence 1?

    (A) A scientific journal   (D) A popular magazine

    (B) A book   (E) A website

    (C) A media report

2. Which of the following is missing from sentence 3?

    (A) Further details about the content of *A Nation at Risk*

    (B) A critique of the central thesis of *A Nation at Risk*

    (C) Citation information for *A Nation at Risk*

    (D) A note about the relationship between the previous citation and *A Nation at Risk*

    (E) Information about whether *A Nation at Risk* is a book or some other type of source

3. Which of the following best describes the purpose of sentence 5?

    (A) To qualify the statement made in sentence 4

    (B) To illustrate the assertions made in sentence 6

    (C) To include a citation for the assertion made in sentence 6

    (D) To provide an example of the statement made in sentence 4

    (E) All of the above

4. Which of the following best describes the purpose of the quotation in sentence 6?

    (A) To contrast NCLB with *A Nation at Risk*

    (B) To support the writer's thesis that the American educational system is in trouble

    (C) To provide a succinct critique of NCLB

    (D) To give some examples of how NCLB impacts educational practice

    (E) To briefly summarize why NCLB was created

5. Which of the following best describes the purpose of the second paragraph (sentences 4–11)?

    (A) To describe one example of federal legislation created in response to concerns about the achievement of American students

    (B) To qualify the argument that a variety of people are concerned about the achievement of American students

    (C) To explain why parents, educators, researchers, and policymakers have been concerned about student achievement

    (D) To critically analyze the role of the federal government in educational practice

    (E) To raise questions about the extent to which federal legislation ultimately translates into effects on student achievement

6. In context, which is best to do with sentence 11 (reproduced below)?

    In this way, federal support targets educational programs that have a rigorous scientific basis.

    (A) Leave it as is.

    (B) Revise it so that it is more similar to sentence 10.

    (C) Add a definition of "scientific."

    (D) Delete it.

    (E) Replace "In this way" with "In sum."

7. Which of the following pieces of information, if added to the second paragraph (sentences 4–11), would most effectively advance the main point of the paragraph?

    (A) A historical example of NCLB-like federal legislation related to education.

    (B) A concrete example of NCLB-related federal support for educational programs.

    (C) A qualifying example that shows how NCLB impacts outcomes other than achievement.

    (D) A contrasting example of how NCLB influences noneducational programs.

    (E) A supplemental example of other purposes served by NCLB.

Questions 8–10 refer to the following passage.

(1) The term "Native American" is somewhat misleading. (2) According to experts, what we call "Native Americans" or "Indians" migrated to our continent from many other places. (3) For example, the ancestors of the Anasazi, who once occupied what is now Colorado, New Mexico, Utah, and Arizona, probably migrated from the Asian continent about 25,000 years ago while the continental land bridge still existed. (4) Other archaeologists have suggested more recent migrations to what is now the United States among peoples from the north (e.g., the so-called "Eskimos"). (5) Likewise, many "Native Americans" originated from more southern regions. (6) This is partly why my best friend, a full-blooded Cherokee and an amateur archaeologist, likes to say that he is not Native American but rather Cherokee.

8.   For which of the following sentences is a citation <u>least</u> necessary?

(A) sentence 1   (D) sentence 4

(B) sentence 2   (E) sentence 5

(C) sentence 3

9.   In context, which of the following is the best replacement for "experts" in sentence 2?

(A) scholars   (D) archaeologists

(B) commentators   (E) critics

(C) scientists

10. In sentence 6, the author's reference to his or her best friend serves what purpose?

(A) It provides an expert view on the main idea expressed in the passage.

(B) It illustrates the main idea of the passage by means of an anecdote.

(C) It qualifies the main idea discussed in the passage.

(D) It contradicts the expert claims that are alluded to in the passage.

(E) It extends the main idea developed in the passage.

<u>Questions 11–12</u> refer to the following sentence.

The U.S. government is based on the principle that elected individuals should represent the entire citizenry (e.g., as political scientists would say, our government is a representative democracy).

11.   Which of the following is the best thing to do with "e.g." in this sentence?

(A)   Leave it as is.

(B)   Delete it.

(C)   Replace it with "n.p."

(D)   Replace it with "et al."

(E)   Replace it with "i.e."

12.   In context, what does the information in parentheses convey?

(A)   It provides an example of how the U.S. government operates, according to political scientists.

(B)   On the basis of what political scientists would say, it qualifies the description of the government given in the main portion of the sentence.

(C)   On the basis of what political scientists would say, it extends the description of the government given in the main portion of the sentence.

(D)   It identifies the category of "government" represented by the U.S. government, according to political scientists.

(E)   On the basis of what political scientists would say, it corrects the description of the government given in the main portion of the sentence.

Rhetorical Analysis (25%)

> **DIRECTIONS:** The following questions test your ability to analyze writing. Some questions refer to passages, while other questions are self-contained. For each question, choose the best answer.

<u>Questions 1–6</u> refer to the following passage.

(1) There is a lively debate among musicologists, critics, and fans about what should be considered the first rock and roll recording. (2) Some candidates for the first rock and roll song include Elvis Presley's *That's All Right (Mama)* (1954), Big Joe Turner's *Shake, Rattle, and Roll* (1954), and Bill Haley's *Rock*

Around the Clock (1955). (3) In my opinion, *Rock Around the Clock* is the first true rock and roll song. *That's All Right (Mama)* has a country feel distinctive of the rockabilly tradition from which it springs, while *Shake, Rattle, and Roll* is more of a blues tune. (4) Rockabilly and blues are two of the major sources for the early development of rock and roll, but it is the fusion of these and other sources that distinguishes rock as genre. (5) *Rock Around the Clock* is a perfect example. (6) Based on rockabilly-style melody set to a 12-bar blues progression, the driving rhythm and flamboyant guitar solo of Bill Haley's classic sets it apart as a true rock and roll song.

1. Which of the following best describes sentence 1?

    (A) It summarizes the author's view in a particular debate about music history.

    (B) It explains why the history of rock and roll is an important topic.

    (C) It outlines different positions in the debate about the origins of a particular musical genre.

    (D) It provides a context for the topic addressed in the passage.

    (E) It provides insight into the author's opinion about the first rock and roll song.

2. In context, the word "lively" in sentence 1 emphasizes that the debate in question is

    (A) bitter   (D) positive

    (B) unresolved   (E) useless

    (C) superficial

3. Which of the following best describes the purpose of describing the musical qualities of the two songs named in sentence 3?

    (A) To undermine the claim that they are true rock and roll songs

    (B) To contrast them with other songs from each genre

    (C) To praise their creativity and musical qualities

    (D) To analyze their contributions to rock and roll

    (E) To emphasize limitations in the debate noted in sentence 1

4.   What purpose is served by the first clause of sentence 4 (reproduced below)?

*Rockabilly and blues are two of the major sources for the early develop-
ment of rock and roll*

(A) To emphasize the differences between rock and roll, rockabilly, and
blues

(B) To highlight the author's opinions about what constitutes the first
rock and roll song

(C) To implicitly criticize established views about the history of rock
and roll

(D) To indicate a preference for certain genres among the sources of rock
and roll

(E) To acknowledge that rock and roll is not completely distinct from
rockabilly and blues

5.   In sentence 5, what is *Rock around the Clock* supposed to be a perfect
example of?

(A) A source for the early development of rock and roll

(B) A genre of rock and roll

(C) A fusion of rockabilly and blues

(D) A blues song

(E) A rockabilly song

6.   Which of the following transition words, if inserted at the beginning of
sentence 6 (reproduced below), would increase the coherence of the sentence in the context of this passage?

*Based on rockabilly-style melody set to a 12-bar blues progression, the
driving rhythm and flamboyant guitar solo of Bill Haley's classic sets it
apart as a true rock and roll song.*

(A) Although   (D) Nevertheless

(B) If   (E) Since

(C) However

7. This passage is primarily concerned with

    (A) criticizing alternative views

    (B) tracing a historical progression

    (C) summarizing the positions of a debate

    (D) expressing an opinion

    (E) drawing connections between facts

Questions 8–13 refer to the following passage.

(1) Published in 1925, F. Scott Fitzgerald's classic novel *The Great Gatsby* is both a reflection of and a commentary on its time. (2) The great prosperity and rapid cultural change in America during the 1920s invited the nickname "The Roaring Twenties." (3) Not all Americans embraced the new attitudes and lifestyles of the age. (4) The Roaring Twenties embodied a gigantic clash between traditional and contemporary moral views. (5) Thus, Prohibition was established in the midst of a party atmosphere internationally renowned for its flappers, jazz, and general indulgence. (6) *The Great Gatsby* embraces such contradictions. (7) Nick Carraway, the protagonist, both idolizes and worries about the unrestrained excess of the age.

8. Which of the following best characterizes sentence 1?

    (A) It introduces a claim that is questioned in later sentences.

    (B) It describes a theory of the relationship between literature and history.

    (C) It summarizes the theme of the passage.

    (D) It presents a statement about a particular historical period.

    (E) It evaluates a critical claim about a work of literature.

9. Which of the following transition words, if inserted at the beginning of sentence 3 (reproduced below), would be most logical in the context of the passage?

    Not all Americans embraced the new attitudes and lifestyles of the age.

    (A) But   (D) Consequently

    (B) Although   (E) Thus

    (C) Since

10. Which is best to do with the word "gigantic" in sentence 4 (reproduced below)?

    The Roaring Twenties embodied a gigantic clash between traditional and contemporary moral views.

    (A) Leave it as is.

    (B) Delete it.

    (C) Replace it with "enormous."

    (D) Replace it with "heavy."

    (E) Replace it with "magnificent."

11. The purpose of sentence 5 is to

    (A) Qualify the assertion made in sentence 3.

    (B) Comment on the historical trend described in sentence 4.

    (C) Illustrate the point raised in sentence 4.

    (D) Outline evidence for the main thesis of the passage.

    (E) Provide examples of the idea conveyed in sentence 6.

12. In context, a synonym for "embraces" in sentence 6 would be

    (A) rejects   (D) encompasses

    (B) advocates   (E) questions

    (C) ignores

13. Which of the following would be best to add after sentence 7?

    (A) An example of the "unrestrained excess" of the 1920s.

    (B) A hypothesis about the real-life model for Nick Carraway.

    (C) A comment on another novel written during the 1920s.

    (D) A brief discussion of F. Scott Fitzgerald's life.

    (E) An anecdote illustrating Nick Carraway's ambivalence.

ESSAYS

TIME: 70 Minutes

You will have a total of 70 minutes to write two argumentative essays. You will have 30 minutes to complete the first essay, which is to be based on your own reading, experience, or observations, and 40 minutes to complete the second essay, which requires you to synthesize two sources that are provided. Although you are free to begin writing at any point, it is better to take the time you need to plan your essays and to do the required reading than it is to begin writing immediately.

First Essay

DIRECTIONS: According to Mark Twain, "Clothes make the man." Write an essay in which you discuss what you think Twain meant by this sentence. Then, discuss whether you agree or disagree. Support your discussion with specific reasons and examples from your reading, experience, or observations.

Second Essay

DIRECTIONS: The following assignment requires you to write a coherent essay in which you synthesize the two sources provided. Synthesis refers to combining the sources and your position to form a cohesive, supported argument. You must develop a position and incorporate both sources. **You must cite the sources whether you are paraphrasing or quoting.** Refer to each source by the author's last name, or by any other means that adequately identifies it.

Introduction

Social networks like Facebook and MySpace have changed our educational system. Some observers consider the changes beneficial. These observers note that it is desirable for teachers to make use of social networks as a way of facilitating communication among learners, as well as among learners, teachers, and outside experts. Other observers are concerned that these changes undermine the learning process. They argue that pedagogy (i.e., the way teaching is carried out) should determine how teachers use social networks, but in actual practice, social networks are influencing pedagogy, a concern because social networks are created for profit rather than for educational purposes.

Assignment

Read the following sources carefully. Then write an essay in which you develop a position on whether social networks should or should not be used in the classroom. Be sure to incorporate and cite both of the accompanying sources as you develop your position.

McIntosh, Ewan. Web. 15 Jan. 2008. <http://www.economist.com/debate/days/view/127>

Social networking in all its forms has already begun to transform the way teachers teach, learners learn, and education managers lead learning, and will continue to do so. Social networking has arrived in hundreds of thousands of classrooms and is attempting to show that technology in education is less about anonymous chips and bytes filling up our children with knowledge, less about teachers reinforcing a "chalk and talk" style with an interactive whiteboard, and less about death by PowerPoint bullets. It's more about helping learners become more world-aware, more communicative, learning from each other, and understanding firsthand what makes the world go around.

Bugeja, Michael. Web. 15 Jan. 2008. <http://www.economist.com/debate/days/view/127>

[Social networks] are programmed for revenue generation, especially the vending of marketing data and the advertising base that can be established because of that data. To do so, those networks rely on technology developed by military (to surveil) and industry (to sell).... [Technology has] altered education in every conceivable facet. I have seen it used as delivery system, then as content in the classroom, and finally as classroom, building, and campus itself, and in every case, pedagogy changed to accommodate the interface. Shouldn't it be the other way around? Unless we impose that logic on social networks, they will align educational methods with corporate motives....

Practice Test 1

Answer Key

Conventions of Standard Written English

1. **D** The correct phrase would be "that have."

2. **C** The correct word would be "an."

3. **E** This sentence contains no errors.

4. **D** The correct phrase would be "following the."

5. **B** The correct word would be "show."

Revision Skills

1. **B** Sentences 2 and 6 introduce each side of the debate. "Educators" is the specific group referred to in Sentence 6.

2. **A** Option A is the only grammatically correct option in which letters and groups of letters are depicted as constituents of words.

3. **D** Option D is the only option that reflects the way each instructional approach is named in the passage.

4. **B** In Sentence 4, reference to the popularity of phonics-based methods does not fit the other content of the passage, which pertains to the nature of the two instructional methods.

5. **C** Option C is the only option that accurately reflects the meaning of the passage.

6. **E** Option E is the only option that is both coherent and grammatically correct.

7. **D** Option D is the only option that is both coherent and grammatically correct.

8. **D** In Option D, the reference to Santiago's struggle points back to the courage and strength attributed to him in Sentence 1, while also describing the landing of the marlin whose loss is noted in Sentence 2.

9. **B** In context, the phrase "express and" is redundant.

10. **A** In Option A, the reference is clearest.

11. **D**   Option D is the only option that provides a comparative phrase for "deeper water."

12. **E**   Option E is the only option that is both coherent and grammatically correct.

13. **C**   Option C is the only option that is both coherent and grammatically correct.

14. **C**   Option C is the only option that is both coherent and grammatically correct.

15. **E**   Since the emphasis here is on the risk-taking of other riders, reference to these riders as "daredevils" will convey the message of Sentence 3 most clearly.

16. **B**   Option B is the only option that is both coherent and grammatically correct.

17. **C**   The admonition in Sentence 5 does not fit the content of the passage.

18. **A**   Option A reflects the theme of the second paragraph.

19. **E**   Option E is the only option that is both coherent and grammatically correct.

20. **D**   Option D is the only option that is both coherent and idiomatic.

Ability to Use Source Materials

1. **B**   Examination of the references reveals that the source is a book.

2. **C**   Citation information is needed for *A Nation at Risk*.

3. **D**   The first clause of Sentence 5 indicates that what follows is an example of the statement made in Sentence 4.

4. **E**   Option E is the only accurate option.

5. **A**   All of the second paragraph following Sentence 1 describes NCLB, one example of the kind of federal legislation in question.

6. **D**   In context, Sentence 11 is redundant.

7. **B**   Although Sentences 9–11 indicate that NCLB enables federal support for educational programs, no examples are given.

8. **A**   Unlike Sentence 1, Sentences 2–5 each assert specific facts and hypotheses.

9. **D**   "Archaeologists" is the more specific term also used in Sentence 4.

10. **B**   Option B is the only accurate option.

11. **E** The information in parentheses clarifies the meaning of the main portion of the sentence, and thus "i.e." is the appropriate phrase.

12. **D** Option D is the only accurate option.

Rhetorical Analysis

1. **D** Option D is the only accurate option.

2. **B** In context, "lively" implies that the debate is energetic—and, therefore, unresolved.

3. **A** Option A is the only accurate option.

4. **E** Option E is the only accurate option.

5. **C** Sentence 5 refers back to Sentence 4, and thus *Rock Around the Clock* is meant to be a perfect example of the fusion described in Sentence 4.

6. **A** "Although" is a necessary term, because the first clause of Sentence 6 is meant to acknowledge the influences of rockabilly and blues on the song, while the second clause indicates that in spite of those influences, it represents a distinctive genre (rock and roll).

7. **D** Option D is the only accurate option.

8. **C** Option C is the only accurate option.

9. **A** Sentence 3 is meant to qualify the characterization presented in Sentence 2. Thus, "but" serves as an appropriate comparative term.

10. **B** In context, the term "clash" is sufficient to describe the relationship between traditional and contemporary views. The term "gigantic" and the adjectives in options C–E are exaggerated and distracting.

11. **C** Option C is the only accurate option.

12. **D** In context, option D is the only accurate option.

13. **E** Sentence 7 presents a general description that would be clearer if accompanied by a concrete example.

Answer Key for Essays

Sample First Essay

I think that Twain's sentence, "Clothes make the man," is a concise way of saying that appearances play an important role in the impressions people make on others. In the ideal world, people would be judged on the basis of their inner merits. Whether we are deciding to offer someone a job, to be his or her friend, or to forgive a crime that he or she has committed, the ideal would be to know every detail of the person's heart and mind before making a judgment. After all, the person's potential as an employee, friend, or reformed criminal should not depend on his or her appearance. But we cannot see directly into people's hearts and minds, and in any case, our time is limited. In a job interview, at a party, or during a legal trial, we judge people on the basis of limited information available during a limited amount of time. Thus, our judgments must rely on appearances. We examine specific behaviors, for example. A person who does not look us in the eye will inspire less trust than a person who readily meets our gaze. Another aspect of a person's appearance is their clothing. Often we look at what a person is wearing and make inferences about what type of person he or she is. Here again, we make judgments on the basis of limited information (a particular outfit) available during a limited amount of time (a quick glance). In this sense, clothes do make the man (or woman). You are, to an extent, what you wear.

Although I agree with Twain's observation, I also feel that, like many other catchy phrases, it is too simplistic. Yes, clothes help make the man (or woman). This is inevitable, as I pointed out in the previous paragraph, and to some extent, it is desirable. During a twenty-minute job interview, I do want to consider my potential employee's outfit. Clothing that is dirty, inappropriate, or garishly mismatched would be a clue that the person might not be a careful worker, or be sufficiently aware of his or her impact on others. However, I would also want to consider the person's qualifications. In the case of a supremely qualified applicant, I might be willing to forgive a small soup stain on the shirt or a magenta-colored tie. So, yes, clothes would make or break the man (or woman), but so would their inner qualities. Arguably, in some cases, the inner qualities are more important.

The limitations of Twain's comment are evident when we consider some of the leading entrepreneurs of computer technology over the past three decades. Bill Gates, the founder of Microsoft, Sergey Brin, the cofounder of Google, and Mark Zuckerberg, the founder of Facebook, all have something in common besides their colossal influence on electronic technology: All of them, at least early in their careers, dressed informally, regardless of who they were with. I have read that some of the more traditional members of the industry were startled, or took offense, when these individuals showed up at business meetings wearing t-shirts, jeans, and sneakers. However, their casual clothing did not limit the success of these three superstars. Each one of them had ideas that were innovative and insightful, and it was the quality of these ideas rather than the cut of their clothing that determined their success. For people like Gates, Brin, and Zuckerberg, brilliance makes the man, in spite of the clothes.

Commentary

Look back at the directions for this essay. You will see that the directions include three requests:

1. *Write an essay in which you discuss what you think Twain meant by this phrase.*

2. *Then, discuss whether you agree or disagree.*

3. *Support your discussion with specific reasons and examples, etc.*

The author of the essay addresses the first request in the first paragraph of the essay. The discussion there is detailed, and the author shows some thoughtfulness by linking Twain's observation about clothes to appearances more generally, and by then distinguishing appearances from the underlying substance.

The author addresses the second request by agreeing with Twain's comment (paragraph 1) but then describing the limitations of that comment (paragraphs 2 and 3). The reasons for agreeing with Twain, and for finding his comment simplistic, are clearly explained and supported by examples.

The author addresses the third request by providing a rationale for each idea developed in the essay, and by providing general examples (paragraphs 1 and 2) as well as specific examples (paragraph 3) of these ideas.

Notice that the essay is clear, well-organized, grammatically varied, and free of errors. In the last sentence or two of each paragraph, the author shows good command of the language in playing with variants of Twain's comment.

Suggestions for Essay Development for the Second Essay

A good place to begin is to read these quotes, to be sure you understand the similarities and differences between the positions that McIntosh and Bugeja express, and then to think about the position you will develop in your own essay. Will you side with one of the authors? Will you develop a position that represents a compromise between their positions? Or will you develop a third position that is to some extent separate from theirs?

The next step is to plan your essay. Although your time is limited, you should take a few minutes to create an informal outline that will guide your writing. The outline should identify key points and examples and indicate the order in which they will be discussed.

Below you will see an outline for one particular essay that could be written. This outline is based on the premise that while McIntosh and Bugeja each make good points, other points should be considered when judging the desirability of using social networks in educational settings. The conclusion will be that social networks should be incorporated into classroom instruction, but only if used carefully.

The outline below is relatively detailed and written in complete sentences so that you can follow the progression of ideas. An outline written during the actual test would not need to be as elaborate.

1.   Social networks (SNs) are here to stay, as McIntosh notes; we couldn't ban them from classrooms even if we wanted to.

2.   SNs have advantages and disadvantages as classroom tools.

   (a)   Advantages: SNs connect learners to each other and to more knowl-edgeable sources (McIntosh). And, SN are fast and powerful.

   (b)   Disadvantages: SNs are created by corporations that have profit motives, and these SNs drive pedagogy rather than vice versa (Bugeja). In addition, SNs can be a source of distraction.

3.   No technology is perfect. However, a technology will be desirable if its advantages outweigh its disadvantages. Bugeja does not make a strong case against SNs.

   (a)   Bugeja is correct that SNs are motivated by corporate interests, but so are other materials used in the classroom. Textbooks and other curricular materials are created for a profit. The same may be true of teacher training programs.

   (b)   Bugeja is correct that pedagogy is altered by the use of SNs, but is this really a bad thing? Shouldn't teachers be flexible when incorpo-rating new tools into their instruction? And, isn't the way that SNs are used in the classroom determined by teachers rather than con-trolled by the technology?

4. Since we can't ban SNs from the classroom, we should consider how to maximize their advantages and minimize their disadvantages. McIntosh is correct about the advantages but does not acknowledge the disadvantages that Bugeja notes.

5. SNs are a desirable part of the classroom if used carefully.

    (a) Teachers can help students recognize profit motives, and to understand that exposure to advertising and pressure to purchase applications are among the distractions that come with superior connectivity to other learners and experts.

    (b) Teachers can incorporate SN in a sensible and discriminating way into their classroom instruction rather than allowing SNs to completely determine their pedagogical approach.

Sample Second Essay

Social networks are here to stay, as McIntosh notes. They are becoming prevalent in our society and, like other technological innovations; we can expect them to have an increasing presence in the classroom.

Social networks (SNs) have distinct advantages as classroom tools. They connect learners to each other and to more knowledgeable sources, as McIntosh points out, and they do so in a rapid and efficient way. Through SNs, students can work collaboratively even if they do not attend the same school, and if they need a question answered in a hurry, they may have better luck using SNs to consult with an expert rather than attempting to answer the question themselves through research.

Key disadvantages of SNs are identified by Bugeja. Because SN are created for profit, they reflect some of the characteristics of products that are not very conducive to learning. These characteristics include the presence of advertising, which is a distraction to the learner, as well as a "fun" atmosphere that places emphasis on entertaining rather than educating the user.

No technology is perfect. A technology will be desirable if its advantages outweigh its disadvantages. Thus, we might ask: In a classroom setting, do the speed and interactivity of SNs outweigh the potential problems created by their fun and distracting characteristics?

I do not believe that Bugeja makes a very strong case for the disadvantages of SNs. Although SNs are motivated by a corporate desire for profit, so are other materials used in the classroom, from pencils to desks to textbooks. And although SNs influence pedagogy, this is not necessarily a bad thing. Teachers should be flexible when incorporating new tools into classroom instruction. If electronic technologies such as SNs can make some aspects of teaching easier or more effective, then teachers should take advantage of them. This does not mean that teachers "align educational methods with corporate motives," as Bugeja puts it, but simply that they use technology to improve their educational methods.

SNs are a desirable part of classroom instruction, but only if used carefully. McIntosh's optimism should be tempered by thoughtful integration of SNs into instruction. For example, teachers can help students recognize profit motives, and to understand that exposure to advertising and pressure to purchase applications are among the distractions that come with superior connectivity to other learners and experts. By imposing some limits on the usage of SNs, teachers can incorporate SNs in a sensible and discriminating way into their classroom instruction rather than allowing SNs to completely determine their pedagogical approach.

CLEP College Composition
Practice Test 2

TIME: 50 Minutes

Conventions of Standard Written English (10%)

> **DIRECTIONS:** The following sentences test your knowledge of grammar, usage, diction (choice of words), and idiom. Note that some sentences are correct, and no sentence contains more than one error. Read each sentence carefully, paying particular attention to the underlined portions. You will find that the error, if there is one, is underlined. Assume that elements of the sentence that are not underlined are correct and cannot be changed. In choosing answers, follow the requirements of standard written English. If there is an error, select the one underlined part that must be changed to make the sentence correct. If there is no error, select No error.

1. <u>A group of</u> students <u>were</u> chosen <u>to represent</u> Wilson High School in the <u>annual</u>
   A   B   C   D
   Thanksgiving parade. <u>No error</u>
                         E

2. "What <u>was</u> that?" asked the woman when <u>a</u> tree limb scraped <u>up</u> against <u>her</u>
        A   B   C   D
   window. <u>No error</u>
             E

3. Monetarism is the economic theory <u>holding that</u> a <u>nation's</u> money supply
                                     A   B
   <u>is the</u> key to its <u>economic health</u>. <u>No error</u>
    C   D   E

4. Chinese children love to hear <u>stories about</u> Sun Wukong, the fabulous monkey <u>who</u>
                              A   B
   mastered every martial art <u>and could</u> perform <u>tricks of</u> magic too. <u>No error</u>
                          C   D   E

5. After <u>listening to</u> Mr. Smith complain <u>for at</u> least ten <u>minutes, the</u> clerk began
       A   B   C
   <u>to lose</u> patience with him. <u>No error</u>
    D   E

Revision Skills (40%)

DIRECTIONS: The following passages are early drafts of essays. Read each passage and then answer the questions that follow. Some questions refer to particular sentences or parts of sentences and ask you to improve sentence structure or diction (word choice). Other questions refer to the entire essay or parts of the essay and ask you to consider the essay's organization, development or effectiveness of language. In selecting your answers, follow the conventions of standard written English.

Questions 1–5 are based on the following draft of an essay.

(1) Jake grew up in a small town in a country area of Oklahoma. (2) His parents owned the only drugstore in town. (3) Jake's grandfather had worked on an oil rig. (4) Jake spent early years wandering through the aisles of the drugstore, admiring the different products, a happy time for Jake. (5) By the time he was in ninth grade, Jake was spending most of his afternoons and weekends operating the cash register. (6) No wonder that when he reached his junior year, Jake began to think about attending college. (7) For Jake, college was his ticket away from the small town and the drugstore that had become so oppressive to him.

1. In context, which of the following is the best substitute for "a country area of" in sentence 1?

   (A) local

   (B) part of

   (C) rural

   (D) country

   (E) urban

2. The coherence of the passage would be increased by the removal of which sentence?

   (A) Sentence 1

   (B) Sentence 2

   (C) Sentence 3

   (D) Sentence 4

   (E) Sentence 5

3. Which of the following is best to do with sentence 4 (reproduced below)?

Jake spent early years wandering through the aisles of the drugstore, admiring the different products, a happy time for Jake.

(A) Jake spent his early years wandering through the aisles of the drugstore and admiring the different products, and it was a happy time for Jake.

(B) Jake spent his early years wandering through the aisles of the drugstore and admiring the different products. It was a happy time for Jake.

(C) Jake spent his early years wandering through the aisles of the drugstore, admiring the different products. A happy time for Jake.

(D) Jake spent his early years wandering through the aisles of the drugstore, and admiring the different products, and a happy time for Jake.

(E) Jake spent his early years wandering through the aisles of the drugstore, admiring the different products; a happy time for Jake.

4. Which of the following, if inserted between sentences 5 and 6, would increase the coherence of the passage?

(A) Jake felt proud of himself for being able to operate the register.

(B) Jake's parents appreciated the work that he did at their drugstore.

(C) Jake also enjoyed spending time with his girlfriend whenever he could.

(D) Jake began to grow weary of his responsibilities at the drugstore.

(E) Jake made a number of friends through his work at the drugstore.

5. Which of the following is best to do with the underlined portion of Sentence 7 (reproduced below)?

For Jake, college was his ticket <u>away from</u> the small town and the drugstore that had become so oppressive to him.

(A) Leave it as it is.

(B) Delete it.

(C) Replace it with "to."

(D) Replace it with "transporting him from."

(E) Replace it with "out of."

Questions 6–11 are based on the following draft of an essay.

(1) In James Joyce's short story *Eveline*, the key character's fearful personality paralyzes her in all aspects of her life. (2) Both at home and at work, Eveline submits passively to the will of others, making no effort to better her situation but simply allowing herself to respond to circumstances. (3) Eveline is a very interesting character. (4) In the midst of this inert existence, Eveline is presented with an opportunity to escape. (5) Her lover Frank asks her to be his wife and accompany him to Buenos Aires. (6) There he has a home. (7) She agrees, but then, at the dock where their ship is about to depart, she is unable to join him.

6. In sentence 1 (reproduced below), which is best to do with the word "key"?

   In James Joyce's short story Eveline, *the key character's fearful personality paralyzes her in all aspects of her life.*

   (A) Leave it as is.

   (B) Delete it.

   (C) Replace it with "title."

   (D) Replace it with "sad."

   (E) Replace it with "passive."

7. In context, which is best to do with the underlined portion of sentence 2 (reproduced below)?

   Both at home and at work, Eveline submits passively to the will of others, making no effort to better her situation but simply allowing herself to respond to circumstances.

   (A) Leave it as is.

   (B) Delete it.

   (C) Replace it with "manage."

   (D) Replace it with "make note of."

   (E) Replace it with "be buffeted by."

8. In context, which of the following is closest in meaning to the word "inert" in sentence 4?

   (A) passive

   (B) stable

   (C) quiet

   (D) reflective

   (E) cautious

9. The coherence of the essay would be increased by the deletion of which sentence?

    (A) Sentence 1   (D) Sentence 4

    (B) Sentence 2   (E) Sentence 5

    (C) Sentence 3

10. Which of the following is the best way to combine sentences 5 and 6?

    (A) Her lover Frank asks her to be his wife and accompany him to Buenos Aires; there he has a home.

    (B) Her lover Frank asks her to be his wife and accompany him to Buenos Aires, where he has a home.

    (C) Her lover Frank asks her to be his wife and accompany him to Buenos Aires, there he has a home.

    (D) Her lover Frank asks her to be his wife and accompany him to Buenos Aires; where he has a home.

    (E) Her lover Frank asks her to be his wife and accompany him to Buenos Aires; he has a home there.

11. With which of the following sentences would it be best to end the passage?

    (A) The ship leaves and Frank returns to Buenos Aires, where presumably he has a happy life without her.

    (B) Given how typical this is of the way she lives her life, it is no surprise that Eveline chooses not to accompany Frank.

    (C) She stands at the dock, watching Frank call to her from the ship, once again paralyzed and unable to choose a better life.

    (D) What then must have been going through her mind as she watched Frank sail off toward a life in Buenos Aires without her.

    (E) She could have joined him, and enjoyed a better life in Buenos Aires, but she chose to stay behind.

Questions 12–15 are based on the following draft of an essay.

(1) In the social sciences, most interventions designed to help poor children succeed in school consist of: individual programs that nurture a few key skills. (2) Researchers acknowledge that poor children and their families have a variety of different needs that cannot be met by a single program, or even by

multiple programs available at only one stage of development. (3) Practitioners have also called for multiple programs available throughout children's development. (4) For example, programs such as the Harlem Children's Zone help disadvantaged children reach their educational potential by providing various support from the prenatal period through graduation from high school and beyond.

12. Which of the following is the best revision of sentence 1 (reproduced below)?

In the social sciences, most interventions designed to help poor children succeed in school consist of: individual programs that nurture a few key skills.

(A) In the social sciences, most interventions designed to help poor children succeed in school consist of: Individual programs that nurture a few key skills.

(B) In the social sciences most interventions designed to help poor children succeed in school consist of individual programs that nurture a few key skills.

(C) In the social sciences, most interventions designed to help poor children succeed in school consist of individual programs, that nurture a few key skills.

(D) In the social sciences, most interventions designed to help poor children succeed in school consist of individual programs that nurture a few key skills.

(E) In the social sciences most interventions, designed to help poor children succeed in school, consist of individual programs that nurture a few key skills.

13. In context, which of the following, if added to the beginning of sentence 2, would make the meaning of the sentence clearer?

(A) However,   (D) All things considered,

(B) Nevertheless,   (E) Clearly,

(C) Even so,

14. Which is best to do with the underlined portion of sentence 4 (reproduced below)?

    For example, programs such as the Harlem Children's Zone help disad-vantaged children reach their educational potential by providing <u>various support</u> from the prenatal period through graduation from high school and beyond.

    (A) Leave it as is.

    (B) Delete "various."

    (C) Replace it with "much support."

    (D) Replace it with "various kinds of support."

    (E) Replace it with "the most support."

15. Which of the following sentences, if inserted between sentences 3 and 4, would increase the coherence of the passage?

    (A) There is evidence that such programs are effective.

    (B) Demand for such programs is steadily increasing.

    (C) Researchers and practitioners agree on the need for such programs.

    (D) The hope is that such programs would benefit poor children.

    (E) Such programs are sorely needed in American communities.

Questions 16–20 are based on the following draft of an essay.

(1) Edgar Allan Poe is credited for originating the detective story. (2) But Poe did not invent the mystery. (3) This genre had flourished long before Poe's time. (4) Poe's famous detective Dupin was the first literary detective. (5) Although Poe only wrote three stories featuring Dupin, the detective was an instant hit among readers. (6) What is it about Dupin that made him so popular? (7) In a word, his ratiocination. (8) When investigating a case, Dupin was never inter-ested in merely solving the mystery, but analyzing the motives and thought processes of other characters.

16. Which of the following is the best revision of the underlined portion of sentence 1 (reproduced below)?

Edgar Allan Poe is credited <u>for originating</u> the detective story.

(A) for creating

(B) in originating

(C) by producing

(D) as developing

(E) with originating

17. Which of the following is the best way to combine sentences 2 and 3?

(A) But Poe did not invent the mystery; because this genre had flourished long before his time.

(B) But Poe did not invent the mystery, as this genre had flourished long before his time.

(C) But Poe did not invent the mystery, however, this genre had flourished long before his time.

(D) But Poe did not invent the mystery; a genre that had flourished long before his time.

(E) But Poe did not invent the mystery; since the genre had flourished long before his time.

18. Which of the following is the best substitute for the underlined word of sentence 1 (reproduced below)?

Poe's famous <u>detective</u> Dupin was the first literary detective.

(A) man

(B) figure

(C) fictional device

(D) character

(E) creation

19. In context, which of the following is most closely synonymous with the word "ratiocination" in sentence 7?

(A) sympathy

(B) attractiveness

(C) reasoning

(D) leadership

(E) sociability

20. Which is best to do with the underlined portion of sentence 8 (reproduced below)?

When investigating a case, Dupin was never interested in merely solving the mystery, but <u>he was also interested</u> in analyzing the motives and thought processes of other characters.

(A) Leave it as is.

(B) Delete it.

(C) Replace it with "although he was interested in."

(D) Replace it with "also interested in."

(E) Replace it with "he was also interested in."

Ability to Use Source Materials (25%)

DIRECTIONS: The following questions test your familiarity with basic research, reference, and composition skills. Some questions refer to passages, while other questions are self-contained. For each question, choose the best answer.

Questions 1–5 refer to the following draft of a letter to the editor of a campus newspaper.

(1) While many people claim that there is no such thing as bad publicity, the *Daily Campus* article about our football team proves otherwise. (2) Although we appreciate someone trying to justify our losses, she diminishes the hard work we put into practice every day. (3) Anyone who has actually attended one of our games would see an entire team of players sprinting, not "limping," onto the field. (4) To conclude that the football team has not shown improvement in the past four years is to reduce us to numbers that are not at all accurate. (5) This year we won eight games. (6) Has our team ever shown that much improvement in a single year?

1. Which of the following is most needed in sentence 1?

(A) Information about the main theme of the article.

(B) The name of the football team discussed in the article.

(C) The date that the article appeared in the *Daily Campus*.

(D) A citation for the claim that people make about bad publicity.

(E) Further details about the impact of the article on team spirit.

2. In context, which of the following is the best replacement for "she" in sentence 2?

    (A) The more inclusive phrase "he or she."

    (B) The name of the person who wrote the *Daily Campus* article.

    (C) The name of the author of this letter to the editor.

    (D) The word "everyone."

    (E) The word "it."

3. In sentence 3, who appears to have used the word "limping"?

    (A) The author of this letter to the editor.

    (B) The person who wrote the *Daily Campus* article.

    (C) A spectator at one of the football games.

    (D) The coach of the football team.

    (E) An anonymous person referred to as "she."

4. Which of the following, if added to sentence 5, would best support the claim made in sentence 4?

    (A) The margin of victory for each of the eight wins in the current year.

    (B) The names of the teams that had been defeated in the current year.

    (C) Information about how many games had been won in previous years.

    (D) Details about the strategy for winning implemented in the current year.

    (E) Discussion of school support for the team in previous years.

5. In context, which of the following would be preferable to sentence 6?

    (A) A statement that owing to the improvement observed in the current year, the prognosis for the upcoming season is good.

    (B) A rhetorical question about whether it is fair to criticize such a hard-working, successful team.

    (C) A prediction that the team will most likely win all of its games in the upcoming season.

    (D) An acknowledgment that, in spite of recent improvement, the team could still do much better, and will do so in the next five years.

    (E) A remark that the recent improvement is attributable to a team effort rather than the contributions of any one individual.

Questions 6–8 refer to the following entry from the *Oxford English Dictionary*.

flob (flob), *v.* [onomatopoeic var. of FLOP *v.*, indicating a softer movement and duller sound (see FLABBY).] *intr.* To move heavily or clumsily, with a dull heavy sound.

6. Which of the following statements about the word "flob" is supported by the entry above?

   (A) It is the source of the word "flabby."

   (B) It is a transitive verb.

   (C) It is a very ancient word.

   (D) It is a variant of the word "flop."

   (E) All of the above.

7. In the entry above, what does "onomatopoeic" indicate about the word "flob"?

   (A) The word has a very pleasant sound.

   (B) The word is composed of poetic sounds.

   (C) The word contains a single vowel sound.

   (D) The word is relatively easy to pronounce.

   (E) The word sounds like what it represents.

8. In the entry above, what does the phrase "see FLABBY" suggest that the reader should do?

   (A) Note the visual resemblance between "flob," "flop," and "flabby."

   (B) Observe how the word "flabby" is currently used.

   (C) Consult the dictionary's entry for "flabby."

   (D) Examine a reference work entitled "Flabby."

   (E) None of the above.

Questions 9–12 refer to the following quotation from Jussim, L. & Harber K. D. (2005). Self-fulfilling prophecies: Knowns and unknowns, resolved and unresolved controversies. *Personality and Social Psychology Review,* 9(2), 131-155.

"There is nothing false in the aforementioned, oversimplified summary of Rosenthal and Jacobson (1968). It is true, and to this day, the study is often described in this manner (Fiske & S. Taylor, 1991; Gilbert, 1995; Myers, 1999;

Schultz & Oskamp, 2000). Nonetheless, Rosenthal and Jacobson's (1968) pattern of results was not quite as straightforward as the summary suggests."

9. The paragraph immediately preceding this quotation most probably contained

    (A) a critique of a theory by Rosenthal and Jacobson.

    (B) a summary of a debate between Rosenthal and Jacobson.

    (C) an evaluation of an experiment by Rosenthal and Jacobson.

    (D) a description of a study by Rosenthal and Jacobson.

    (E) an analysis of a claim by Rosenthal and Jacobson.

10. What was Jussim and Harber's purpose in citing authors such as Fiske and Taylor?

    (A) To alert the reader to differences in the way Rosenthal and Jacobson's study has been interpreted.

    (B) To refer the reader to typical summaries of Rosenthal and Jacobson's study.

    (C) To provide the reader with descriptions of flaws in Rosenthal and Jacobson's study.

    (D) To show the reader that other studies are consistent with the results of Rosenthal and Jacobson's study.

    (E) To help the reader understand why summaries of Rosenthal and Jacobson's study are oversimplified.

11. How would Jussim and Harber's summary of the Rosenthal and Jacobson study differ from summaries provided by the authors cited in parentheses (Fiske and Taylor, etc.)?

    (A) Jussim and Harber's summary would probably be simpler than the other summaries.

    (B) Jussim and Harber's summary would probably be completely inconsistent with the other summaries.

    (C) Jussim and Harber's summary would probably focus on different details than explored in the other summaries.

    (D) Jussim and Harber's summary would probably reflect greater complexity than found in the other summaries.

    (E) Jussim and Harber's summary would probably be identical to the other summaries.

12. What would most likely be presented in the paragraph immediately following this quotation?

(A) A refutation of Rosenthal and Jacobson's findings.

(B) A discussion of recent evidence that supports Rosenthal and Jacobson's findings.

(C) A summary of Rosenthal and Jacobson's findings.

(D) A review of recent critiques of Rosenthal and Jacobson's findings.

(E) An outline of historical precursors to Rosenthal and Jacobson's
findings.

Rhetorical Analysis (25%)

DIRECTIONS: The following questions test your ability to analyze writing.
Some questions refer to passages, while other questions are self-contained.
For each question, choose the best answer.

All questions in this section refer to the following essay.

(1) Thus polar bears have evolved physical characteristics that help them
survive in freezing temperatures. (2) The natural habitat of polar bears is
mostly north of the Arctic circle. (3) They have water-repellent fur and pads
of dense, stiff fur on the soles of their snowshoe-like feet. (4) Their feet give
them good traction when walking or running across ice. (5) Polar bears have
such thick layers of fat beneath their fur that infrared photos show no detectable
heat other than their breath. (6) Polar bears are the largest land-based carnivores. (7) They are deadly hunters. (8) Because their fur is mostly white, they
are difficult to spot on ice floes, their favorite hunting ground. (9) With their
small heads, long necks, and long bodies, polar bears are efficient swimmers.
(10) And they have sharp claws that help them hunt. (11) Polar bears have
no natural enemy other than man. (12) Increased human activity in the Arctic region has caused a decline in the polar bear population. (13) Organizations such as the Polar Bear Specialist Group have been formed to help
preserve the species. (14) Polar bears need assistance from these organizations. (15) These organizations are among the contributors to a recent spike
in the polar bear population. (16) At present the population is estimated to be
around 25,000.

1. Which of the following is best to do with sentences 1 and 2?

    (A) Divide each of them into two sentences.

    (B) Reverse their order.

    (C) Delete them.

    (D) Combine them using a semicolon.

    (E) Move them to the end of the paragraph.

2. Sentence 5 primarily serves to

    (A) qualify the observation made in Sentence 3.

    (B) provide a transition to Sentence 6.

    (C) extend the idea given in Sentence 2.

    (D) contrast with the observation in Sentence 4.

    (E) illustrate the statement made in Sentence 1.

3. The coherence of the first paragraph would be increased by deleting which of the following sentences?

    (A) Sentence 1   (D) Sentence 4

    (B) Sentence 2   (E) Sentence 5

    (C) Sentence 3

4. Which of the following would be the best way to combine sentences 6 and 7 (reproduced below)?

    Polar bears are the largest land-based carnivores. They are deadly hunters.

    (A) Polar bears, the largest land-based carnivores: they are deadly hunters.

    (B) Polar bears, the largest land-based carnivores, are deadly hunters.

    (C) Polar bears are the largest land-based carnivores, and are deadly hunters.

    (D) Polar bears are the largest land-based carnivores: they are deadly hunters.

    (E) Polar bears are the largest land-based carnivores; and they are deadly hunters.

5.   Which of the following would contribute most to the coherence of the second paragraph?

   (A)   Further details on the physical dimensions and behaviors of polar bears

   (B)   A discussion of the hunting behavior of other types of bears

   (C)   An explanation or example of why polar bears are described as deadly hunters

   (D)   Additional examples of places where polar bears engage in hunting

   (E)   A comment or discussion about the evolution of polar bears' physical features

6.   In context, adding which of the following to the end of sentence 9 would increase the coherence of the sentence?

   (A)   and can hunt underwater as well.

   (B)   and can be found in the Arctic Ocean.

   (C)   and can outswim most land-based carnivores.

   (D)   and good at maneuvering under the water.

   (E)   and enjoy spending time in the water.

7.   In context, which of the following would most improve sentence 10?

   (A)   A remark about what types of animals polar bears hunt.

   (B)   A comparison between polar bear claws and those of other bears.

   (C)   An explanation of how sharp claws aid polar bears in hunting.

   (D)   A description of the size, shape, and color of polar bear claws.

   (E)   A comment about other purposes served by the sharp claws.

8.   Which of the following is most clearly suggested by sentences 11 and 12?

   (A)   Polar bears are the reason for increased human activity in the Arctic region.

   (B)   Humans and polar bears cannot coexist under any circumstances.

   (C)   The decline in the polar bear population was exclusively caused by human activity.

   (D)   Humans naturally wish to reduce the polar bear population.

   (E)   If not for human influence, the polar bear population would continue to expand.

9. Which of the following, if inserted at the beginning of sentence 13, would provide the best transition between sentences 12 and 13?

    (A) However,

    (B) Nevertheless,

    (C) Even so,

    (D) Meantime,

    (E) As a result,

10. The coherence of the third paragraph would be increased by deleting which of the following sentences?

    (A) Sentence 11

    (B) Sentence 12

    (C) Sentence 13

    (D) Sentence 14

    (E) Sentence 15

11. In context, the word "spike" in sentence 15 most nearly means

    (A) decline

    (B) trend

    (C) interest

    (D) change

    (E) increase

12. Which of the following details, inserted before or after sentence 16, would increase the meaningfulness of that sentence?

    (A) Information on how the reader can contribute to the organizations that support the preservation of polar bears.

    (B) The size of the polar bear population at a time when it was smaller than it is at present.

    (C) An example of what organizations such as the Polar Bear Specialist Group do to support polar bears.

    (D) A projection about the size of the polar bear population in the near and distant future.

    (E) The number of organizations that have been created to help preserve the polar bear species.

13. Which of the following best captures the overall meaning of the passage?

   (A) Polar bears have developed a number of physical characteristics that both help them survive in cold weather and contribute to their prowess as hunters.

   (B) Polar bears have adapted well to their natural habitat, but their survival as a species continues to be influenced by human activity.

   (C) Polar bears have distinctive physical characteristics that help them survive yet fail to protect them from human influence.

   (D) Polar bears are an important and interesting species, but their survival is threatened by human activity in the Arctic region.

   (E) Polar bears would be the dominant predators in the Arctic region if not for the detrimental impact of human activity.

ESSAYS

TIME: 70 Minutes

You will have a total of 70 minutes to write two argumentative essays. You will have 30 minutes to complete the first essay, which is to be based on your own reading, experience, or observations, and 40 minutes to complete the second essay, which requires you to synthesize two sources that are provided. Although you are free to begin writing at any point, it is better to take the time you need to plan your essays and to do the required reading than it is to begin writing immediately.

First Essay

DIRECTIONS: Sir Winston Churchill once said that "Success is the ability to go from one failure to another with no loss of enthusiasm." Write an essay in which you discuss what you think Churchill meant by that comment. Then, discuss whether you agree or disagree. Support your discussion with specific reasons and examples from your reading, experience, or observations.

Second Essay

DIRECTIONS: The following assignment requires you to write a coherent essay in which you synthesize the two sources provided. Synthesis refers to combining the sources and your position to form a cohesive, supported argument. You must develop a position and incorporate both sources. You must cite the sources whether you are paraphrasing or quoting. Refer to each source by the author's last name, or by any other means that adequately identifies it.

Introduction

"Concealed carry" (CC) refers to the practice of carrying a concealed weapon in public. The practice is controversial, particularly with respect to handguns.

Pro-CC View

Supporters of CC argue that it promotes safety, in that criminals are less likely to attack a person if they assume the person is armed. CC supporters also argue that having a gun allows one to protect oneself when actually attacked.

Anti-CC View

Critics of CC argue that it fosters greater crime, including unplanned shootings that occur during arguments. CC critics also argue that carrying a gun increases the frequency of unintended injuries.

Assignment

Consider the pro- and anti-CC arguments carefully. Then write an essay in which you develop a position on the practice of CC. Be sure to incorporate and cite arguments from both sides of the debate as you develop your position.

Practice Test 2

Answer Key

Conventions of Standard Written English

1. **B** The correct word would be "was."

2. **C** The word "up" should simply be deleted.

3. **A** The correct phrase would be "which holds that."

4. **D** The correct phrase would be "feats of."

5. **E** This sentence contains no errors.

Revision Skills

1. **C** In context, option C is the only option that is both coherent and idiomatic.

2. **C** The information in Sentence 3 does not fit the rest of the sentence.

3. **B** Option B is the only option that is both grammatically correct and idiomatic.

4. **D** Option D is the only option that provides a sensible transition between Sentences 5 and 6.

5. **E** Option E is the only option that is both coherent and idiomatic.

6. **C** Option C provides the clearest reference to the character discussed in Sentence 1.

7. **E** Option E is most accurate in light of details given earlier in the sentence.

8. **A** Option A is most accurate in light of details given in the first paragraph.

9. **C** Sentence 3 contributes nothing to the essay other than to distract from the main theme.

10. **B** Option B is the only grammatically correct option.

11. **C** Option C remains closest to the story while reiterating the main theme of the essay.

12. **D**   Option D is the only grammatically correct option.

13. **A**   Option A is the only option that captures the relationship between the first two sentences.

14. **D**   Option D is the only option that allows the content of Sentence 4 to illustrate the idea expressed in Sentence 3.

15. **A**   Option A provides the clearest transition between the third and fourth sentences.

16. **E**   Option E is the only grammatically correct and idiomatic option.

17. **B**   Option B is the only grammatically correct option.

18. **D**   Option D is the most idiomatic option.

19. **C**   Sentence 8 illustrates the meaning of "ratiocination."

20. **E**   Option E is grammatically correct and the option that relates the last two clauses of the sentence most clearly.

Ability to Use Source Materials

1. **C**   Although all of the options convey potentially interesting details, it is most critical to provide the reader with a citation for the original article.

2. **B**   Since the intended reference is to the author of the article, the author should be named.

3. **B**   In context, the quotation marks indicate that this term was used in the *Daily Campus* article.

4. **C**   Contrasting the current year's performance with that of previous years would be a direct approach to demonstrating improvement.

5. **A**   In context, Option A provides the best connection between the observations expressed in Sentences 4 and 5, and a reasonable inference that can be made from those observations.

6. **D**   Option D is the only correct option.

7. **E**   Option E is the only correct option.

8. **C**   Option C is the only correct option.

9. **D**   The term "aforementioned" in the first sentence and the term "study" in the second sentence are among the details indicating that Option D is correct.

10. **B**   In context, Option B is the only correct option.

11. **D**   Details from the entire passage indicate that Option D is correct.

12. **C**   The final sentence of the passage is likely to serve as a transition to Jussim and Harber's own summary of Rosenthal and Jacobson's study.

Rhetorical Analysis

1. **B**   In context, the sentences would make more sense if their order were reversed.

2. **E**   Sentence 5 provides another example of the physical characteristics alluded to in Sentence 1.

3. **D**   Sentence 4 is the only sentence that does not fit the theme of the first paragraph.

4. **B**   Option B is the only grammatically correct option.

5. **C**   No information is provided as to why polar bears are described as deadly hunters.

6. **A**   Option A would relate Sentence 9 most clearly to the hunting theme of the second paragraph.

7. **C**   Option C would add specificity to the vague statement in Sentence 10.

8. **C**   Although not directly stated, Sentences 11 and 12 strongly imply that human activity was the sole cause of the decline in the polar bear population.

9. **E**   The passage strongly implies that organizations such as the Polar Bear Specialist Group were formed in response to the decline in the polar bear population.

10. **D**   Sentence 14 contributes nothing to the paragraph other than a vague statement of an idea that the paragraph arguably already conveys.

11. **E**   In context, Option E makes most sense.

12. **B**   In context, the statistic in Sentence 16 is not informative without details about population size in earlier years.

13. **B**   Option B captures all of the major points expressed in the passage.

Answer Key for Essays

Sample First Essay

Failure is a part of life. Nobody reaches adulthood without having failed in at least some things. But there are many different ways that one can react to personal failures. Some people give up and simply assume that failure is inevitable. For these people, their pessimism becomes a self-fulfilling prophecy: They continue to fail because they expect to do so. Other people maintain a more positive attitude. Failure does not deter these individuals. Rather, they react to failure by continuing to pursue success with enthusiasm. These are the people who are truly successful, according to Churchill. In his view, success is the ability to maintain enthusiasm following failure.

However, there is more to Churchill's observation. He refers to the process of going "from one failure to another" as if failure were not just an occasional event in the life of a successful person, but rather the norm. Does it make sense to say that successful people are the ones who are merely enthusiastic in response to repeated failures? Is this the best way to define success?

Certainly, as I noted earlier, even the most successful people must contend with failure. Michael Jordan is an excellent example. Widely considered the greatest basketball player in the history of the game, Jordan attained every possible form of success in basketball, including numerous scoring records, six championship rings, two Olympic gold medals, and admission to the NBA Hall of Fame. Outside the court, Jordan earned more money than any other athlete for product endorsements, and upon retirement he became a successful businessman and owner of the Charlotte Bobcats. However, this most stellar of careers was not without setbacks. As a sophomore in high school, Jordan failed to make the varsity basketball team. He persevered in spite of a serious injury in his second pro season, repeated losses during the playoffs early in his career, and an inability to succeed in professional baseball while taking a break from the NBA. By all accounts Jordan is a highly competitive person. It appears that his enthusiasm for basketball was not diminished by the failures and setbacks that occurred during his career.

At the same time, enthusiasm would not have helped Michael Jordan much if he had lacked the talent and the work ethic that brought him success following his specific failures. In my view there is an important difference between someone like Jordan, who was phenomenally successful, versus the people who fail repeatedly but maintain an enthusiastic attitude. Both types of people are enthusiastic, but only one type experiences tangible success.

Thus, I have to disagree somewhat with Churchill's comment. The ability to go from failure to failure with no loss of enthusiasm is a good thing, in that it shields people from the misery that can accompany personal failures. However, maintaining an enthusiastic attitude is not the same thing as success. Success, in my opinion, is a form of accomplishment that is acknowledged and rewarded by others. It is not guaranteed by enthusiasm, although I am sure it is much sweeter if accompanied by an enthusiastic attitude.

In sum, I would modify Churchill's comment as follows: Success is the ability to go from one failure to another with no loss of enthusiasm, and to succeed in spite of earlier failures.

Commentary

Look back at the directions for this essay. You will see that the directions include three requests:

1. Write an essay in which you discuss what you think Churchill meant by that comment.

2. Then, discuss whether you agree or disagree.

3. Support your discussion with specific reasons and examples from your reading, experience, or observations.

The author of the essay addresses the first request in the first paragraph of the essay. The discussion there is very analytical. This analytical approach is continued in the second paragraph, in which the author examines Churchill's comment closely and draws out one of its apparent assumptions.

The remainder of the essay addresses the second request listed above. The author ends up disagreeing with Churchill's comment without entirely rejecting the comment as unfounded. In the final paragraph, the author incorporates Churchill's view into his or her own position on the topic.

Throughout the essay the writing is clear, well-organized, grammatically varied, and free of errors. The ideas that are ultimately expressed in the final two paragraphs are carefully developed. The extended discussion of Michael Jordan's career allows the author to address the third request listed above while developing the central thesis of the essay.

Suggestions for Essay Development for the Second Essay

A good place to begin is to think about the content of the pro- and anti-CC positions, as summarized above. Do you agree with one position more than the other? If so, how strong is the extent of your agreement? Do you find any of the arguments in favor of one of the other position to be especially convincing or unconvincing? Can you think of other arguments for or against either position that are not mentioned here?

The next step is to plan your essay. Although your time is limited, you should take a few minutes to create an informal outline that will guide your writing. The outline should identify key points and examples and indicate the order in which they will be discussed.

Below you will see an outline for one particular essay that could be written. This outline reflects a largely anti-CC point of view. The outline is relatively detailed and written in complete sentences so that you can follow the progression of ideas. An outline written during the actual test would not need to be as elaborate.

1. The world is a dangerous place, owing in part to criminal activity.

2. Guns do promote safety in several ways.

    (a) The pro-CC view seems correct in asserting that criminals are less likely to attack someone who is armed.

    (b) The pro-CC view also seems correct in asserting that when criminals do attack, the intended victims can protect themselves by means of a gun.

3. Although guns do promote safety, the pro-CC view is misguided. Just because an action has benefits, it doesn't follow that the action is desirable. Criminals are probably less likely to attack a person who is wearing a vest of hand grenades, but it doesn't follow that people should be allowed to walk around wearing hand grenades.

4. CC has many undesirable consequences.

    (a) As noted in the Introduction, CC allows people to go virtually anywhere with a concealed gun. This makes it easier to commit premeditated crimes such as robbery, muggings, and murder. And, it enables unpremeditated violence by making it easy for an angry or intoxicated person to shoot someone else.

    (b) As noted in the Introduction, CC opens the door to accidental injuries to oneself and to others.

5. In sum, the anti-CC view is more sensible, because the risks of CC outweigh the benefits.

CLEP College Composition Modular

Practice Test 1

TIME: 90 Minutes

Conventions of Standard Written English (10%)

> **DIRECTIONS:** The following sentences test your knowledge of grammar, usage, diction (choice of words), and idiom. Note that some sentences are correct, and no sentence contains more than one error. Read each sentence carefully, paying particular attention to the underlined portions. You will find that the error, if there is one, is underlined. Assume that elements of the sentence that are not underlined are correct and cannot be changed. In choosing answers, follow the requirements of standard written English. If there is an error, select the one underlined part that must be changed to make the sentence correct. If there is no error, select "No error."

1. "What do I know?" <u>was</u> the motto of the influential French essayist Michel
                   A
  de <u>Montaigne, who</u> was born <u>on</u> 1533 and <u>lived for</u> 59 years. <u>No error</u>
        B   C   D   E

2. John <u>Steinbeck more</u> than any other writer, <u>sparked</u> the young <u>author's</u>
        A   B   C
  interest <u>in 20th-</u>century American literature. <u>No error</u>
           D   E

3. <u>As soon as</u> the boxing match <u>ended and</u> the referee <u>announced</u> the winner,
     A   B   C
  the crowd began to <u>quickly move</u> toward the exit. <u>No error</u>
                 D   E

4. <u>Confronted with</u> the choice of either <u>cleaning up</u> his room or <u>cleaning out</u>
    A   B   C
  the garage, the teenager <u>became</u> angry with his parents. <u>No error</u>
                 D   E

5. <u>Of all</u> the important contributions to history that he <u>might have made,</u>
   A   B
  John Montagu, the Earl of Sandwich, is <u>better</u> known for a lunch of meat
                                 C
  inserted <u>between</u> two slices of bread. <u>No error</u>
         D   E

6. One reason <u>astronomers</u> study quasars is <u>because</u> these small, quasi-stellar
    　　　　　　 A　　　　　　　　　　　　 B
    objects <u>might</u> provide <u>clues</u> to the origin of the universe. <u>No error</u>
    　　　　　 C　　　　　 D　　　　　　　　　　　　　　　　　　 E

7. Jerry <u>found</u> it <u>more difficult</u> to <u>divide</u> exponents than <u>adding</u> exponents. <u>No error</u>
    　　　 A　　　 B　　　　　　　 C　　　　　　　　　 D　　　　　　　　　 E

8. The kindergarten teacher <u>was so tired</u> after her first day on the job <u>that</u>
    　　　　　　　　　　　　　 A　　　　　　　　　　　　　　　　　　　　 B
    thoughts of sleep <u>was all</u> that <u>went</u> through her mind. <u>No error</u>
    　　　　　　　　　 C　　　　 D　　　　　　　　　　　　 E

9. Ramon y Cajal's 1904 monograph <u>on</u> the human nervous system, <u>still</u>
    　　　　　　　　　　　　　　　　 A　　　　　　　　　　　　　　　 B
    considered a seminal work in neurobiology, <u>infers</u> that neural connections
    　　　　　　　　　　　　　　　　　　　　　　 C
    <u>in the brain</u> are highly structured. <u>No error</u>
    　 D　　　　　　　　　　　　　　 E

Revision Skills (40%)

DIRECTIONS: The following passages are early drafts of essays. Read each passage and then answer the questions that follow. Some questions refer to particular sentences or parts of sentences and ask you to improve sentence structure or diction (word choice). Other questions refer to the entire essay or parts of the essay and ask you to consider the essay's organization, development, or effectiveness of language. In selecting your answers, follow the conventions of standard written English.

<u>Questions 1–6</u> are based on the following draft of an essay.

(1) This year, paleontologists discovered two new species of dinosaurs in southern Utah, Kosmoceratops richardsoni and Utahceratops gettyi. (2) Paleontologists believe that the two rhino-sized dinosaurs are closely related to the Triceratops. (3) However, the Kosmoceratops had 15 horns on its head, the Utahceratops had 5 horns, in contrast to the three-horned Triceratops. (4) Each horn was about 6 to 12 inches in length. (5) The horns were used, according to paleontologists, to attract females and to intimidate rivals for females. (6) However, the females of these species also had horns. (7) Paleontologists speculate that females evolved horns to ward off predators. (8) Kosmoceratops and Utahceratops lived about 76 million years ago. (9) Kosmoceratops and Utahceratops are two of the dinosaur species recently discovered in the

Grand Staircase-Escalante National Monument. (10) Which occupies a large area in southern Utah. (11) This part of the country is rocky and arid now, it would have been a swamp during the time that Kosmoceratops and Utahceratops flourished. (12) The ongoing discovery of new dinosaur species in areas such as the Grand Staircase-Escalante National Monument shows that the fossil record is constantly emerging rather than fixed.

1.   In context, which of the following words should be used to replace the second comma in sentence 3 (immediately following the word "head")?

(A) but   (D) though

(B) and   (E) then

(C) as

2.   Which of the following is the best way to reorder sentence 5 (reproduced below)?

The horns were used, according to paleontologists, to attract females and to intimidate rivals for females.

(A) The horns were, according to paleontologists, used to attract females and to intimidate rivals for females.

(B) The horns, according to paleontologists, were used to attract females and to intimidate rivals for females.

(C) According to paleontologists, the horns were used to attract females and to intimidate rivals for females.

(D) The horns were used to attract females and, according to paleontologists, to intimidate rivals for females.

(E) The horns were used to attract females and to intimidate rivals, according to paleontologists, for females.

3.   Where would be the best place to relocate sentence 8?

(A) After Sentence 1   (D) After Sentence 10

(B) After Sentence 2   (E) After Sentence 12

(C) After Sentence 3

4. In context, which of the following is the best way to combine sentences 9 and 10 (reproduced below)?

Kosmoceratops and Utahceratops are two of the dinosaur species recently discovered in the Grand Staircase-Escalante National Monument. Which occupies a large area in southern Utah.

(A) Kosmoceratops and Utahceratops are two of the dinosaur species recently discovered in the Grand Staircase-Escalante National Monument; which does occupy a large area in southern Utah.

(B) Kosmoceratops and Utahceratops are two of the dinosaur species recently discovered in the Grand Staircase-Escalante National Monument, which is a large area in southern Utah.

(C) Kosmoceratops and Utahceratops are two of the dinosaur species recently discovered in the Grand Staircase-Escalante National Monument, a monument that occupies a large area in southern Utah.

(D) Kosmoceratops and Utahceratops are two of the dinosaur species recently discovered in the Grand Staircase-Escalante National Monument, and this occupies a large area in southern Utah.

(E) Kosmoceratops and Utahceratops are two of the dinosaur species recently discovered in the Grand Staircase-Escalante National Monument, occupying a large area in southern Utah.

5. Which of the following words added to the beginning of sentence 11 would make the sentence both grammatically correct as well as coherent?

(A) However

(B) Since

(C) Although

(D) Because

(E) As

6. In context, which is the best replacement for "emerging" in sentence 12 (reproduced below)?

The ongoing discovery of new dinosaur species in areas such as the Grand Staircase-Escalante National Monument shows that the fossil record is constantly emerging rather than fixed.

(A) scintillating

(B) vacillating

(C) translating

(D) adding

(E) growing

<u>Questions 7–14</u> are based on the following draft of an essay.

(1) Although most new homes are finished in brick in the United States, stucco is becoming an increasingly popular finish. (2) Stucco finishes are composed of sand, water, and a binding material. (3) Traditionally, the binding material was lime; cement is widely used. (4) The first coat or two is 3/8 of an inch thick, while the final is coat about 1/4 to 1/8 of an inch thick. (5) Stucco is applied with a trowel. (6) It is quick and easy. (7) Stucco has many advantages, one advantage being energy efficiency. (8) A waterproof, low-maintenance exterior is produced by coating the final application of stucco with a clear acrylic finish. (9) Because colors can be mixed into stucco finishes, home owners and designers can select a color. (10) Finally, stucco is lightweight and quite inexpensive, too.

7. In context, which of the following is the best way to reorder sentence 1 (reproduced below)?

    Although most new homes are finished in brick in the United States, stucco is becoming an increasingly popular finish.

    (A) In the United States, although most new homes are finished in brick, stucco is becoming an increasingly popular finish.

    (B) Although in the United States most new homes are finished in brick, stucco is becoming an increasingly popular finish.

    (C) Although most new homes in the United States are finished in brick, stucco is becoming an increasingly popular finish.

    (D) Although most new homes are, in the United States finished in brick, stucco is becoming an increasingly popular finish.

    (E) Although most new homes are finished in the United States in brick, stucco is becoming an increasingly popular finish.

8. Which is best to do with sentence 3 (reproduced below)?

    Traditionally, the binding material was lime; cement is widely used.

    (A) Leave it as is.

    (B) Change "was" to "is."

    (C) Replace the semicolon with a comma.

    (D) Add "nowadays" at the end of the sentence.

    (E) Break it into two sentences.

9. In context, which of the following is the best way to relate sentences 4 and 5?

    (A) Reverse their order.

    (B) Combine them into a single sentence separated by a semicolon.

    (C) Place them both inside one set of parentheses.

    (D) Combine them using the word "and."

    (E) Combine them using the word "but."

10. Which of the following is the best revision of sentence 6 (reproduced below)?

    It is quick and easy.

    (A) Stucco is quick and easy.

    (B) It is a quick and easy thing.

    (C) Stucco: quick and easy.

    (D) Applying stucco is quick and easy.

    (E) It is quick and easy, the stucco.

11. Which of the following is the best revision of the underlined portion of sentence 7 (reproduced below)?

    Stucco has many advantages, one advantage being energy efficiency.

    (A) and one of those advantages is

    (B) including

    (C) like the

    (D) but

    (E) and one being

12. In context, which word or phrase, added to the beginning of sentence 8, makes the purpose of the sentence clearer?

    (A) However   (D) Nevertheless

    (B) In addition   (E) Even so

    (C) But

13. In context, which revision to the underlined portion of sentence 9 (reproduced below) would make the sentence more persuasive?

    Because colors can be mixed into stucco finishes, home owners and designers can select <u>a color</u>.

    (A) from a variety of colors.

    (B) from at least one color.

    (C) an interesting color.

    (D) a preferred color.

    (E) one color or more.

14. For which of the following audiences is this passage most likely to have been written?

    (A) A person who owns a stucco house.

    (B) A recently retired stucco manufacturer.

    (C) A manufacturer of brick finish.

    (D) A potential buyer of stucco finish.

    (E) An architect who specializes in stucco materials.

Improving Sentences

DIRECTIONS: The following sentences test correctness and effectiveness of expression. In choosing your answers, follow the requirements of standard written English: that is, pay attention to grammar, diction (choice of words), sentence construction, and punctuation. In each of the following sentences, part of the sentence or the entire sentence is underlined. Beneath each sentence you will find five versions of the underlined part. The first option repeats the original; the other four options present different versions. Choose the option that best expresses the meaning of the original sentence. If you think the original is better than any of the alternatives, choose the first option; otherwise, choose one of the other options. Your choice should produce the most effective sentence—one that is clear and precise.

15. The Arctic Ocean is the <u>smallest, but shallowest</u> of the world's five major oceans.

    (A) smallest, but shallowest

    (B) smallest and shallowest

    (C) smallest, and the shallowest

    (D) smallest shallowest

    (E) smallest, yet shallowest

16. <u>The</u> Great Chicago Fire of 1871 was one of the largest U.S. disasters of the 19th century, the reconstruction that took place afterward helped Chicago become one of the most prominent American cities.

    (A) The

    (B) Surely the

    (C) Knowing that the

    (D) Since the

    (E) Although the

17. Nobody was surprised when Sandra won the race, <u>given she</u> had won so many races in the past.

    (A) given she

    (B) given when she

    (C) given that she

    (D) given where she

    (E) given the knowledge she

18. Madeleine L'Engle, a prominent writer of young adult <u>fiction, was born</u> in New York City on November 29, 1918.

    (A) fiction, was born

    (B) fiction; born

    (C) fiction. She was born

    (D) fiction was born

    (E) fiction, born

19. Although most professional basketball coaches believe that their players desire to win, some coaches doubt whether <u>they have</u> the necessary skills.

    (A) they have

    (B) their team have

    (C) they do have

    (D) their players have

    (E) they will have

20. Finding a book on top of the desk, <u>it was placed on the shelf with the others by the librarian</u>.

    (A) it was placed on the shelf with the others by the librarian.

    (B) it was placed with the others on the shelf by the librarian.

    (C) the librarian placed it on the shelf with the others.

    (D) and placing it on the shelf with the others was the librarian.

    (E) the librarian placed it on the shelf, with the others.

21. The musicians carried four instruments <u>which is needed for the musical program</u>.

    (A) which is needed for the musical program.

    (B) that is needed for the musical program.

    (C) as are needed for the musical program.

    (D) they are needed for the musical program.

    (E) that are needed for the musical program.

22. In writing *A Tale of Two Cities*, <u>Dickens produced one of the best-sellers of the Victorian Period</u>.

    (A) Dickens produced one of the best-sellers of the Victorian Period.

    (B) one of the best-sellers of the Victorian Period was produced.

    (C) the Victorian Period witnessed the production of one of Dickens's best-sellers.

    (D) Dickens in the Victorian Period produced one of its best-sellers.

    (E) production of one of the best-sellers of the Victorian Period was created by Dickens.

23. If a person needs to leave the testing area during the test, <u>they should obtain</u> verbal permission as well as a pass from the proctor.

    (A) they should obtain   (D) they could obtain

    (B) he or she should obtain   (E) you could obtain

    (C) you should obtain

24. In *The Music Man,* Robert Preston portrays a fast-talking salesman who comes to a small town in Iowa <u>inadvertently falling in love with</u> the librarian.

    (A) inadvertently falling in love with

    (B) and inadvertently falls in love with

    (C) and afterwards he inadvertently falls in love with

    (D) then falling inadvertently in love with

    (E) when he inadvertently falls in love with

25. Two-thirds of American 17-year-olds do not know that the Civil War <u>takes place</u> between 1850–1900.

    (A) takes place   (D) took place

    (B) have taken place   (E) is taking place

    (C) has taken place

26. Father Junipero Serra, a Franciscan missionary sent from Spain to Mexico, <u>where he taught and worked among the Indians</u> and then founded many missions in California that later became cities.

    (A) where he taught and worked among the Indians

    (B) there he taught and worked among the Indians

    (C) he taught and worked among the Indians

    (D) taught and worked among the Indians

    (E) teaching and working among the Indians

27. He went to the meeting eager to explain his point of view but <u>had fear of public speaking</u>.

    (A) had fear of public speaking

    (B) having fear of public speaking

    (C) having fear he would have to speak in public

    (D) fearing the public speaking

    (E) afraid of public speaking

28. Reducing calories <u>are ways to lose weight</u>.

    (A) are ways to lose weight.   (D) weight is lost.

    (B) is a way to lose weight.   (E) is a loss of weight.

    (C) loses weight.

29. After having written many books, <u>the author was made popular</u>.

    (A) the author was made popular

    (B) the author is popular

    (C) the author became a popular author

    (D) the author will become popular

    (E) the author became popular

30. Patricia noticed that <u>some</u> button on her shirt had popped off.

    (A) some   (D) that

    (B) this   (E) any

    (C) a

31. As she read through Plato's early dialogues, the philosophy student found Socrates <u>a</u> brilliant and intriguing character.

    (A) a   (D) to be a

    (B) as a   (E) to be the

    (C) the

32. Without warning, the sky darkened and <u>the rain</u>.

    (A) the rain.   (D) came the rain.

    (B) then the rain.   (E) it was the rain.

    (C) it began to rain.

33. In 1905, Theodore Roosevelt played the role of mediator between Russia and Japan <u>during</u> negotiations that resulted in the Treaty of Portsmouth.

    (A) during   (D) considering

    (B) among   (E) overseeing

    (C) around

34. Walking down Main Street, <u>the trees</u> were especially lovely.

    (A) the trees   (D) he noticed that the trees

    (B) there were many trees   (E) it was the trees

    (C) she considered the trees

35. If <u>I'd have been</u> paying closer attention, I wouldn't have overcooked the soup.

    (A) I'd have been   (D) I'd've been

    (B) I had been   (E) I been

    (C) I would have been

36. Mary reached down to pick up the <u>pencil, that</u> had fallen underneath her desk.

    (A) pencil, that

    (B) pencil as

    (C) pencil, what

    (D) pencil which

    (E) pencil that

Ability to Use Source Materials (25%)

> **DIRECTIONS:** The following questions test your familiarity with basic research, reference, and composition skills. Some questions refer to passages, while other questions are self-contained. For each question, choose the best answer.

Questions 1–6 refer to the following passage.

(1) During his two terms as president of the United States, George Washington established a number of precedents that subsequent presidents are known to have followed. (2) For example, Washington decided that his official title should be "Mr. President," choosing this designation over more formal options that Congress had considered, such as "His Highness" and "His High Mightiness" (Ellis, 2004). (3) Washington also delivered an inaugural speech and refused to serve as president for more than two terms, a practice that was later made law by means of the Twenty-second Amendment to the U.S. Constitution. (4) Other aspects of Washington's presidency were more idiosyncratic. (5) He did not belong to a political party, for example, and he advocated neutrality in foreign affairs (Grizzard, 2005). (6) Ellis (2004) and many other historians suggest that the precedents established by Washington, whether or not adopted by future presidents, all reflected Washington's commitment to the strength and well-being of the United States, as well as the characteristics of his own distinctive personality.

References

Ellis, J. 2004. *His Excellency: George Washington*. New York: Random House.

Grizzard, F. 2005. *George! A Guide to All Things Washington*. Buena Vista and Charlottesville, VA: Mariner Publishing.

1. Which is best to do with the underlined portion of sentence 1 (reproduced below)?

    During his two terms as president of the United States, George Washington established a number of precedents that subsequent presidents <u>are known to have followed</u>.

    (A) Leave it as is.

    (B) Delete "are known to."

    (C) Replace it with "have clearly followed."

    (D) Add ", according to scholars" at the end.

    (E) Replace it with "will follow."

2. Must each of the quoted phrases in sentence 2 be attributed to a separate source?

    (A) No.

    (B) Yes, but only if the source was one of Washington's contemporaries.

    (C) Yes, but only if a primary source is cited.

    (D) Yes, but only if the source is a professional historian.

    (E) Yes, but only if the source is an expert on Washington.

3. Which of the following best describes the purpose of sentence 3?

    (A) To qualify an earlier statement

    (B) To establish an overarching theme

    (C) To summarize an idea expressed earlier

    (D) To provide concrete examples of an earlier point

    (E) To criticize a general assumption

4. The information in parentheses at the end of sentence 5 most clearly indicates that

    (A) the sentence is a quotation from a work by Grizzard.

    (B) Grizzard has written a work that focuses on political affiliation and foreign affairs.

    (C) Grizzard has written a work that includes information about Washington's views on political affiliation and foreign affairs.

(D) Grizzard was a contemporary of Washington who wrote a work about Washington's views of political affiliation and foreign affairs.

(E) details about Washington's views on political affiliation and foreign affairs can be found on page 2005 of a work by Grizzard.

5. In context, the reference to Ellis (2004) at the beginning of sentence 6 informs the reader that

(A) Ellis is a famous historian who has written extensively about U.S. presidents.

(B) Ellis is the most important historian who has expressed the idea summarized in Sentence 6.

(C) Ellis has a unique perspective on Washington's political views.

(D) Ellis is a historian who does not agree with the idea summarized in Sentence 6.

(E) Ellis is one of numerous historians who have expressed the idea summarized in Sentence 6.

6. Which of the following kinds of information added to the end of this passage would increase the coherence of sentence 6?

(A) A general analysis of how a leader's personality can influence his or her leadership style.

(B) A concrete example of how Washingtonian precedents reflected Washington's distinctive personality.

(C) A critique of the ways that Washington's personality impacted his key decisions as president.

(D) A theoretical discussion of how Washington might have conducted his presidency differently.

(E) An exhortation for scholars to pay greater attention to the role of each president's personality in policy decisions.

Questions 7–8 refer to the following citation.

Bronfenbrenner, U. 1986. Ecology of the family as a context for human development: Research perspectives. *Developmental Psychology 22*: 723-742.

7. In the citation above, what is *"Developmental Psychology"*?

   (A) The name of a book

   (B) The name of an edited volume

   (C) The name of a journal

   (D) The name of Bronfenbrenner's academic department

   (E) The name of a field of inquiry

8. In the citation above, what is the "22"?

   (A) It is part of the name of the source.

   (B) It is the total page length of the work cited.

   (C) It is the ranking of the source in a professional database.

   (D) It is the number of publications contributed by the author.

   (E) It is the volume number of the source.

Questions 9–17 refer to the following passage.

(1) A tree is a perennial woody plant...that has many secondary branches supported clear of the ground on a single main stem or trunk with clear apical dominance. (2) A minimum height specification at maturity varying from 3 m to 6 m is cited by some authors; some authors set a minimum of 10 cm trunk diameter (30 cm girth). (3) Woody plants that do not meet these definitions by having multiple stems and/or small size are called shrubs. (4) Compared with most other plants, trees are long-lived, some reaching several thousand years old and growing to up to 115 m (379 ft) high. (5) Trees are an important component of the natural landscape because of their prevention of erosion and the provision of a weather-sheltered ecosystem in and under their foliage.... (6) Wood from trees is a building material, as well as a primary energy source in many developing countries. (7) Trees also play a role in many of the world's mythologies (see trees in mythology).

Quoted from *Wikipedia: The Free Encyclopedia*. Wikimedia Foundation, Inc. Web. 27 Sept. 2010. <http://en.wikipedia.org/wiki/Tree>

9. What kind of information does sentence 1 provide?

   (A) A definition

   (B) A hypothesis

   (C) A theme

   (D) A theory

   (E) A synthesis

10. In sentence 1, which of the following is most likely indicated by the ellipsis immediately following "plant"?

   (A) Overt omission of factually incorrect information

   (B) Deliberate censorship of objectionable material

   (C) Accidental omission of a sentence

   (D) Inadvertent loss of text from original source

   (E) Intentional omission of words

11. Which of the following information, if inserted at the end of sentence 1, would increase the understandability of Sentence 1?

   (A) A description of one particular species of tree

   (B) A contrast between the features of various types of plant

   (C) A definition of the phrase "apical dominance"

   (D) A citation for the details given in sentence 1

   (E) A summary of the information to come in sentence 2

12. How does sentence 2 appear to contribute to the passage?

   (A) It shows that certain dimensions of trees are not fully understood.

   (B) It describes two possible criteria for the definition of a tree.

   (C) It contrasts the relative dimensions of trees versus shrubs.

   (D) It illustrates controversies about how trees have been defined.

   (E) It reflects natural variability in the physical dimensions of trees.

13. In context, which of the following is most clearly implied by the two references to "some authors" in sentence 2?

   (A) Not all authors agree that trees are classifiable in terms of physical dimensions.

   (B) Not all authors who discuss trees provide a concrete definition for this category.

   (C) Not all authors consider physical dimensions among the criteria for being a tree.

   (D) Not all authors agree about all of the criteria for the definition of a tree.

   (E) Not all trees fit the definitional criteria for a tree described by some authors.

14. Which of the following is the best revision to the underlined portion of sentence 2 (reproduced below)?'

    A minimum height specification at maturity is cited by some authors, varying from 3 m to 6 m; some authors set a minimum of 10 cm trunk diameter (30 cm girth).

    (A) other authors

    (B) these authors

    (C) a few authors

    (D) as well as authors

    (E) the many authors

15. Which of the following is the best revision of sentence 3 (reproduced below)?

    Woody plants that do not meet these definitions by having multiple stems and/or small size are called shrubs.

    (A) Woody plants that have multiple stems and/or small size and therefore do not meet these definitions are called shrubs.

    (B) Woody plants that do not meet these definitional criteria owing to multiple stems and/or small size are called shrubs.

    (C) Woody plants that do not meet these definitions owing to their multiple stems and small size are called shrubs.

    (D) Woody plants that do not meet these definitional criteria by their having multiple stems and/or small size are called shrubs.

    (E) Woody plants having multiple stems and/or small size that do not meet these definitions are called shrubs.

16. What is the contribution of the second paragraph (sentences 5–7) to the passage?

    (A) It shows that the scientific definition of a tree is inadequate.

    (B) It describes some of the natural functions and cultural uses of trees.

    (C) It explains why trees are more important than shrubs.

    (D) It illustrates why the conservation and management of trees is controversial.

    (E) It analyzes the role of trees in human society.

17. In sentence 7, the underlined phrase ("trees in mythology") is a hyperlink that will most probably lead to

   (A) an online book.

   (B) a hypermedia display concerning trees.

   (C) a separate Wikipedia entry.

   (D) a slideshow.

   (E) a Greek mythology website.

Questions 18–22 refer to the following passage.

   (1) 131 breeds of dog are currently recognized by the American Kennel Club. (2) Dalmatians are a particularly interesting breed. (3) They are quite popular, and they have risen in popularity recently from 24th to 19th. (4) Although scholars are unsure of their exact origin, the breed may have originated in Dalmatia, a narrow strip of land along the Adriatic Sea that is populated mostly by Croatians. (5) Most scholars believe that when bands of Gypsies migrated westward to settle in Yugoslavia, the dogs traveled with them. (6) Dog-lovers are grateful now that they did.

18. Which of the following information would be most appealing to the reader who wishes to know more about the facts presented in sentence 1?

   (A) The name of a classic book about Dalmatians

   (B) The website of the American Kennel Club

   (C) The name of a book of photography that concerns Dalmatians

   (D) The reference for a classic article about Dalmatian breeding

   (E) The name of an essay about the joys of Dalmatian ownership

19. Which of the following kinds of information would contribute most to the understandability of sentence 3?

   (A) A description of why Dalmatians are popular

   (B) An analysis of whether the difference between 24th and 19th is statistically meaningful

   (C) A summary of which dogs are greater than 19th in popularity

   (D) An explanation of how the popularity of different breeds is measured

   (E) A characterization of the typical Dalmatian owner

20. Which details of sentence 4 and/or sentence 5 are in greatest need of clarification?

    (A) The geographic location of the possible origins of Dalmatians

    (B) The reasons why Dalmatians would have accompanied the Gypsies during a migration

    (C) The historical basis for the assertion that Dalmatians originated in Dalmatia

    (D) The alternative accounts of the origins of Dalmatians, as proposed by other scholars

    (E) The connections between Gypsies and Croatians, and between Yugoslavia and Dalmatia

21. Sentence 6 best serves as a transition to a paragraph that

    (A) describes and praises the characteristics of Dalmatians.

    (B) analyzes the geographical origins of other breeds.

    (C) discusses the features of the Adriatic Sea.

    (D) summarizes key issues in the care of Dalmatians.

    (E) advocates for the humane treatment of Dalmatians and other animals.

22. Which sentence is <u>least</u> clearly in need of a citation?

    (A) Sentence 1   (D) Sentence 4

    (B) Sentence 2   (E) Sentence 5

    (C) Sentence 3

Rhetorical Analysis (25%)

DIRECTIONS: The following questions test your ability to analyze writing. Some questions refer to passages, while other questions are self-contained. For each question, choose the best answer.

<u>Questions 1–6</u> refer to the following passage.

(1) The return of peace did not bring contentment to the Americans. (2) Because Congress had no means of raising a revenue or enforcing its decrees, it was unable to make itself respected either at home or abroad.

(3) For want of pay, the army became very troublesome. (4) In January 1781, there had been a mutiny of Pennsylvania and New Jersey troops, which at one moment looked very serious. (5) In March 1783, inflammatory appeals were made to the officers at the headquarters of the army at Newburgh. (6) In the spring of 1782 some of the officers, disgusted with the want of efficiency in the government, seem to have entertained a scheme for making Washington king; but Washington met the suggestion with a stern rebuke. (7) It seems to have been intended that the army should overawe Congress and seize upon the government until the delinquent states should contribute the money needed for satisfying the soldiers and other public creditors. (8) Gates either origi-nated this scheme or willingly lent himself to it, but an eloquent speech from Washington prevailed upon the officers to reject and condemn it. (John Fiske, *The War of Independence*. Boston: Houghton Mifflin and Company, 1889, pp. 182-183.)

1. The purpose of sentence 1 is to

    (A) introduce the general theme of the passage.

    (B) demonstrate the writer's authority on the subject of the passage.

    (C) describe an idea that the author refutes later in the passage.

    (D) undermine the central claim of the passage.

    (E) present the idea that peace equals contentment.

2. In context, which of the following revisions of sentence 2 (reproduced below) would be preferable?

    Because Congress had no means of raising a revenue or enforcing its decrees, it was unable to make itself respected either at home or abroad.

    (A) Because Congress had no means of enforcing its decrees, it was unable to make itself respected either at home or abroad.

    (B) Because Congress had no means of raising a revenue, it was unable to make itself respected either at home or abroad.

    (C) Because Congress had no means of enforcing its decrees, it was unable to make itself respected.

    (D) Because Congress had no means of raising a revenue, it was unable to make itself respected.

    (E) Congress was unable to make itself respected.

3. What does sentence 4 contribute to the passage?

   (A) It provides for a transition between Sentences 3 and 5.

   (B) It provides an example of the statement made in Sentence 3.

   (C) It qualifies the assertion made in Sentence 3.

   (D) It provides background for Sentence 5.

   (E) It contributes nothing to the passage.

4. In context, "want" in sentences 3 and 6 most nearly means

   (A) desire   (D) standards

   (B) interest   (E) lack

   (C) abundance

5. Which of the following seems <u>least</u> clearly conveyed by the passage?

   (A) The reason for the army's discontent.

   (B) Details of concerns about the government's efficiency.

   (C) The nature of the events that occurred between 1781 and 1783.

   (D) The potential for significant political instability.

   (E) Washington's personal view on a proposed increase in the army's power.

6. Which of the following summarizes the relationship between Washington and the army most clearly implied by this passage?

   (A) Washington and the army had a perpetually adversarial relationship.

   (B) The army did not respect Washington's authority.

   (C) Washington had considerable influence over the army.

   (D) The army regularly consulted with Washington about matters of national importance.

   (E) Washington was not interested in the army's views of political matters.

Questions 7–13 refer to the following essay.

(1) Most teenagers do not get in trouble on a regular basis, and few of us actually commit crimes. (2) The news media should give teenagers the publicity

we deserve, instead of just focusing on our bad behavior. (3) For example, in my home town recently, a local youth group visited a retirement home one day in order to sing songs and chat with the residents. (4) This story was only reported on the second page of the local paper. (5) Another example is the Eagle Scout project of a teenager named Jay Jones, who made beautiful signs for the city to denote locations of public buildings such as city hall, the library, and the police station. (6) Did anyone from the news show up for the dedication of the signs? (7) A reporter was across town that day gathering information on a traffic accident caused by a teen-aged driver. (8) The story of the accident made the front page of the newspaper, of course, while the Eagle Scout's signs were not mentioned anywhere. (9) These examples show that the news media is totally unfair and that adults don't respect teenagers. (10) Our good works are passed over. (11) Truly, we deserve recognition for our positive contributions to society.

7. Which of the following, if inserted between sentences 1 and 2, would increase the persuasiveness of the first paragraph.

    (A) The crime rate among teenagers is actually pretty low.

    (B) We are not all bad; in fact, some of us are good.

    (C) At the same time, many of us do good works for which we receive little or no publicity.

    (D) Moreover, it is rare to see a teenager convicted of a highly serious crime.

    (E) We are trying our best every day to be good citizens.

8. In context, which of the following terms, inserted before the phrase "bad behavior" in sentence 2, would increase the coherence of the sentence?

    (A) well-known   (D) frequent

    (B) occasional   (E) notoriously

    (C) underreported

9. Why do sentences 3 and 4 fail to help the author develop the main theme of the essay?

    (A) The author does not acknowledge that the teenagers' visit might have been mandatory rather than voluntary.

    (B) Since the teenagers' visit took place in the author's home town, the author might be biased.

(C) The fact that the teenagers' visit was reported on the second rather than first page of the newspaper suggests that they were ignored.

(D) It is difficult to understand why the teenagers' visit can be considered an example of good behavior.

(E) The fact that the teenagers' visit was reported in the newspaper seems to contradict the main theme of the passage.

10. Which of the following sentences could be deleted without affecting the coherence of the essay?

(A) Sentence 2

(B) Sentence 3

(C) Sentence 4

(D) Sentence 6

(E) Sentence 8

11. In context, sentence 8 serves to

(A) introduce a new theme into the essay.

(B) indicate similarities in the way that the news media covers stories that involve teenagers.

(C) juxtapose two anecdotes that cast teenagers in an unflattering light.

(D) provide a concrete illustration of the idea discussed in the previous sentence.

(E) emphasize differences in the way the news media covers desirable versus undesirable behavior on the part of teenagers.

12. What is the main shortcoming of sentence 9?

(A) The conclusion it draws is much broader than warranted by the examples in the passage.

(B) It fails to acknowledge any of the benefits of the news media noted in the passage.

(C) The two assertions in it contradict each other.

(D) It reflects a somewhat negative tone regarding the news media and adults in general.

(E) It is inaccurate concerning the relationship between adults and teenagers.

13. Which of the following best describes the organization of the passage as a whole?

    (A) A problem is described and solutions are discussed.

    (B) An assertion is made and examples are provided.

    (C) A hypothesis is presented and challenged by available data.

    (D) Two theories are proposed and evidence in support of one theory is discussed.

    (E) A question is developed and answers are evaluated.

Questions 14–19 refer to the following essay.

(1) Born in Crete in 1541, Domenikos Theotokopoulos grew up to become one of the world's great painters. (2) Known as *El Greco,* meaning "The Greek," he moved to Spain around 1577 after several frustrating years in Venice and Rome and eventually became known as a Spanish painter. (3) El Greco's relocation to Toledo, Spain, was probably due to his inability to obtain important commissions in Italy. (4) However, at first he had no better luck in Spain. (5) Paintings were supposed to inspire prayer and teach religious doctrine, but El Greco did not always adhere to scripture. (6) For example, he painted three Marys in *The Disrobing of Christ,* set biblical scenes in Toledo, and depicted Roman soldiers in 16th-century armor. (7) As a result, he lost the patronage of the Toledo Cathedral. (8) Later, he was able to gain the respect and patronage of Toledo's intellectuals. (9) Support from this liberal audience probably allowed the artist more freedom in developing his own style, which is characterized by elongated forms, graceful lines, and metallic colors with white highlights.

14. Which of the following words, inserted at the beginning of sentence 2, smoothes the transition between the first two sentences?

    (A) Although   (D) Therefore

    (B) Clearly   (E) Once

    (C) Better

15. The purpose of Sentence 3 is to

    (A) explain an action that was introduced in sentence 2.

    (B) evaluate a theory about the painter's life.

    (C) contrast two different points of view.

(D) analyze the relationship between individual and society.

(E) illustrate key influences on the painter's style.

16. Which of the following phrases, added to the beginning of sentence 5, most improves the clarity of the sentence?

(A) According to some,

(D) At that time,

(B) As often asserted,

(E) Arguably,

(C) Thus,

17. Which of the following is <u>not</u> explained in the first six sentences?

(A) Why the painter is called El Greco

(B) Where the painter was born

(C) Why the painter struggled to obtain commissions

(D) Where the painter flourished

(E) Why the painter did not adhere to scripture

18. Which of the following is most clearly implied by the term "probably" in sentences 3 and 9?

(A) The author has not read biographical portraits of El Greco very closely.

(B) El Greco experienced much uncertainty in his development as an artist.

(C) Some details of El Greco's life and personal choices are not known with certainty.

(D) El Greco rarely spoke definitively about his career as an artist.

(E) The author does not wish to speak very decisively about the topic.

19. Sentence 9 is most likely to serve as a transition to

(A) a description of late 16th-century Toledo.

(B) a discussion of El Greco's paintings.

(C) an analysis of the artist's role in society.

(D) an account of El Greco's voyage from Italy to Spain.

(E) a critique of religious influences on the visual arts.

Questions 20–23 refer to the following essay.

(1) Alexander the Great's boyhood was shaped by two strong parents. (2) Alexander's father, King Philip of Macedonia, was a consummate general whose armies conquered Greece and made Macedonia a powerful force in the ancient world. (3) Taught to read, sing, and debate in Greek before he was ten, Alexander was tutored by the philosopher Aristotle from ages thirteen to sixteen. (4) As a young man, Alexander was fearless and showed great promise. (5) He was evidently perceptive as well. (6) At age thirteen, he was given a horse that no one had been able to touch, much less ride. (7) After noticing that the horse shied every time it saw its own shadow, Alexander turned it toward the sun and was able to tame it. (8) He called the horse Bucephalus, meaning ox-head, and kept the horse for many years, riding him into numerous battles.

20. Which of the following would be most critical to include in the first paragraph?

    (A) Discussion of what Alexander learned from Aristotle

    (B) Anecdotes about Macedonian culture

    (C) Information about Alexander's other strong parent

    (D) Commentary on Macedonia's role in the ancient world

    (E) Description of King Phillip's personality

21. In sentence 2, "consummate" most nearly means

    (A) hesitant   (D) skilled

    (B) overbearing   (E) inexperienced

    (C) modest

22. Which of the following would most improve sentence 4?

    (A) A description of the areas in which Alexander showed promise

    (B) The use of a flashier adjective other than "great"

    (C) Replacement of "young man" with "youth"

    (D) An explanation of what "fearless" means

    (E) The addition of "reportedly" after "was"

23. In sentence 5, what does the word "evidently" allude to?

    (A) The tutoring that Alexander received from Aristotle

    (B) The name that Alexander gave to his horse

    (C) The author's personal opinion of Alexander

    (D) The military talent of King Phillip

    (E) The anecdote described in Sentences 6 and 7

ESSAYS

TIME: 70 Minutes

You will have a total of 70 minutes to write two argumentative essays. You will have 30 minutes to complete the first essay, which is to be based on your own reading, experience or observations, and 40 minutes to complete the second essay, which requires you to synthesize two sources that are provided. Although you are free to begin writing at any point, it is better to take the time you need to plan your essays and to do the required reading than it is to begin writing immediately.

First Essay

DIRECTIONS: The old saying, "Experience is the best teacher," suggests that people will benefit more from learning on the job or in the world than from formal education in the academic setting of the classroom. Write an essay in which you discuss the relative importance of academic and experiential learning. Support your discussion with examples from your reading, observations, or personal experience.

Second Essay

Introduction

There are many different views on the meaning of patriotism (i.e., love of one's country). Some writers assert that patriotism is expressed by devotion and service to one's country. Other writers hold that patriotism is expressed in the form of dissent that inspires other citizens to question their beliefs and actions. Both views assume that patriotism is motivated by the desire to improve the moral strength of one's country; the views differ as to whether support or dissent tends to be the preferable means of improvement.

Assignment

Read the following quotations carefully. Then write an essay in which you develop a position on whether support or dissent is closer to the true meaning of patriotism. Be sure to incorporate and cite both of the accompanying quotations as you develop your position.

"He loves his country best who strives to make it best." —Robert G. Ingersoll

"Dissent is the highest form of patriotism." —Howard Zinn

Practice Test 1

Answer Key

Conventions of Standard Written English

1. **C** The correct word would be "in."

2. **A** A comma is needed after "Steinbeck," given that one already appears after "writer."

3. **E** The sentence contains no errors.

4. **E** This sentence contains no errors.

5. **C** The correct word would be "best."

6. **B** The correct word would be "that."

7. **D** The correct phrase would be "to add."

8. **C** The correct phrase would be "were all."

9. **C** Authors can "imply," "indicate," or otherwise convey an idea. It is the reader who makes inferences.

Revision Skills

1. **B** "And" is needed, since Sentence 3 presents a contrast between the two recently discovered dinosaurs and Triceratops.

2. **C** Option C is the only option in which the entire statement about the horns and their functions are clearly attributed to paleontologists.

3. **A** Relocation of Sentence 8 after Sentence 1 is the only place where Sentence 8 fits into the passage without disrupting the narrative flow.

4. **B** Option B is the only option that is both grammatically correct and stylistically desirable.

5. **C** "Although" emphasizes the contrast between the two clauses in Sentence 11.

6. **E** In context, Option E is the only option that makes sense.

7. **C** Option C is the only option that is both grammatically correct and stylistically desirable.

8. **D** Option D is the only option that is both grammatically correct and supportive of the contrast between the two parts of the sentence.

9. **A** Reversing the order allows the action of applying of stucco to be mentioned before the thickness of the applied stucco is discussed.

10. **D** Option D is the only option that is both grammatically correct and coherent.

11. **B** Option B is the only option that is both grammatically correct and stylistically desirable.

12. **B** Option B is the only option that correctly indicates the relationship between Sentence 8 and the preceding sentence.

13. **A** Reference to a "variety" of colors makes Option A most persuasive concerning the merits of stucco.

14. **D** Since the passage extols the virtues of stucco finish, Option D is the best choice.

Improving Sentences

15. **B** Option B is the only option that is grammatically correct.

16. **E** Option E is the only option that is both grammatically correct and coherent.

17. **C** Option C is the only option that is grammatically correct.

18. **A** Option A is the only option that is grammatically correct.

19. **D** Option D is the only option that is grammatically correct and unambiguous as to who has the necessary skills.

20. **C** Option C is the only option that is grammatically correct and makes use of active voice.

21. **E** Option E is the only option that is grammatically correct.

22. **A** Option A is the only option that is both grammatically correct and stylistically desirable.

23. **B** Option B is the only option that is grammatically correct.

24. **B** Option B is the only option that is grammatically correct.

25. **D** Option D is the only option that is grammatically correct.

26. **D** Option D is the only option that is grammatically correct.

27. **E** Option E is the only option that is both grammatically correct and stylistically desirable.

28. **B**   Option B is the only option that is both grammatically correct and stylistically desirable.

29. **E**   Option E is the only option that is both grammatically correct and stylistically desirable.

30. **C**   Option C is the only option that is both grammatically correct and stylistically desirable.

31. **D**   Option D is the only option that is both grammatically correct and stylistically desirable.

32. **C**   Option C is the only option that is grammatically correct.

33. **A**   Option A is the only option that is both grammatically correct and coherent.

34. **D**   Option D is the only option that is grammatically correct.

35. **B**   Option B is the only option that is grammatically correct.

36. **E**   Option E is the only option that is grammatically correct.

Ability to Use Source Materials

1. **B**   "Are known to" does not contribute any information that is not already implicit in the sentence.

2. **A**   The quoted phrases are evidently noted in Ellis (2004).

3. **D**   Sentences 2 and 3 each provide examples of the statement made in Sentence 1.

4. **C**   Options A and E are inaccurate. Evidently, Grizzard discussed the two facts about Washington described in Sentence 5, and thus Option C is most likely to be accurate.

5. **E**   Option E is the only accurate option.

6. **B**   Although Sentence 6 asserts that Washingtonian precedents were, in part, reflections of his personality, no examples are given.

7. **C**   Given the citation format, it is evident that *Developmental Psychology* is a journal.

8. **E**   Option E is the only accurate option.

9. **A**   Option A is the only accurate option.

10. **E**   Option E is the only accurate option.

11. **C**   The phrase "apical dominance" is unlikely to be understood by anyone other than an expert reader.

12. **B** Option B is the only accurate option.

13. **D** Since each use of the word "some" refers to different authors, it is clear that not all authors agree about the physical dimensions that should be included in the definition of a tree.

14. **A** Use of the phrase "other authors" clarifies the fact that two sets of authors are compared.

15. **B** Option B is the only grammatically correct and sensible option.

16. **B** Option B is the only accurate option.

17. **C** In context, Option C is most likely to be correct.

18. **B** Since the American Kennel Club is mentioned as the source of the information in Sentence 1, the website of this organization would be most appealing to interested readers.

19. **D** No information about the definition or measurement of popularity is given in Sentence 3.

20. **E** Relationships between Gypsies and Croatians, and between Yugoslavia and Dalmatia, are hinted at in these sentences but not made clear.

21. **A** Option A seems most likely in light of the favorable allusion to Dalmatians in Sentence 6.

22. **B** Sentence 2 presents a highly general opinion expressed by the author.

Rhetorical Analysis

1. **A** Option A is the only accurate option.

2. **D** The discussion that follows Sentence 2 focuses on military unrest arising from lack of pay. Option D is preferable owing to its sole focus on revenue and on lack of respect for Congress at home.

3. **B** Option B is the only accurate option.

4. **E** In context, Option E is the only accurate option.

5. **B** No information is provided about governmental efficiency.

6. **C** Support for Option C can be found in Sentences 6 and 8.

7. **C** Option C succinctly expresses the theme of the passage.

8. **B** Since the sentence appears to assert that the news media should focus on good behavior rather than just negative behavior, the assertion will be clearer if it is emphasized that the bad behavior is occasional.

9. **E**   Option E is the only accurate option.

10. **D**   Sentence 6 presents a rhetorical question that disrupts the narrative flow from Sentence 5 to Sentence 7.

11. **E**   Option E is the only accurate option.

12. **A**   In Sentence 9, the description of the news media as "totally" unfair, and the reference to "adults" in general following a discussion that had been restricted to the news media, both render the conclusion of the sentence much too broad relative to the examples discussed in the passage.

13. **B**   Option B is the only accurate option.

14. **C**   Given that El Greco's original name is given in Sentence 1, Option C is preferable.

15. **A**   Option A is the only accurate option.

16. **D**   Option D would make explicit the fact that the sentence pertains to El Greco's time, and would thus help the reader understand Sentences 6 and 7.

17. **E**   Option E is the only accurate option.

18. **C**   Option C is the only option that can be safely inferred.

19. **B**   Option B is most likely to be accurate, given the focus of Sentence 9 on the details of El Greco's style.

20. **C**   Since "two" strong parents are mentioned in Sentence 1 but only one parent is described in the first paragraph, Option C is correct.

21. **D**   In context, Option D is the only accurate option.

22. **A**   Options B–E would contribute virtually nothing to the passage.

23. **E**   Perceptiveness is implied by Alexander's behavior in the anecdote described in Sentences 6 and 7.

Answer Key for Essays

Sample First Essay

Perhaps I am old-fashioned, but I believe that academic learning is essential to personal growth. Nothing can substitute for the information we obtain from the classroom. Our capacity to be informed, productive citizens relies on what we have learned in school, from basic reading and math skills acquired during the early years all the way up to sophisticated information about nature and society we learn in high school. Academic learning is not infallible, of course. When I was a child, I learned that there are nine planets. Now there are eight, according to astronomers. But the fact that there are nine or eight planets is not something one could learn by walking outside at night and looking up into the sky. We learn such facts in school, and we would need to attend school for many years before we could examine the sky with a telescope and formulate an experienced-based opinion about the number of planets. Along the way, we would also need to learn how to use the telescope, how to make astronomical calculations, and how to do a number of other things we could not figure out on our own.

Although academic learning is critical, I believe that learning from experience is important, too. Each type of learning is important in a different way. School prepares us for life. It gives us the foundation for safe, happy, productive lives. But outside of the classroom, we must continue to learn about life as we live it, and a critical source of learning after graduation will be experience. We would not be able to function without experiential learning. My father is a typical example. He is a police officer, and he is fond of saying that he learned more in his first six days on the job than he did during his entire six months of training at the police academy. When he makes comments like this, he means to say that he has learned things on the street that he wasn't taught in the police academy. His point is that academic learning is insufficient. But it is still the foundation for what he does. He wouldn't deny the importance of his academic training.

Although experiential learning becomes the main source of learning once we finish school, there will continue to be opportunities to advance our knowledge that are more academic than experiential. When we read a book or consult with an experienced co-worker, for example, we are engaging in what might be called academic learning rather than just acquiring information through direct personal experience. These examples show that academic learning is not limited to classroom settings. I believe that becoming an informed, productive citizen depends on continuing to learn in the academic sense and not just experiential learning. Academic learning can enrich our personal experiences, just as our experiences can extend what we learn through academic methods.

Commentary

Look back at the directions for this essay. You will see that the directions include two requests:

1. *Discuss the relative importance of experiential and academic learning.*

2. *Support your discussion with examples from your reading.*

The author of this essay addresses the first request throughout the essay. Paragraph 1 describes the importance of academic learning. Paragraph 2 describes the separate importance of experiential learning. Paragraph 3 continues to contrast the two types of learning, and closes with a brief comment on how they are related.

The author addresses the second request by describing examples in each paragraph of the essay, including personal examples (paragraphs 1 and 2) as well as general examples (paragraph 3).

Notice that the essay is clear, well-organized, grammatically varied, and free of errors. The author shows good command of the language in the choice of words and phrases.

Suggestions for Essay Development for the Second Essay

A good place to begin is to read these quotes, to be sure you understand the similarities and differences between each point of view, and then to think about the position you will develop in your own essay. Will you side with one of the authors? Will you develop a position that represents a compromise between their views? Or will you develop a third position that is to some extent separate from theirs.

The next step is to plan your essay. Although your time is limited, you should take a few minutes to create an informal outline that will guide your writing. The outline should identify key points and examples and indicate the order in which they will be discussed.

Below you will see an outline for one particular essay that could be written. This outline is based on the premise that the points of view represented in the two quotations are not as inconsistent as they might seem at first glance.

The outline below is relatively detailed and written in complete sentences so that you can follow the progression of ideas. An outline written during the actual test would not need to be as elaborate.

1.	Patriotism consists of more than just words. Anybody can talk the talk. True patriotism means serving one's country through action, as Ingersoll suggests.

2.	At first glance, Ingersoll and Zinn seem to present opposing views: Ingersoll's patriot supports his or her country, while Zinn's patriot expresses dissent. For example, when the country is at war, Ingersoll's patriot would do extra work to support the war effort, while Zinn's patriot would openly question the rationale for war.

3.	A deeper interpretation of Ingersoll's comment shows that the two writers do not necessarily have opposing views. What does it mean to "strive" to make one's country "best"? It could mean supporting the country's actions blindly, of course. But it could also mean promoting the country's interests through everything that one says and does. Arguably, the greatest good one can do for one's country is to dissent from mainstream views whenever possible, so that other citizens can question their assumptions and consider whether to alter their behavior. Even if the dissenter does not change anything, dissent keeps other citizens thinking and amenable to ideas for improvement they may not have considered. In a time of war, for example, the dissenter helps other citizens question whether involvement in the war continues to be best for the country. Dissent in such cases can be effective if the dissenter is tactful, coherent, and persuasive.

4.	In sum, Zinn can be thought of as describing a method (i.e., dissent) by which a person can meet Ingersoll's criterion for patriotism (i.e., striving to make one's country best). The true meaning of patriotism is striving to make one's country best by means of tactful, coherent, and persuasive dissent from mainstream views.

CLEP College Composition Modular

Practice Test 2

TIME: 90 Minutes

Conventions of Standard Written English (10%)

DIRECTIONS: The following sentences test your knowledge of grammar, usage, diction (choice of words), and idiom. Note that some sentences are correct, and no sentence contains more than one error. Read each sentence carefully, paying particular attention to the underlined portions. You will find that the error, if there is one, is underlined. Assume that elements of the sentence that are not underlined are correct and cannot be changed. In choosing answers, follow the requirements of standard written English. If there is an error, select the one underlined part that must be changed to make the sentence correct. If there is no error, select "No error."

1. He enjoyed <u>the music of</u> Muddy Waters more than that <u>of</u> other blues artists
             A   B

   <u>such as</u> Albert Collins <u>and</u> Robert Cray. <u>No error</u>
     C   D   E

2. People <u>can become</u> very <u>susceptible to</u> colds if <u>they</u> do not get <u>enough</u>
           A   B   C   D

   rest. <u>No error</u>
       E

3. Estuaries <u>are bodies of water</u> that are <u>found</u> at <u>the mouth</u> of rivers <u>that empty</u>
            A   B   C   D

   into the ocean. <u>No error</u>
           E

4. <u>Although he</u> is now one of the <u>luminescents</u> of world literature, Kafka published
     A   B

   <u>very</u> little <u>during his lifetime</u>. <u>No error</u>
     C   D   E

5. <u>When adults</u>, they recalled <u>their nine years</u> in Chicago with <u>a mixture of</u>
       A   B   C

   contentment <u>and</u> nostalgia. <u>No error</u>
         D   E

6. "Always forgive your enemies," <u>wrote</u> Oscar Wilde <u>in</u> the <u>late</u> 19th <u>century,</u> "as

                                     A   B   C   D

    nothing annoys them so much." <u>No error</u>

                                     E

7. The sound <u>that a</u> functioning wind turbine <u>makes</u> does not <u>come from</u> its gear

                   A   B   C

    box but <u>because of</u> the movement of its blades through the air. <u>No error</u>

                 D   E

8. Tuna, salmon, and halibut are <u>among</u> the many <u>types of</u> fish <u>that is</u> especially

                                  A   B   C

    popular <u>in</u> sushi restaurants. <u>No error</u>

          D   E

9. The mother <u>asked her</u> toddler <u>to stop interrupting</u> <u>whereas</u> the child <u>refused</u>.

                 A   B   C   D

    <u>No error</u>

    E

Revision Skills (40%)

> **DIRECTIONS:** The following passages are early drafts of essays. Read each passage and then answer the questions that follow. Some questions refer to particular sentences or parts of sentences and ask you to improve sentence structure or diction (word choice). Other questions refer to the entire essay or parts of the essay and ask you to consider the essay's organization, development, or effectiveness of language. In selecting your answers, follow the conventions of standard written English.

<u>Questions 1–6</u> refer to the following passage.

(1) The bolero inspired Maurice Ravel to create the ballet *Bolero*. (2) An impassioned folk dance popular in Spain. (3) The sister of the legendary Russian dancer Vaslav Nijinsky choreographed this classic ballet created by Ravel. (4) The bolero as we know it is credited to Anton Bolsche and Sebastian Cerezo around the mid-1700s. (5) Although almost no one has seen Ravel's *Bolero*, the music from this ballet continues to enjoy immense popularity and is performed regularly throughout the world. (6) The driving force of this musical composition is the snare drum. (7) The percussionist begins by playing the rhythm of the bolero dance, a pattern consisting of two measures and six beats, as quietly as possible. (8) At the beginning, other instruments pick up the rhythm as the intensity builds. (9) The first flute then introduces the melody, while instruments such as the clarinet, bassoon, and piccolo contribute individual parts.

1. In context, which of the following is the best way to combine sentences 1 and 2?

    (A) The bolero inspired Maurice Ravel to create the ballet *Bolero*, an impassioned folk dance popular in Spain.

    (B) The bolero is an impassioned folk dance popular in Spain, and the bolero inspired Maurice Ravel to create the ballet *Bolero*.

    (C) The bolero, an impassioned folk dance popular in Spain, inspired Maurice Ravel to create the ballet *Bolero*.

    (D) An impassioned folk dance popular in Spain inspired Maurice Ravel to create the ballet *Bolero,* and it was the bolero.

    (E) An impassioned folk dance popular in Spain, it was the bolero that inspired Maurice Ravel to create the ballet *Bolero*.

2. In context, which of the following is the best revision of the underlined portion of sentence 3 (reproduced below)?

    The sister of the legendary Russian dancer Vaslav Nijinsky choreographed this classic ballet created by Ravel.

    (A) this classic ballet

    (B) this classic ballet of Ravel's

    (C) this classic ballet that Ravel created

    (D) this classic ballet from Ravel's oeuvre

    (E) this classic ballet inspired by the bolero

3. In sentence 5, the word "enjoy" most nearly means

    (A) appreciate   (D) create

    (B) have   (E) receive

    (C) deserve

4. Which sentence, if deleted, would increase the coherence of the passage?

    (A) Sentence 1   (D) Sentence 5

    (B) Sentence 3   (E) Sentence 6

    (C) Sentence 4

5. In context, which of the following revisions to the underlined portion of sentence 8 (reproduced below) would increase the coherence of the sentence?

At the beginning, other instruments pick up the rhythm as the intensity builds.

(A) At the outset, other

(B) Then, these

(C) At the beginning, the

(D) Then, other

(E) At this point, the

6. In context, the deletion of which word or phrase in sentence 9 (reproduced below) would make the passage clearer?

The first flute then introduces the melody, while instruments such as the clarinet, bassoon, and piccolo contribute individual parts.

(A) first

(B) then

(C) instruments such as

(D) such as the clarinet, bassoon, and piccolo

(E) individual

Questions 7–17 refer to the following essay.

(1) Although most historical accounts state that the birthplace of Christopher Columbus was Genoa, Italy, writers have argued that Columbus was born elsewhere. (2) Spain, Portugal, and France have each been cited. (3) Which is to say each has been considered the birthplace of the famous explorer. (4) Contrary to popular myth, most educated people of the 1400s believed that the world is round. (5) Columbus didn't have to sell his benefactors on that idea. (6) What he was trying to sell was a faster route to Asia. (7) In his day, trade with China and India either required a traditional overland route, or a newer route by ship around the southern tip of Africa. (8) His four voyages between Spain and the Americas were all motivated by a desire to reach Asia. (9) Through his life, Columbus always believed that he had reached Asia on those voyages. (10) Another common myth is that Queen Isabella of Spain had to sell her jewels in order to underwrite the four voyages. (11) King Ferdinand and Queen Isabella were experiencing financial difficulties. (12) They were able to cover their share of Columbus's expenses through funds from the royal treasury. (13) Columbus's first landing site in America was probably the Bahama Islands, although there are disagreements about which island Columbus reached first, Samana Cay or San Salvador being two possibilities that scholars have debated. (14)

Easily the most famous myth about Columbus is that he was the first outsider to set foot in the Americas. (15) Approximately 500 years before Columbus, for example, Leif Ericson not only landed on the northeastern coast of Canada but established a settlement there.

7. Which of the following is the best revision of the underlined portion of sentence 1 (reproduced below)?

    Although most historical accounts state that the birthplace of Christopher Columbus was Genoa, Italy, <u>writers</u> have argued that Columbus was born elsewhere.

    (A) these writers

    (B) although writers

    (C) no writers

    (D) most writers

    (E) a few writers

8. Which of the following is the best way to combine sentences 2 and 3 (reproduced below)?

    Spain, Portugal, and France have each been cited. Which is to say each has been considered the birthplace of the famous explorer.

    (A) Spain, Portugal, and France have each been considered the birthplace.

    (B) Spain, Portugal, and France have each been cited; each has been considered the birthplace of the famous explorer.

    (C) Spain, Portugal, and France have each been cited; each has been considered.

    (D) Spain, Portugal, and France have each been cited as the birthplace of the famous explorer.

    (E) Spain, Portugal, and France have each been cited; which is to say each has been considered the birthplace of the famous explorer.

9. What is the "popular myth" referred to in sentence 4?

    (A) The world is flat.

    (B) Educated people in the 1400s considered the world to be flat.

    (C) Columbus had to convince his benefactors that the world is round.

    (D) A faster route to Asia would not be useful.

    (E) Columbus reached Asia on his voyages.

10. Which of the following can be inferred from sentences 6 and 7?

    (A) The overland route from Europe to Asia was not as fast as the route by ship around the southern tip of Africa.

    (B) The route Columbus hoped to find would take the same amount of time as the route by ship around the southern tip of Africa.

    (C) The overland route from Europe to Asia was not as fast as the route Columbus hoped to find.

    (D) The route Columbus hoped to find would take the same amount of time as the overland route from Europe to Asia.

    (E) The overland route from Europe to Asia took the same amount of time as the route by ship around the southern tip of Africa.

11. Which of the following sentences can be deleted without diminishing the coherence of the passage?

    (A) Sentence 4   (D) Sentence 8

    (B) Sentence 5   (E) Sentence 9

    (C) Sentence 6

12. Which of the following is the best revision of the underlined portion of sentence 9 (reproduced below)?

    Through his life, Columbus always believed that he had reached Asia on those voyages.

    (A) Across   (D) During

    (B) Over   (E) Throughout

    (C) In

13. In sentence 10, the closest synonym for "underwrite" would be

    (A) finance   (D) motivate

    (B) initiate   (E) justify

    (C) popularize

14. In context, which of the following is the best way to combine sentences 11 and 12 (reproduced below)?

    King Ferdinand and Queen Isabella were experiencing financial difficulties. They were able to cover their share of Columbus's expenses through funds from the royal treasury.

    (A) King Ferdinand and Queen Isabella were experiencing financial difficulties; they were able to cover their share of Columbus's expenses through funds from the royal treasury.

    (B) King Ferdinand and Queen Isabella were experiencing financial difficulties, and were able to cover their share of Columbus's expenses through funds from the royal treasury.

    (C) Although King Ferdinand and Queen Isabella were experiencing financial difficulties, they were able to cover their share of Columbus's expenses through funds from the royal treasury.

    (D) Even so, King Ferdinand and Queen Isabella were experiencing financial difficulties, but they were able to cover their share of Columbus's expenses through funds from the royal treasury.

    (E) If King Ferdinand and Queen Isabella were experiencing financial difficulties, they were also able to cover their share of Columbus's expenses through funds from the royal treasury.

15. Which of the following is the best way to divide sentence 13 (reproduced below) into separate sentences?

    Columbus's first landing site in America was probably the Bahama Islands, although scholars disagree about which island Columbus reached first, Samana Cay and San Salvador being two possibilities that scholars have debated.

    (A) Columbus's first landing site in America was probably the Bahama Islands. There are disagreements about which island Columbus reached first, two possibilities that scholars have debated being Samana Cay and San Salvador.

    (B) Columbus's first landing site in America was probably the Bahama Islands, although there are disagreements about which island Columbus reached first. Two possibilities that scholars have debated are Samana Cay and San Salvador.

    (C) Columbus's first landing site in America was probably the Bahama Islands, although there are disagreements about which island

Columbus reached first, and there are two possibilities. The possibilities that scholars have debated are Samana Cay and San Salvador.

(D) Columbus's first landing site in America was probably the Bahama Islands. There are disagreements about which island Columbus reached first, two possibilities that scholars have debated being Samana Cay and San Salvador.

(E) Columbus's first landing site in America was probably the Bahama Islands, although there are disagreements about which island Columbus reached first, and two possibilities that scholars have debated. These possibilities are Samana Cay and San Salvador.

16. In context, the best synonym for the word "Easily" in sentence 14 would be

(A) Rightfully   (D) By far

(B) Perhaps   (E) Simply

(C) Some say

17. Which of the following is best to revise the underlined portion of sentence 15 (reproduced below)?

Approximately 500 years before Columbus, for example, Leif Ericson not only landed at the northeastern coast of Canada but established a settlement there.

(A) landed in   (D) arrived on

(B) reached   (E) came upon

(C) sailed

Improving Sentences

DIRECTIONS: The following sentences test correctness and effectiveness of expression. In choosing your answers, follow the requirements of standard written English: that is, pay attention to grammar, diction (choice of words), sentence construction, and punctuation. In each of the following sentences, part of the sentence or the entire sentence is underlined. Beneath each sentence you will find five versions of the underlined part. The first option repeats the original; the other four options present different versions. Choose the option that best expresses the meaning of the original sentence. If you think the original is better than any of the alternatives, choose the first option; otherwise, choose one of the other options. Your choice should produce the most effective sentence—one that is clear and precise.

18. There are many kinds of bullying, <u>they include</u> gossip, physical aggression, and cyberbullying.

    (A) they include

    (B) including

    (C) these kinds include

    (D) that include

    (E) these are including

19. Last year, the Cincinnati team <u>play</u> especially well.

    (A) play

    (B) plays

    (C) played

    (D) do play

    (E) had play

20. In the photograph, Monet <u>is standing beside his lily pond, in the sunlight</u>.

    (A) is standing beside his lily pond, in the sunlight.

    (B) is in the sunlight standing beside his lily pond.

    (C) is standing beside, in the sunlight, his lily pond.

    (D) is standing, beside his lily pond, in the sunlight.

    (E) is standing in the sunlight beside his lily pond.

21. Cecilia is smarter than most children her age, <u>and she is especially</u> sweet-natured as well.

    (A) and she is especially

    (B) and especially

    (C) and, she is especially

    (D) and she especially

    (E) especially

22. Socrates's most famous student <u>is as we know Plato</u>.

    (A) is as we know Plato

    (B) is Plato as we know

    (C) is, as we know, Plato

    (D) is as we know, Plato

    (E) is, Plato as we know

23. Yesterday he told me that of all the Belgian cities he visited last year, Antwerp was his <u>favorite city</u>.

    (A) favorite city

    (B) favorite of all of them

    (C) favorite out of all the cities

    (D) favorite

    (E) favorite among the cities

24. The governor's indifference to our political crises <u>are</u> increasingly problematic.

    (A) are

    (B) were

    (C) seem

    (D) is

    (E) sound

25. Pixar Studios has created many animated feature <u>films, *Finding Nemo*</u> was my son's favorite film.

    (A) films, *Finding Nemo*

    (B) films; *Finding Nemo*

    (C) films and *Finding Nemo*

    (D) films but *Finding Nemo*

    (E) films, though *Finding Nemo*

26. John is an especially <u>thinking</u> man.

    (A) thinking

    (B) thinkful

    (C) thought-of

    (D) thoughtful

    (E) thinkable

27. Sheronica became a scientist, <u>whereas</u> her sister Mary pursued a career in business.

    (A) whereas

    (B) likewise

    (C) notwithstanding

    (D) still

    (E) while

28. Thanksgiving <u>is</u> an annual tradition in the United States since 1863.

    (A) is

    (B) was

    (C) has been

    (D) would be

    (E) will be

29. In the 14th century, Chaucer invented a poetic <u>form known as</u> rhyme royal.

    (A) form known as

    (B) form, and it is known as

    (C) form, known as

    (D) form, that is known as

    (E) form, which is known as

30. Near the end of the game, with time running <u>away</u>, the coach made a critical substitution.

    (A) away

    (B) off

    (C) out

    (D) on

    (E) low

31. Who could say <u>if</u> the girl had been wise in choosing to attend Harvard rather than Yale?

    (A) if

    (B) as

    (C) but

    (D) whether

    (E) then

32. Because the soldier had fought with so much courage and selflessness, his platoon unanimously agreed that the medal of valor he received was <u>well-determined</u>.

    (A) well-determined

    (B) well-justified

    (C) well-conceived

    (D) well-considered

    (E) well-earned

33. In the field of psychology, the analysis of dreams was dominated at one time by Freud's classic 1899 monograph *The Interpretation of Dreams,* <u>but</u> in recent years the influence of this text has waned.

    (A) but

    (B) still

    (C) however

    (D) nonetheless

    (E) thus

34. She loves hockey and <u>lacrosse and</u> other sports intrigue her as well.

   (A) lacrosse and

   (B) lacrosse;

   (C) lacrosse,

   (D) lacrosse; and,

   (E) lacrosse; and;

35. Baseball is popular in the United States now, but not to the extent that it <u>was once</u>.

   (A) was once.

   (B) had once been.

   (C) used to have been.

   (D) was at one time.

   (E) had one time been

36. My favorite bands and her favorite bands are almost identical; they are <u>both</u> typical of the music that was cutting-edge during the early 1990s.

   (A) both

   (B) jointly

   (C) all

   (D) only

   (E) each

Ability to Use Source Materials (25%)

> **DIRECTIONS:** The following questions test your familiarity with basic research, reference and composition skills. Some questions refer to passages, while other questions are self-contained. For each question, choose the best answer.

<u>Questions 1–5</u> refer to the following passage.

(1) Physicians are now encouraging the public to pay attention to their triglyceride levels, as high levels of triglycerides are associated with an increased risk of heart disease. (2) For example, the American Heart Association has set guidelines for triglyceride levels, defining levels of 200 or above as indicating high risk (American Heart Association, 2010). (3) Triglyceride levels may be raised by diets high in carbohydrates, and by heavy alcohol consumption (American Heart Association, 2010).

1. In context, which of the following is most needed in, immediately before, or immediately after, Sentence 1?

    (A) An indication of what constitutes high triglyceride levels.

    (B) A sense of how clearly the relationship between triglyceride levels and heart disease is understood.

    (C) A definition of triglycerides that a layperson could understand.

    (D) An example of how physicians are encouraging the public to pay attention to their triglyceride levels.

    (E) A list of foods that contribute to high triglyceride levels.

2. What kind of source is given in parentheses at the end of Sentence 2?

    (A) Website   (D) Pamphlet

    (B) Book   (E) Cannot tell

    (C) Journal article

3. What additional information would contribute most to the meaningfulness of Sentence 2?

    (A) An explanation of what the American Medical Association is.

    (B) A description of the kind of risk that is associated with triglyceride levels above 200.

    (C) A comment as to whether other medical organizations have set guidelines for triglyceride levels.

    (D) An identification of the unit of measurement to which "200" refers.

    (E) An indication of how high triglyceride levels can be.

4. In context, what is best to do with Sentence 3?

    (A) Leave it as it is.

    (B) Delete the entire sentence.

    (C) Delete the citation as well as the reference to alcohol.

    (D) Delete the citation as well as the reference to carbohydrate consumption.

    (E) Delete the citation.

5. Which of the following information, added to the end of the passage, would be most helpful to the interested reader?

    (A) Recommended levels of carbohydrate and alcohol consumption.

    (B) Strategies for reducing triglyceride levels.

    (C) Information about how and when to have triglyceride levels checked.

    (D) Description of other influences on triglyceride levels.

    (E) All of the above.

Questions 6–9 refer to the following entry from *Webster's New World Thesaurus, 3rd Edition*, 1997.

ingress, *n*. 1. [The act or right of entering] - Syn. entrance, admission, access; see **entrance** 1, **intrusion**. 2. [opening] - Syn. doorway, entry, portal; see **door** 1, **entrance** 2, **gate**.

6. What information is provided in each set of brackets?

    (A) A synonym   (D) An antonym

    (B) A definition   (E) An example

    (C) A related concept

7. What part of speech is "ingress"?

    (A) Noun   (D) Adverb

    (B) Adjective   (E) Preposition

    (C) Verb

8. In the entry above, what are the words "entrance," "admission," and "access"?

    (A) Definitions   (D) Appendix items

    (B) Examples   (E) Antonyms

    (C) Related entries

9. What does "**entrance** 2" imply?

    (A) Synonyms for "ingress" are only given in the second thesaurus entry for "entrance."

    (B) Synonyms for "ingress" can be found in the "entrance 2" subsection of "door 1."

(C) There are at least two synonyms given in the dictionary entry for "entrance."

(D) There are at least two entries given in the thesaurus for "entrance."

(E) There are at least two antonyms given in the thesaurus for "entrance."

Questions 10–22 refer to the following passage.

(1) After-school programs (ASPs) for children are increasingly viewed as a means of supporting physical, academic, social, and behavioral development. (2) According to a survey, about 15% of American students participate in some sort of structured, supervised program outside of school, and an additional 30% would participate if quality programming were available in their community (Afterschool Alliance, 2009). (3) Owing in part to growing federal support, the number of ASPs continues to expand in ways that have been clearly documented. (4) This is an important trend. (5) As ASPs proliferate, so do studies of their impact on the children they serve. (6) From a community perspective, these studies are important not only for improving program quality, but also because federal support is increasingly tied to empirically substantiated benefits (Watts, Witt, & King, 2008). (7) The psychosocial benefits of ASPs are well-documented and include, among other things, enhanced social skills (Darling, Caldwell, & Smith, 2005), greater motivation (Mahoney, Lord, & Carryl, 2005), better classroom behavior (Martin, Martin, Gibson, & Wilkins, 2007), lower rates of substance abuse (Tebes et al., 2007), and less delinquency (ibid.). (8) However, evidence for the academic benefits of ASPs is mixed. (9) Some studies show benefits for grades or achievement test scores, while others do not. (10) This is an interesting twist.

10. In context, which of the following could be justifiably included before the word "survey" in sentence 2?

    (A) extensive

    (B) local

    (C) prominent

    (D) recent

    (E) careful

11. According to the Afterschool Alliance, about what percentage of American students would be participating in ASPs now if quality programming were universally available?

    (A) 15%

    (B) 30%

    (C) 45%

    (D) 60%

    (E) 100%

12. In sentence 6, the phrase "empirically substantiated benefits" most likely refers to

(A) benefits that are substantial rather than minimal

(B) benefits that are documented by studies

(C) benefits that are federally supported

(D) benefits that have no negative side effects

(E) benefits that are understandable

13. What does the "et al." in the next-to-last parentheses of sentence 7 indicate?

(A) Tebes's work in 2007 is an example of a study on the impact of ASPs on substance abuse.

(B) Tebes is the author of many studies concerning the impact of ASPs on substance abuse, and one such study was published in 2007.

(C) Tebes wrote about many topics in 2007, including a study on the impact of ASPs on substance abuse.

(D) Tebes was the first of many authors to study the impact of ASPs on substance abuse, beginning in 2007.

(E) Tebes is the first of several authors of a 2007 study on the impact of ASPs on substance abuse.

14. What does the "ibid." in the final parentheses of sentence 7 indicate about the impact of ASPs on delinquency?

(A) Other topics have been studied, too.

(B) The topic has been studied by Tebes et al.

(C) The topic has been studied by all authors cited in Sentence 7.

(D) The topic has been studied by authors who are not cited in the sentence.

(E) The topic has not been studied but simply discussed.

15. In sentence 7, why did the author choose not to place all of the citations together at the end of the sentence?

(A) The entire group of citations would be too long.

(B) The author wished to provide citations in chronological order.

(C) Each citation refers to a study on a different topic.

(D) The author wished to provide citations in alphabetical order.

(E) The narrative flow would be disrupted by a group of citations.

16. In context, which of the following is the best synonym for the word "mixed" in sentence 8?

(A) varied

(B) inconsistent

(C) ambiguous

(D) uncertain

(E) diverse

17. In context, which of the following sentences is in greatest need of a citation?

(A) Sentence 1

(B) Sentence 3

(C) Sentence 4

(D) Sentence 5

(E) Sentence 8

18. Which of the following sentences could be deleted without undermining the coherence of the passage?

(A) Sentence 4

(B) Sentence 6

(C) Sentence 7

(D) Sentence 8

(E) Sentence 9

19. Which of the following is most clearly indicated by the passage?

(A) Federal support for ASPs is not currently available.

(B) Studying the impact of ASPs can lead to improvements in program quality.

(C) Little is known about the psychosocial benefits of ASPs.

(D) The availability of ASPs is sufficient to meet current demand.

(E) There are more ASPs and studies of ASPs now than there used to be.

20. Which authors would you consult in order to learn more about the effects of ASPs on children's compliance with teachers' instructions?

(A) Watts, Witt & King

(B) Darling, Caldwell & Smith

(C) Mahoney, Lord & Carryl

(D) Martin, Martin, Gibson & Wilkins

(E) Tebes et al.

21. If the studies cited in the passage can be trusted, what can be concluded about the impact of ASPs on children's development?

(A) ASPs do not have clear benefits for any aspect of development.

(B) ASPs benefit academic development, but it is unclear whether they benefit psychosocial development.

(C) ASPs benefit psychosocial development, but it is unclear whether they benefit academic development.

(D) ASPs have a positive impact on all aspects of development.

(E) None of the above

22. Which of the following would you expect to see in the paragraph immediately following the passage?

(A) An elaboration of the psychosocial benefits of participation in ASPs

(B) A discussion of specific kinds of federal support for ASPs

(C) An analysis of recent trends in the development of new ASPs

(D) An anecdote illustrating how ASPs ordinarily operate

(E) A summary of studies on the academic effects of participation in ASPs

Rhetorical Analysis (25%)

DIRECTIONS: The following questions test your ability to analyze writing. Some questions refer to passages, while other questions are self-contained. For each question, choose the best answer.

Questions 1–9 refer to the following passage.

(1) A growing number of businesses providing day care facilities for the children of their employees. (2) Some companies charge a standard fee, but most provide day care free or at a nominal cost. (3) The day care programs that they do provide reflect a genuine effort to meet the needs of employees with children. (4) Typically, these programs serve children from infancy through the

teenage years. (5) Many companies are trying to decide if they should help with day care at all. (6) Most programs stay open late on weekdays, and some even provide day care on the weekends for especially hard-working parents. (7) One might ask whether this kind of care is really necessary, should businesses be in the business of day care? (8) There are many advantages to employer-provided day care. (9) As company loyalty is fostered, so the morale of employees increases. (10) Studies show that when a company begins to provide day care services for children of employees, they witness a decline in both absenteeism and tardiness. (11) In addition, employees feel that the company has taken more of a personal interest in them, and their loyalty to the company increases. (12) Turnover declines. (13) Finally, human resource managers estimate that every $1 that companies spend on their day care programs returns $2 or more in increased productivity.

1. In context, which of the following is the best substitute for the underlined portion of sentence 1 (reproduced below)?

    A growing number of businesses <u>providing</u> day care facilities for the children of their employees.

    (A) provided

    (B) are providing

    (C) will provide

    (D) have provided

    (E) had provided

2. In context, which of the following is the best synonym for the word "nominal" in sentence 2?

    (A) moderate

    (B) predetermined

    (C) variable

    (D) minimal

    (E) nonstandard

3. What is the purpose of sentence 4?

    (A) To illustrate the assertion made in Sentence 3

    (B) To qualify the observation made in Sentence 1

    (C) To provide a transition to Sentence 5

    (D) To explain the rationale for the facts noted in Sentence 2

    (E) To qualify the statements made throughout the paragraph

4. Which sentence clashes with the theme of the first paragraph?

    (A) Sentence 1

    (B) Sentence 2

    (C) Sentence 3

    (D) Sentence 4

    (E) Sentence 5

5. What purpose is served by the word "even" in sentence 6?

    (A) To underscore the fact that day care programs provided by businesses were created in order to reward employee productivity

    (B) To help emphasize the earlier point that day care programs provided by businesses represent a genuine effort to meet employee needs

    (C) To show that accurate statements about the nature of day care programs provided by businesses must be nuanced

    (D) To illustrate the extent of devotion and hard work among employees of day care programs provided by businesses

    (E) To clarify the fact that there is some flexibility in the availability of day care programs provided by businesses

6. In context, which is best to do with sentence 7?

    (A) Leave it as is.

    (B) Delete it.

    (C) Divide it into two sentences by changing the comma to a period.

    (D) Replace the comma with a dash.

    (E) Switch the order of clauses.

7. Where is the best place to relocate sentence 9?

    (A) Before Sentence 8

    (B) After Sentence 10

    (C) After Sentence 11

    (D) After Sentence 12

    (E) After Sentence 13

8. Which of the following is the best revision of the underlined portion of sentence 10 (reproduced below)?

   Studies show that when a company begins to provide day care services for children of employees, they witness a decline in both absenteeism and tardiness.

   (A) both absenteeism and tardiness decline

   (B) a decline in both absenteeism and tardiness exist

   (C) one can witness a decline in both absenteeism and tardiness

   (D) both absenteeism and tardiness can be seen to decline

   (E) a decline in absenteeism and tardiness is the consequence

9. In context, which of the following phrases should be added to the end of sentence 12?

   (A) unquestionably

   (B) though

   (C) in any case

   (D) nevertheless

   (E) as well

Questions 10–17 refer to the following passage.

(1) Marathon runners love to worry about their knees. (2) For years we have been told that running such long distances will cause knee problems as we get older. (3) Now there are studies questioning whether running is as hard on the knees as once believed. (4) One of the major concerns that marathoners have about our knees is arthritis. (5) Of course, we are also concerned about a variety of knee injuries that can occur as a result of training for and running such long distances. (6) These injuries are often preventable, and when they do occur, the body will typically heal given proper care. (7) Running has a more insidious connection to arthritis, in that running may contribute to the progression of the disease without the runner realizing it, and once it has developed, it is not readily cured. (8) Although we used to believe that extensive running causes arthritis, recent studies do not provide clear support for this belief. (9) One reviewer observed that in many studies, extensive running does not lead to narrower space between joints, which is one of the precursors to arthritis. (10) However, a few studies show that extensive running causes other changes in the knee area that are related to development of arthritis, even though extensive running is not always directly linked to a greater incidence of arthritis in study participants.

10. In context, what is misleading about the phrase "love to" in sentence 1?

   (A) It is an overly casual phrase that clashes with the highly formal tone of the passage.

   (B) It implies that runners worry about their knees simply because doing so is enjoyable.

   (C) The second paragraph suggests that runners no longer worry about their knees.

   (D) Runners most probably worry about other aspects of their health besides their knees.

   (E) The rest of the passage does not support the idea that runners worry about their knees.

11. Which of the following is most clearly implied by sentence 2?

   (A) The author of the passage is an expert on knee injuries.

   (B) Distance running is the only kind of running that has been linked to knee problems.

   (C) The author of the passage is convinced that running causes knee problems.

   (D) In the past, experts disagreed about the link between running and knee problems.

   (E) The author of the passage is a marathon runner.

12. What is the purpose of sentence 4?

   (A) To assure readers that runners' concerns about their knees are serious

   (B) To describe the problem that the passage resolves

   (C) To help distinguish arthritis from other kinds of knee problems

   (D) To introduce the specific problem that the passage focuses on

   (E) To suggest a limitation in recent studies of relevance

13. Which sentence contains the main theme of the passage?

   (A) Sentence 1   (D) Sentence 4

   (B) Sentence 2   (E) Sentence 5

   (C) Sentence 3

14. What is the relationship between the two paragraphs of this passage?

    (A) The first paragraph introduces a claim that is analyzed and evaluated in the second paragraph.

    (B) The second paragraph presents an alternative to the key ideas described in the first paragraph.

    (C) The first paragraph discusses a possibility that is substantiated by evidence presented in the second paragraph.

    (D) The second paragraph shifts to a different topic of indirect relevance to the theme of the first paragraph.

    (E) The first paragraph presents a summary that is described in greater detail in the second paragraph.

15. The discussion of running injuries in sentences 5 and 6 primarily serves to

    (A) present a complete picture of the kinds of concerns runners share.

    (B) encourage the reader to view runners sympathetically.

    (C) illustrate by contrasting why arthritis is a major concern.

    (D) remind the reader of the importance of injuries.

    (E) demonstrate by example why running can be dangerous.

16. In context, which of the following would be best to insert at the beginning of sentence 6?

    (A) But

    (B) Nevertheless

    (C) Thus

    (D) Still

    (E) Meanwhile

17. In sentence 7, the word "insidious" most nearly means

    (A) internal

    (B) undesirable

    (C) damaging

    (D) stealthy

    (E) complex

18. Which of the following conclusions is suggested by the information presented in sentences 9 and 10?

(A) Some recent studies show that extensive running clearly contributes to arthritis.

(B) Recent studies are inconclusive as to the connection between extensive running and arthritis.

(C) Some recent studies show that extensive running causes arthritis while others do not.

(D) Recent studies do not suggest anything about links between extensive running and arthritis.

(E) Recent studies show no link whatsoever between extensive running and arthritis.

Questions 19–23 refer to the following passage.

(1) Throughout life, the American poet Robert Frost endured considerable personal tribulations. (2) Among his tribulations was the loss of numerous family members to mental or physical illness. (3) His younger sister and one of his daughters were both committed to psychiatric institutions, and one of his sons committed suicide. (4) Of his six children, two outlived him. (5) These tragic events aside, Frost had a long and productive career as one of America's greatest poets.

19. Which is best to do with the underlined portion of sentence 1 (reproduced below)?

Throughout life, the American poet Robert Frost endured considerable personal hardship.

(A) Leave it as is.

(B) Delete it.

(C) Insert "his" before "life."

(D) Insert "a" before "life."

(E) Insert "this" before "life."

20. Which of the following is the best way to combine sentences 1 and 2 (reproduced below)?

Throughout life, the American poet Robert Frost endured considerable personal tribulations. Among his tribulations was the loss of numerous family members to mental or physical illness.

(A) Throughout life, the American poet Robert Frost endured considerable personal tribulations: the loss of numerous family members to mental or physical illness.

(B) Throughout life, the American poet Robert Frost endured considerable personal tribulations; among these tribulations was the loss of numerous family members to mental or physical illness.

(C) Throughout life, the American poet Robert Frost endured considerable personal tribulations and the loss of numerous family members to mental or physical illness.

(D) Throughout life, the American poet Robert Frost endured considerable personal tribulations, including the loss of numerous family members to mental or physical illness.

(E) Throughout life, the American poet Robert Frost endured considerable personal tribulations, among them the loss of numerous family members to mental or physical illness.

21. The primary purpose of sentence 3 is to

(A) give an example illustrating the main point of the passage.

(B) elicit genuine sympathy from the reader.

(C) add to the biographical sketch being developed.

(D) provide a transition to ideas expressed later in the passage.

(E) comment on the perilous nature of life.

22. In context, which of the following revisions to the underlined portion of sentence 4 (reproduced below) would be most consistent with the sentence's purpose?

Of his six children, two outlived him.

(A) two children

(B) two ultimately

(C) two of them

(D) there were two that

(E) only two

23. In context, which of the following revisions to the underlined portion of sentence 5 (reproduced below) would be best?

These tragic events aside, Frost had a long and productive career as one of America's greatest poets.

(A) These tragic events occurred, but

(B) Along with these tragic events,

(C) While these tragic events were taking place,

(D) In spite of these tragic events,

(E) Yes, there were tragic events, but

ESSAYS

TIME: 70 Minutes

You will have a total of 70 minutes to write two argumentative essays. You will have 30 minutes to complete the first essay, which is to be based on your own reading, experience, or observations, and 40 minutes to complete the second essay, which requires you to synthesize two sources that are provided. Although you are free to begin writing at any point, it is better to take the time you need to plan your essays and to do the required reading than it is to begin writing immediately.

First Essay

DIRECTIONS: Napoleon Hill once commented that "Action is the real measure of intelligence." Write an essay in which you discuss what you think Hill meant by this phrase. Then, discuss whether you agree or disagree. Support your discussion with specific reasons and examples from your reading, experience, or observations.

Second Essay

DIRECTIONS: The following assignment requires you to write a coherent essay in which you synthesize the two sources provided. Synthesis refers to combining the sources and your position to form a cohesive, supported argument. You must develop a position and incorporate both sources. **You must cite the sources whether you are paraphrasing or quoting.** Refer to each source by the author's last name, or by any other means that adequately identifies it.

Assignment

Read the following quotations carefully. Then write an essay in which you develop a position on the nature of winning. Be sure to incorporate and cite both of the accompanying quotations as you develop your position.

"Winning isn't everything; it's the only thing."—Henry Sanders

"[It's] not that you won or lost, but how you played the game."—Grantland Rice

Practice Test 2
Answer Key

Conventions of Standard Written English

1. **B** The correct phrase would be "that of."
2. **E** This sentence contains no errors.
3. **C** The correct phrase would be "the mouths."
4. **B** The correct word would be "luminaries."
5. **A** The correct phrase would be "As adults."
6. **E** This sentence contains no errors.
7. **D** The correct word would be "from."
8. **C** The correct phrase would be "that are."
9. **C** The correct word would be "but."

Revision Skills

1. **C** Option C is the only grammatically correct and idiomatic option.
2. **A** It is not necessary to repeat the fact that Ravel created this ballet.
3. **B** Option B is the only correct option.
4. **C** Details about the origin of the folk dance do not fit the theme of the paragraph.
5. **D** Option D is the only clearly accurate option, since the instruments that are alluded to would begin to play after the percussionist has opened the piece.
6. **B** Since the instruments named in this sentence are the "other instruments" noted in the previous sentence, Option B is correct.
7. **E** In context, E is the only accurate option.
8. **D** Option D is the only grammatically correct and idiomatic option.
9. **B** Option B is correct in light of the meaning of Sentence 4.
10. **C** Only Option C can be safely inferred from the sentence.

11. **E** Although Sentence 9 is not irrelevant to the passage, it can be deleted without affecting the coherence of the passage.

12. **E** Option E is the only grammatically correct and idiomatic option.

13. **A** Option A is the only accurate option.

14. **C** Option C is the only accurate and grammatically correct option.

15. **B** Option B is the most idiomatic option.

16. **D** In context, Option D is the only accurate option.

17. **B** Option B is the most idiomatic option.

Improving Sentences

18. **B** Option B is the only grammatically correct option.

19. **C** Option C is the only grammatically correct option.

20. **E** Option E is the only grammatically correct and idiomatic option.

21. **A** Option A is the only grammatically correct option.

22. **C** Option C is the only grammatically correct option.

23. **D** Option D is the only grammatically correct and idiomatic option.

24. **D** Option D is the only grammatically correct option.

25. **B** Option B is the only grammatically correct and idiomatic option.

26. **D** Option D is the only grammatically correct and idiomatic option.

27. **E** Option E is the only grammatically correct option.

28. **C** Option C is the only grammatically correct option.

29. **A** Option A is the only grammatically correct option.

30. **C** Option C is the only grammatically correct and idiomatic option.

31. **D** Option D is the only grammatically correct option.

32. **E** Option E is the only grammatically correct and sensible option.

33. **A** Option A is the only grammatically correct option.

34. **B** Option B is the only grammatically correct option.

35. **D** Option D is the only grammatically correct option.

36. **C** Option C is the only grammatically correct option.

Ability to Use Source Materials

1. **C** Since the passage focuses on a scientific term (i.e., triglycerides), a definition of the term is needed.

2. **E** The nature of the source is unknown without further information.

3. **D** Although all of the options would convey useful information, the number provided makes no sense without knowing the unit of measurement.

4. **A** The sentence contributes some useful information to the passage.

5. **E** All of the options would provide helpful information to interested readers.

6. **B** Option B is the only correct option.

7. **A** The italicized *"n"* in the entry indicates that the word is a noun.

8. **C** Option C is the only correct option.

9. **D** Option D is the only correct option

10. **D** All that can be determined is that the survey was published recently.

11. **C** 15% currently participate, and if quality programming were available, an additional 30% would participate.

12. **B** Option B is the only correct option.

13. **E** Option E is the only correct option.

14. **B** "Ibid." refers back to the immediately preceding citation.

15. **C** Each citation indicates a study on the type of ASP benefit described in the clause.

16. **B** Evidently, the results concerning academic benefits have not been consistent.

17. **B** The sentence contains reference to documentation that is not provided.

18. **A** This sentence contributes very little to the passage.

19. **E** Option E is the only correct option.

20. **D** In light of the information given in Sentence 7, Option D is the only correct option.

21. **C** Option C is the only correct option.

22. **E** Given the level of detail in the discussion of psychosocial benefits, Sentences 8 and 9 appear to be transitional to a deeper discussion of evidence concerning academic benefits.

Rhetorical Analysis

1. **B**   In context, Option B is the most sensible answer.

2. **D**   In context, Option D is the most sensible answer.

3. **A**   The fact that these programs typically serve youth of all ages illustrates the genuineness of efforts to meet their parents' needs.

4. **E**   Sentence 5 implies uncertainty on the part of companies that is inconsistent with the message of the first paragraph.

5. **B**   The term "even" emphasizes the extent of day care services provided.

6. **C**   Option C is the only option that is grammatically correct.

7. **C**   Sentence 9 naturally follows the discussion of loyalty in Sentence 11.

8. **A**   Option A is the most idiomatic option.

9. **E**   Option E is the most sensible option, given the content of Sentence 11.

10. **B**   The passage implies that concerns about knee damage are justifiable and serious.

11. **E**   Use of the term "we" implies that the author is a marathon runner.

12. **D**   Option D is the only correct option.

13. **C**   Sentence 3 refers to both the prior beliefs as well as the current evidence that are discussed in the passage.

14. **E**   Option E is the only correct option.

15. **C**   Sentences 5 and 6 suggest that the injuries are more noticeable and less permanent than arthritis.

16. **A**   Option A is the only option consistent with the purpose of Sentence 6.

17. **D**   Option D is the only correct option.

18. **B**   Option B is the only correct option.

19. **C**   Option C is the only grammatically correct and idiomatic option.

20. **D**   In context, Option D is the only option that is both grammatically correct and combines the two sentences accurately.

21. **A**   Option A conveys the primary purpose of the sentence.

22. **E**   Option E is the option most consistent with the purpose of the sentence.

23. **D**   Option D is the only idiomatic and sensible option.

Answer Key for Essays

Sample First Essay

One of my earliest memories is watching a pot boil over on the stove. I was about four years old at the time, and my mother had left me alone in the kitchen for some reason. I remember seeing the lid of the pot begin to rise and shimmy. I remember hearing the lid rattle against the rim of the pot. And I remember seeing a thick fluid begin to pour over the sides. Even then, I knew it was a bad thing. I knew somehow that I should call my mother immediately, but instead I stood in the middle of the kitchen, watching this unusual event unfold for what seemed like a very long time until she came rushing in.

In my opinion, Hill's comment that "Action is the real measure of intelligence" means not just that intelligence is expressed in actions, but also that a person's level of intelligence is measurable through his or her actions. I suspect that what Hill would say about my anecdote is that I did not show much intelligence. The smartest thing I could have done, given my age, would have been to call my mother. A less intelligent strategy would have been to remove the pot myself. One could argue that my actual behavior reflects the least amount of intelligence because I chose not to act. Instead I stood and watched, recognizing the existence of a problem but failing to act on that knowledge.

For the most part I agree with Hill's observation. Intelligence is an inner quality, presumably instantiated somewhere in the brain. We cannot observe it before a person acts. (As someone once said, thinking is not a spectator sport.) Then, once the person has acted, we can evaluate the intelligence implicit in the action, even if all he or she did was to answer a question.

Although I agree in general terms with Hill's comment, I also find it a bit too broad. What constitutes intelligence varies from situation to situation. Passively observing a pot boil over may not be very smart, but there are situations in which inaction is arguably the most intelligent form of behavior. Consider, for example, the citizens of highly oppressive regimes such as North Korea, where the slightest dissent from prevailing dogma can result in extreme punishment. If I were a North Korean citizen, I would be very cautious about my words and actions. I would not want to jeopardize my own well-being and that of my family by speaking up every time I disagreed with a comment made by one of my leaders, even if I were convinced that the leader was in error. In such situations, inaction might be considered the real measure of intelligence.

Commentary

Look back at the directions for this essay. You will see that the directions include three requests:

1. *Discuss what you think Hill meant by this phrase ["Action is the real measure of intelligence."].*

2. *Discuss whether you agree or disagree.*

3. *Support your discussion with specific reasons and examples from your reading, experience, or observations.*

The author of this essay addresses the first request in the second paragraph of the essay.

The author then applies Hill's apparent meaning to the anecdote described in the first paragraph.

The author addresses the second request in the second paragraph of the essay. However, it becomes clear at the outset of the third paragraph that the author finds some exceptions to Hill's view.

The author addresses the third request throughout the essay. The approach is generally analytical, with sustained examples provided in the first and fourth paragraphs.

Notice that the essay is clear, well-organized, grammatically varied, and free of errors. The author shows good command of the language in the choice of words and phrases.

Suggestions for Essay Development for the Second Essay

A good place to begin is to read these quotes, to be sure you understand the differences between each point of view, and then to think about the position you will develop in your own essay. Will you side with one of the authors? Will you develop a position that represents a compromise between their views? Or will you develop a third position that is to some extent separate from theirs.

The next step is to plan your essay. Although your time is limited, you should take a few minutes to create an informal outline that will guide your writing. The outline should identify key points and examples and indicate the order in which they will be discussed.

Below you will see an outline for one particular essay that could be written. This outline leads to a conclusion that favors Rice's view of winning.

The outline below is relatively detailed and written in complete sentences so that you can follow the progression of ideas. An outline written during the actual test would not need to be as elaborate.

1. In competitive situations, winning isn't literally everything. One must also prepare for the competition and then actually compete. What Sanders probably meant is not that winning is literally the only thing, but simply that it is the most important and desirable aspect of competition.

2. How you play the game isn't everything either. Winning is important, too, because games and other forms of competition wouldn't be interesting or even sensible unless the competitors were trying to win, and unless winners were ultimately recognized. What Rice probably meant is not that how you compete is the only thing, but simply that it is the most important aspect of competition. More specifically, I assume he meant that trying one's best, playing fair, and treating other competitors respectfully are most important and desirable.

3. My own view is closer to that of Rice. One should try one's best to win (and nothing is sweeter than winning), but competition becomes meaningless and brutal if winning takes on so much importance that competitors cannot be honest, fair, and respectful of each other. Whether the competition is between athletic teams, competitors for a job, or businesses vying for a contract, how one plays the game is most important. The best outcome is to play well—and then to win.

Index

A

Abbreviations
  for grammatical information, 115
  for parts of speech, 115
  for usage and etymology, 116–117
Agreement in standard written English
    conventions
  in case, 28–29
  in gender, 26
  in number, 23–25
  in person, 27
Almanac, 112
American Psychological Association
    (APA), style citation, 101–103
Atlas, 112
Audience, 62

B

Bibliography, 112

C

Cause-effect organization, 61. *See also*
    Organization
  illustration of, 143
  outcome, cause of, 142
Chicago Manual of Style (CMS), 105
Chronological organization, 56–57. *See*
    also Organization
  information in order of occurrence, 141
Citation index, 112
Citations, 100–105. *See also Chicago*
    Manual of Style (CMS)
  APA style, 101–103
  Chicago style, 105
  MLA style, 103–105
Coherence
  sentence-level connections
    examples comparison, 73
    repetition of word, 72–73
  topical focus
    defined, 72

College Composition/College Composition
    Modular Examination Guide, 55–56
Comparison organization, 60–61
  contrast, 142
  information about two or more things, 142
Complex sentences, 17–19
Compound-complex sentence, 19
Compound sentences, 17
Concordance, 112
Critical thinking. *See also* Rhetorical
    analysis
  arguments, evaluation of, 130
    authority's conclusions, 135–136
    contradiction, logical, 130
    evidence, misuse of, 132
    fallacious conclusion, 133
    flaws in, 130
    hyperbolic statements, 135
    logical fallacies, examples of, 134
    overstatement, 132–133
    possible fallacies, 132
    questionable assumptions and, 131
    substantive contribution, 135
    understand, ability to, 130
    way to strengthen, 131
  comparing and synthesizing
    missing information, identification,
      136–137
    pertinent information, 136
    theme identification, 136
    views, similarities and differences
      between, 137
  facts and opinions
    accuracy and persuasiveness, evaluation
      of, 129
    distinction between, 127–128
    factual assertion and, 129–130
    means of evidence, verified by, 127
    source and purpose of, 127
  inferences and
    deductive, 137–138
    inductive, 138–139
    logical fallacies, identifying, 139

unfamiliar words, 139–140
writer, purpose and impact of, 137
writing, evaluation of, 140

D

Diction and standard written english
conventions
accept/except, 38
altogether/all together, 38
capitol/capital, 38
compliment/complement, 38
discreet/discrete, 38
effect/affect, 31–32
elicit/illicit, 38
farther/further, 32–33
flaunt/flout, 38
imply/insinuate/infer, 32
lie/lay, 37
principal/principle, 38
stationary/stationery, 38
than/then, 33
there/their/they're, 36
who/that/which, 34–35
who/whom, 35–36
Dictionary, 113
Documentation of sources
additional resources, providing
bibliographic details, use of, 89
topic, information about, 89
credibility and persuasiveness, enhancing
facts and, 87
factual assertions, evidence for, 88
writer's feelings, accurate description
of, 88
ethical requirements
difficult to verify ideas, 92
ideas, originality of, 91
manner of expression, 91
natural selection, reference to, 93
particular statements, credit for, 89
plagiarism and, 89–90
quotation, credit for, 90

E

Emphatic organization, 57–59. *See also*
Organization
information and order, 141

Encyclopedia, 113
Essays
examination and modular option
purpose of, 173–174
structure and scoring, 174–175
writing CLEP argumentative, practice
first essay, 182–185
second essay, 186–190
writing strategies for
errors, avoidance of, 179–181
imagination use and, 177–178
organization of, 178
signal verbs and phrases, 178–179
words frequently misspelled,
181–182
written argument, structure of,
175–177
Ethical requirements for documentation of
sources
difficult to verify ideas, 92
ideas, originality of, 91
manner of expression, 91
natural selection, reference to, 93
particular statements, credit for, 89
plagiarism and, 89–90
quotation, credit for, 90
Evidence evaluation
authority
appeal to, 65–66
distinction between, 66
dimensions of
analogy between, 70
irrelevant statements, 68–69
logical connections, 69
logical fallacy, 69–70
findings
abstinence-only programs, 65
fallacies, 64–65
statistics, 64
observations
credibility of writer, 63
defined, 62
relationship between, 63
writer's goal, 63
reasoning
example of, 67–68
strength of, 68
use of logic, 67

F

Framing, 144–145

G

Generality organization, 59–60. *See also*
    Organization
  information in order of specificity, 141
  thesis, specific discussion of, 142
Grammatical information
  abbreviations for, 115

L

Language
  jargon, 76–77
  slang, 77
  use of, 76
Level of detail
  meaning of, 71
  requirement, 71

M

Modern Language Association (MLA),
    style citation, 103–105
Modifiers in standard written english
    conventions
  adjectives, 39–40
  adverbs, 40–41
  misplaced, 41–42
  reference, 43–44
  squinting and dangling, 42–43

O

Organization
  cause-effect
    departure from, 61
    relationship information about, 61
  chronological, 56
    terms used for, 57
    United States, 57
  comparison, 61
    defined, 60
    uses of, 60
  emphatic, 59
    defined, 57
    formal debate and, 58
      increasing importance, 58
      methodological difference, 57
      results difference, 58
      terms used for, 57
    factors, 56
    generality
      People v. Simpson, 59
      specific-to-general, 59
      writing style and, 59–60

P

Parallelism, 22–23. *See also* Standard
    written english conventions
Parts of speech
  abbreviations for, 115
People v. Simpson, 59
Problem-solution organization
  descriptive writing and, 143–144
  information about problem, 143
  solutions, compare and contrast, 143
Punctuation in standard written english
    conventions
  apostrophes and possessives, 50–51
  commas, 47–50
  periods and exclamation points, 45
  question mark, 45–46
  semicolons and colons, 46–47

R

References, 105. *See also Chicago Manual
    of Style* (CMS)
  abbreviations in, 110–111
  APA style, 106–108
  MLA and Chicago style, 108–110
Revision skills questions
  comma splice, 84
  directions, 78–79
  grammatical problem, 81
  inference about diction, 84–85
  instructions for, 79
  meaning and purpose, 85–86
  options, 80
  organization of, 81–82
  sample CLEP, 79–86
  sentences
    deleting, 82
    reflection, 81

title for, 86
transitions, 83
work through, 80
Rhetorical analysis, 127
  alliteration, 161–162
  CLEP exams and
    questions in, 163–164
    sample questions, 164–169
  critical thinking
    arguments, evaluation of, 130–136
    details, comparing and synthesizing, 136–137
    facts and opinions, analyzing, 127–130
    inferences and, 137–140
  devices
    alliteration, 161–162
    parallelism, 160–161
    statement persuasiveness, increase, 159
  organization, understanding of
    cause-effect, 142–143
    chronological, 141
    comparison, 142
    emphatic, 141
    framing, 144–145
    generality, 141–142
    for non-fiction writing, 140
    problem-solution, 143–144
    transition, 145–147
  parallelism, 160–161
  style, understanding of
    diction, 148–150
    point of view, 152–154
    syntax, 150–152
    writer, choices of, 147
  understanding of
    audience, 154–155
    piece of writing, effects in, 162
    purpose, 156–157
    tone, 157–158
    weaknesses, 163
Rhetorical effects
  approach on, 75–76
  ethos, exclusive reliance on, 75–76
  logos, 75
  pathos, exclusive reliance on, 75–76

S

Sentence-level connections, 72–73
Sentence variety
  illustration of, 74
  structure, 74
Simple sentences, 16
Source materials, 87
  dictionaries and thesauri, use of, 113–115
  documentation of
    additional resources, providing, 89
    credibility and persuasiveness, enhancing, 87–89
    ethical requirements, 89–93
  evaluation of
    author, credibility of, 97
    coverage, relevance of, 97–98
    credibility of, 96–97
    edition, 94
    objectivity, 98–99
    publication, date of, 93–94
    type of, 94–95
  integration of
    bibliographic entries, abbreviations in, 110–111
    citations, 100–105
    references, 105–110
  reference
    almanac, 112
    atlas, 112
    bibliography, 112
    citation index, 112
    concordance, 112
    dictionary, 113
    encyclopaedia, 113
    grammatical information, abbreviations for, 115
    parts of speech, abbreviations for, 115
    thesaurus, 113
    usage and etymology, abbreviations for, 116–117
  sample CLEP questions, 118–125
Standard written english conventions
  agreement
    in case, 28–29

in gender, 26
in number, 23–25
in person, 27
CLEP exams, 52–53
complex sentences, 17–19
compound-complex sentence, 19
compound sentences, 17
diction
  accept/except, 38
  altogether/all together, 38
  capitol/capital, 38
  compliment/complement, 38
  discreet/discrete, 38
  effect/affect, 31–32
  elicit/illicit, 38
  farther/further, 32–33
  flaunt/flout, 38
  imply/insinuate/infer, 32
  lie/lay, 37
  principal/principle, 38
  stationary/stationery, 38
  than/then, 33
  there/their/they're, 36
  who/that/which, 34–35
  who/whom, 35–36
modifiers
  adjectives, 39–40
  adverbs, 40–41
  misplaced, 41–42
  reference, 43–44
  squinting and dangling, 42–43

non-agreement in tense, 29–31
parallelism, 22–23
punctuation
  apostrophes and possessives, 50–51
  commas, 47–50
  periods and exclamation points, 45
  question mark, 45–46
  semicolons and colons, 46–47
sample CLEP questions, 53–54
sentence boundaries, 19–22
simple sentences, 16
Syntax, 15–16

T

Thesaurus, 113
Thesis statement, 75
Tone, 62
Topic sentence, 74
Transitions, 145–147
  previous statement
    consequence of, 77
    contrasting with, 78
    illustrating, 78
    restating or summarizing, 78
    statement adding, 77

U

Usage and etymology
  abbreviations for, 116–117

Notes

INSTALLING REA's TestWare®

SYSTEM REQUIREMENTS

Pentium 75 MHz (300 MHz recommended) or a higher or compatible process. Microsoft Windows 98 or later; 64 MB Available RAM; Internet Explorer 5.5 or higher.

INSTALLATION

1. Insert the CLEP College Composition and College Composition Modular TestWare® CD-ROM into the CD-ROM drive.
2. If the installation doesn't begin automatically from the Start Menu choose the RUN command. When the RUN dialog box appears, type d:\setup (where *d* is the letter of your CD-ROM drive) at the prompt and click OK.
3. The installation process will begin. A dialog box proposing the directory "Program Files\REA\CLEP_College Comp" will appear. If the name and location are suitable, click OK. If you wish to specify a different name or location, type it in and click OK.
4. Start the CLEP College Composition and College Composition Modular TestWare® application by double-clicking on the icon.

REA's CLEP College Composition and College Composition Modular TestWare® is EASY to LEARN AND USE. To achieve maximum benefits, we recommend that you take a few minutes to go through the on-screen tutorial on your computer.

SSD ACCOMMODATIONS FOR STUDENTS WITH DISABILITIES

Many students qualify for extra time to take the CLEP College Composition and College Composition Modular exams, and our TestWare® can be adapted to accommodate your extension. This allows you to practice under the same extended-time accommodations that you will receive on the actual test day. To customize your TestWare® to suit the most common extensions, visit our website at *www.rea.com/ssd*.

TECHNICAL SUPPORT

REA's TestWare® is backed by customer and technical support. For questions about **installation or operation of your software**, contact us at:

Research and Education Association
Phone (732)819-8880 (9 a.m. to 5 p.m. ET, Monday–Friday)
Fax: (732) 819-8808
Website: www.rea.com
E-mail: info@rea.com

Note to Windows XP Users: In order for the TestWare® to function properly, please install and run the application under the same computer administrator-level user account. Installing the TestWare® as one user and running it as another could cause file-access path conflicts.